JOURNAL FOR THE STUDY OF THE OLD TESTAMENT
SUPPLEMENT SERIES
90

Editors
David J.A. Clines
Philip R. Davies

JSOT Press
Sheffield

BIBLICAL HEBREW IN TRANSITION

The Language of the Book of Ezekiel

Mark F. Rooker

Journal for the Study of the Old Testament
Supplement Series 90

Copyright © 1990 Sheffield Academic Press

Published by JSOT Press
JSOT Press is an imprint of
Sheffield Academic Press Ltd
The University of Sheffield
343 Fulwood Road
Sheffield S10 3BP
England

Printed in Great Britain
by Billing & Sons Ltd
Worcester

British Library Cataloguing in Publication Data

Rooker, Mark F.
    Biblical Hebrew in transition.
    1. Bible. O.T.Ezekiel.—Critical studies
    I. Title   II. Series
    224.406

    ISSN 0309-0787
    ISBN 1-85075-230-3

CONTENTS

LIST OF TABLES

FOREWORD

As the present work is a revision of my Brandeis University doctoral dissertation, I am indebted to my mentor Professor Michael Fishbane for his instruction, guidance, and encouragement in seeing the earlier version of this work to completion. Avi Hurvitz of the Hebrew University not only introduced me to the historical study of Biblical Hebrew, but read with great care an earlier version of this work. Many of his suggestions have been incorporated in this final draft. I am grateful to him for his kind help and the interest he has taken in my work. I would also like to convey my gratitude to the editors of the *Journal of Northwest Semitic Languages* and the *Hebrew Annual Review* for permission to utilize the contents of my articles in Chapters 2 and 3 of this study. Special thanks goes to the administration of Dallas Theological Seminary for allowing me free access to their computer facilities and to Mr. Timothy Meyers, a Dallas Seminary student from Melbourne, Australia, who assisted me in preparing the indexes.

To my wife Carole I gratefully express my appreciation both for her encouragement as well as for her commitment to the challenge of caring for our three sons during the time I had to be away working on this study. It is also with gratitude that I remember on this occasion my parents who have stood with me and encouraged me to pursue academic studies. Without their love and support I would not be where I am today. It is thus with deep appreciation and affection that I dedicate this work to my mother and the memory of my father.

קמו בניה ויאשרוה

במותו ציווה לי את החיים

ABBREVIATIONS

BDB	F. Brown, S.R. Driver, and C.A. Briggs, *A Hebrew and English Lexicon of the Old Testament*, Oxford, 1907, reprinted 1974.
BHS	*Biblia Hebraica Stuttgartensia*, Stuttgart, 1966.
BZAW	Beiheft zur Zeitschrift für die alttestamentliche Wissenschaft
CAD	*The Assyrian Dictionary oftheUniversity of Chicago*, Chicago, 1956-
CBQ	Catholic Biblical Quarterly
EncJud	*Encyclopedia Judaica*, Jerusalem, 1971–72.
E M	*Encyclopedia Miqrait*, 1977-82 [In Hebrew].
GKC	*Gesenius' Hebrew Grammar*, ed. E. Kautzsch, Oxford, 1910, reprinted 1974.
HAR	*Hebrew Annual Review*
HTR	*Harvard Theological Review*
IEJ	*Israel Exploration Journal*
JAOS	*Journal of the American Oriental Society*
JANES	*Journal of the Ancient Near Eastern Society of the Columbia University*
JBL	*Journal of Biblical Literature*
JJS	*Journal of Jewish Studies*
JNES	*Journal of Near Eastern Studies*
JQR	*Jewish Quarterly Review*
JPS	*The Holy Scriptures,* The Jewish Publication Society of America, 1955,
KB	L. Koehler and W. Baumgartner, *Lexicon in Veteris Testamenti Libros*, Leiden, 1958
RB	*Revue biblique*
RQ	*Revue de Qumran*

TDOT	*Theological Dictionary of the Old Testament*, 5 vols., Grand Rapids, 1974-86.
VT	*Vetus Testamentum*
ZAW	*Zeitschrift für die altestamentliche Wissenschaft*

Other

BA	Biblical Aramaic	M T	Massoretic Text		
BH	Biblical Hebrew	Q	Qere		
DSS	Dead Sea Scrolls	BT	Babylonian Talmud		
EBH	Early Biblical Hebrew	JT	Jerusalem Talmud		
LBH	Late Biblical Hebrew	M H	Mishnaic Hebrew		
Mek.	Mechilta				

Biblical

CH	Court History
Dtr	Deuteronomic passages
JE	Yahwistic and Elohistic passages of Pentateuch
N1	Nehemiah's memoirs: Neh 1:1-7:5; 12:27-12:31
N2	Non-memoir sections of Neh
P	'Priestly Work' of Pentateuch
Pg	'Groundwork' of Priestly Work
Ps	Alleged secondary additions to Pg

Chapter 1

INTRODUCTION—THE CONCEPT OF LINGUISTIC CHANGE

The premise of this work is that the history of biblical Hebrew is characterized by two successive language states: pre-exilic or Early Biblical Hebrew and post-exilic or Late Biblical Hebrew. This distinction presupposes that the Hebrew Language, as it is represented in the Hebrew Bible, was subject to linguistic change over the course of time.

The postulation that a language should experience change in time is not a novel conception; it is rather, consistent with what is presently known about the history of languages. Bloomfield noted that all languages are subject to change and in fact are subject to constant change: 'A language presents itself to us, at any one moment, as a stable structure of lexical and grammatical habits. This, however, is an illusion. Every language is undergoing, at all times, a slow but unceasing process of *linguistic change*'.[1] Arlotto corroborates:

> Languages change in time. The speech of a given generation is never quite identical to that of its parents or to that of its children. Of course, the differences between adjoining generations are slight and for the most part go unnoticed. However, given a span of time of centuries or millennia, minute differences will have a cumulative effect and often a given language will acquire a very new form.[2]

Readers of English recognize that the English of Beowulf, Chaucer, or Shakespeare differs radically from the English language as it is spoken in the twentieth century. Bloomfield states:

> The English of the King James Bible or of Shakespeare is unlike the English of today. The fourteenth-century English of Chaucer is intelligible to us only if we use a glossary. The ninth-century English of King Alfred the Great, of which we have contemporary manuscript records, seems to us like a foreign language; if we could

---

1. Leonard Bloomfield, *Language* (Chicago, 1983) 281 (italics his). See also Winfred P. Lehman, *Historical Linguistics: An Introduction* (New York, 1962) 1.
2. Anthony Arlotto, *Introduction to Historical Linguistics* (Lanham, 1972) 3.

meet English-speakers of that time, we should not understand their speech, or they ours.[3]

Languages may change gradually over a long period of time or changes may occur quite abruptly. Saussure has noted the unpredictable nature of language change: 'It is possible for a language to change hardly at all over a long span and then to undergo radical transformations within a few years'.[4]

The locus of linguistic change is the point of interaction of the speaker with his speech community:

> It is in speaking that the germ of all change is found. Each change is launched by a certain number of individuals before it is accepted for general use ... In the history of any innovation there are always two distinct moments: (1) when it sprang up in individual usage; and (2) when it became a fact of language, outwardly identical but adopted by the community.[5]

Not only do the changes originate in the speech of individuals within a given speech community, but the procedure by which a linguistic innovation advances from stage one to stage two (in the above quote), is by further adaptation by subsequent speakers who for diverse reasons will adapt their speaking habits to those of their interlocutors. Arlotto notes the requisite role of societal compliance in continued communication:

> The historical linguist views human language as a dynamic, ever-changing phenomenon, stable insofar as it allows communication between speakers at given or nearby points of time, but ever changing as it reflects changing speech habits, as it is subject to internal and external factors, and as it adapts to new situations of the speech community.[6]

It should be stressed, however, that while linguistic change occurs incessantly in all languages it does not interfere with the ability of speakers to communicate. This is due to the orderly nature of language change: 'Language change is not a completely random, unprincipled deviation from a state of pristine perfection, but

3. Bloomfield, *Language*, 281.
4. Ferdinand de Saussure, *Course in General Linguistics*, trans. Wade Baskin (New York, 1959) 101.
5. Saussure, *Course in General Linguistics*, 98.
6. *Introduction to Historical Linguistics*, 5.

proceeds in large measure in a remarkably regular and systematic fashion, without any profound effects on our ability to communicate'.[7]

Having observed the universality of linguistic change, it is necessary to examine the factors or causes which give birth to change, as well as the procedures or mechanisms language change employs. These concerns constitute the intrinsic elements of historical linguistics—a science which studies the differences in languages between two points of time.[8] But, in order to better understand these issues, it is imperative that we first examine the historical context in which these matters came to be discussed.[9] We thus, more immediately turn to the development of the science of historical linguistics.

The Rise of Historical Linguistics

Historically, the field of linguistics can be viewed as having experienced three significant periods of development: (1) the Grammatical Era, (2) the Philological Era, and (3) the Comparative Philological Era.[10]

The Grammatical Era was introduced by the early Greeks. The ancient Greeks made acute grammatical observations as well as discovered parts of speech and inflectional categories. In addition, they noticed many similarities between their language and Latin.[11] Their study, however, was intrinsically restricted by the tendentious presupposition that the structure of Greek language embodied universal forms. On the basis of this ideology they attempted to explain Greek grammar on a philosophical basis. Thus the study of language in the Grammatical Era was unalterably limited to the study of the Greek language.[12]

---

7. Hans Henrich Hock, *Principles of Historical Linguistics* (Berlin, 1986) 2.
8. Lehman, *Historical Linguistics: An Introduction,* 3.
9. The significance of the recognition of linguistic change is summarized by Arlotto: 'The foundation of all modern linguistics, the fact that human language is amenable to scientific analysis, was first shown and accepted on the basis of data drawn from observations of language change'. Arlotto, *Introduction to Historical Linguistics,* 6.
10. Saussure, *Course in General Linguistics,* 1-2.
11. They failed, however, to draw any linguistic conclusions. Saussure, *Course in General Linguistics,* 192.
12. Bloomfield, *Language,* 5.

The second stage in the development of modern linguistics, the
Philological Era, did not arise until the Renaissance, which was
accompanied by an acute interest in language study. More
specifically for our purposes, Renaissance scholars became interested
in the investigation of ancient records. Yet, not unlike the
Grammatical Era, grammatical features were still often explained in
philosophical terms and language distinctions were often thought to
be based on nationalities.[13]

The catalyst of the third stage of modern linguistics, the
Comparative Philological Era, was the discovery and decipherment
of Sanskrit by European scholars. When these scholars recognized
the similarity of this language to European languages, the comparative method of analysis was conceived.[14] The first systematic
comparison of the Indo-European languages comprised an analysis
of the verbal affixes of Sanskrit, Greek, Latin, Persian, and German
verbs by Franz Bopp in 1816.[15] This was soon followed by a phonological study by Rasmus Kristian Rask of Germanic languages in comparison to other Indo-European languages in 1818. It was not long,
before the European scholars, on the basis of the comparative evidence, concluded that Sanskrit, Latin, and Greek were daughter languages of an earlier prototype. Thus the comparative/historical
approach to linguistics had officially begun. The overarching premise
of this comparative method, which led to the recovery of prehistoric
linguistic systems in the nineteenth century, presupposed the
regularity of linguistic change.[16]

13. The latter error was corrected, in part, by the proposal of the 'wave theory'
by Johannes Schmidt in *Verwandtschaftsverhältnisse der Indogermanen*, in
1877. See Saussure, *Course in General Linguistics*, 209.
14. Actually, it could be argued that the method itself began hundreds of years
earlier in medieval times among Jewish scholars in Arab lands who observed
the comparative relationship between Arabic, Aramaic, and Hebrew. This
analysis, however, was not carried through to make historical observations,
e.g. reconstructing the parent language of this related group. This contribution will be discussed more in chapter 2 of this study. For the contribution of
these medieval scholars, see James Barr, 'The Ancient Semitic Languages—
The Conflict between Philology and Linguistics', *Transactions of the Philological Society*, 1968, 43.
15. That Sanskrit was similar to Greek and Latin had been observed shortly
before this time by Sir William Jones, late in the eighteenth century. See
Lehmann, *Historical Linguistics: An Introduction*, 7.
16. Thus Eric P. Hamp, 'Introduction', to *Linguistic Change*, by E.H.
Sturtevant (Chicago, 1917) vi-vii. For the use of the comparative method in

The nineteenth century became the most rigorous period of the study of historical linguistics. One of the earliest European works to analyze the concept of linguistic change was Hermann Paul's *Principles of Linguistic Change* in 1880. In this work Paul built upon the recent work that had been done in the comparative Indo-European studies. He was the first to isolate the language of the individual as the primary object of linguistic inquiry. His work was however limited as he emphasized the comparative study without having an adequate descriptive basis of the languages involved. It was not until the work of Ferdinand de Saussure, often called the father of modern linguistics, that the importance of a thorough examination of languages on the synchronic level (the study of language in its static states) prior to making diachronic conclusions (the study of language in its evolutionary stages) was adequately emphasized for comparative/historical research. He postulated, largely from the study of phonology only, the classification of different linguistic periods of a language as separate and distinct stages, such as Old French, Modern French, etc. Lehmann summarizes Saussure's contribution:

> For these stages Saussure provided an elegant name: *espace de temps*. Admitting that one state of a language is not a point in time he suggested that an *espace de temps* might be as long as ten years, a generation, an age, or more. The assumption of a 'space in time' seemed tenable to him because of the manner in which languages undergo change: during some periods they may evolve little or undergo few changes, at any rate changes of little importance; during other periods they undergo a considerable number of changes rapidly. Periods with few changes would be handled as states; those of many changes would be selected for diachronic study, as the evolutionary phases of a language between its quiescent states.[17]

Bloomfield accurately describes Saussure's contribution in reacting to contemporary linguists who were restricting their studies to the diachronic level without the benefit of a prior, thorough, synchronic analysis:

> The merging of these two streams of study, the historical-comparative and the philosophical-descriptive, has made clear some princi-

reconstructing prehistoric languages, see Lehmann, *Historical Linguistics: An Introduction*, 83-84.

17. W.P. Lehmann, 'Saussure's Dichotomy between Descriptive and Historical Linguistics', in *Directions for Historical Linguistics*, eds. W.P. Lehmann and Yakov Malkiel (Austin, 1968) 7.

ples that were not apparent to the great Indo-Europeanists of the
nineteenth century, as represented, say, by Hermann Paul. All historical study of language is based upon the comparison of two or
more sets of descriptive data. It can be only as accurate and only as
complete as these data permit it to be. In order to describe a language one needs no historical knowledge whatever; in fact, the
observer who allows such knowledge to affect his description, is
bound to distort his data. Our descriptions must be unprejudiced, if
they are to give a sound basis for comparative work.[18]

The historical or diachronic approach to the study of language
arose out of, and is an intrinsic element of, the comparative method of
historical linguistics. Saussure describes the different outlooks of
synchronic and diachronic analysis:

> Synchrony has only one perspective, the speakers', and its whole
> method consists of gathering evidence from speakers; to know to just
> what extent a thing is a reality, it is necessary and sufficient to
> determine to what extent it exists in the minds of speakers.
> Diachronic linguistics, on the contrary, must distinguish two per-
> spectives. One of these, the *prospective*, follows the course of time;
> the other, the *retrospective*, goes back in time; the result is a dupli-
> cation in methodology ...[19]

Thus diachronic linguistics is not concerned with variable terms or
forms which may occur at a particular stage of the language's history. Rather, the diachronic linguist is interested in the relation
between successive terms/forms which are substituted for each other
in time.[20]

18. Bloomfield, *Language*, 19-20. For a fuller, historical discussion see, *ibid.*,
3-20.
19. Saussure, *Course in General Linguistics*, 90 (italics his). This duplication
in methodology, from both the prospective and retrospective view, operates on
an apparent uniformitarian presupposition. That is, the forces operating to
produce language change today, are of the same kind and order of magnitude
as those which operated in the distant past. See, William Labov, 'The Social
Setting of Linguistic Change', in *Current Trends in Linguistics,* vol. 11, ed.
Thomas A. Sebeok (Paris, 1973) 207. For additional information on Saussure's
contribution as well as his discussion of synchronic and diachronic analysis,
see Bergey, *Esther*, 1-14.
20. Saussure, *Course in General Linguistics*, 140. It must be emphasized in
this discussion, that due to the incessant nature of linguistic change, sharp
breaks in continuity between two points in time are nonexistent. It is rather a
matter of convention to speak of languages at different points in their history
as if they were actually two totally separate entities. See Arlotto, *Introduction
to Historical Linguistics*, 22.

As this science developed various issues of the process of linguistic change became the focus of much research and discussion. One of these issues was the important consideration of the factors or causes which effected a linguistic change. Having examined the history of modern linguistics, and particularly the rise of historical linguistics which focused on linguistic change,[21] we now narrow our concentration to the causes of linguistic evolution.

The Factors of Language Change

In an attempt to narrow our focus to examine the causes which lead to language change, we face a semantic problem. Specifically, the problem has to deal with the distinction between what might be considered causes, factors, or mechanisms of linguistic change. Anttila portrays the dilemma:

> It has been almost impossible to separate the factors and mechanisms of change from its causes; indeed, even the consequences of change, that is, various classifications of change, have been given as explanations.[22]

Being cognizant of this semantic difficulty, we believe it is still expedient to cautiously proceed in the discussion of factors, causes, and mechanisms of linguistic change, recognizing that the overlap of these terms will be considerable and their contradistinction sometimes artificial.[23]

---

21. Lightfoot puts forth a dissenting opinion, arguing that the historical linguists' method is fallacious, being in reality 'the exploitation of acquired knowledge to express genetic relations'. David W. Lightfoot, *Principles of Diachronic Syntax* (Cambridge, 1979) 166.
22. *An Introduction to Historical and Comparative Linguistics*, 179.
23. Lass is a representative of those who might believe this to be a futile task:

> Language is not a 'thing', but a congeries of structures and processes in interaction; and since all of the systems involved are to a greater or lesser degree non-deterministic (in the sense of 'free' rather than 'stochastic'), neither the fact of any particular change nor its character can be predicted. If the ontology I have been proposing is plausible, the notion 'cause' in the deductive sense is wholly inappropriate: our explanandum domain is a set of interactions between non-deterministic open systems ... In other words, we are dealing with cultural phenomena, and these are not 'caused'. Language is essentially cultural, and only derivatively biological (and thus even more derivatively and distantly

In order to better understand the factors of linguistic change, we believe it is best to start with general, broad categories. Linguistic change can be restricted to two general but interlocking categories of internal and external factors:

> Linguistic change, then, is governed by two factors: On one hand there are linguistic notions such as naturalness, structure, and function, which provide the 'raw material' for change, plus the notion of perceptibility, which imposes a kind of 'ranking' on the variables of actual speech. On the other hand is a social element which, from the linguistic point of view, arbitrarily selects one of many possible, linguistically motivated, processes for sociolinguistic marking and generalization.[24]

Anttila advances a very similar position:

> One usually speaks of internal and external causation of change. These are extreme poles, a situation we have encountered often before, as it is difficult to draw a line where one ends and the other starts. Language is so integrally connected with the speech community that one has to look at the grammar of the community when studying change, and not at the grammars of individual speakers, the so-called idiolects.[25]

The principal internal factor which effects a linguistic change is the innovation. These changes may become necessary 'for no other reason than that language, as a tool in constant use is (a) liable to constant fluctuation, and/or (b) in need of constant 'repair' or renewal'.[26] An innovation may originate either with the speech of an individual or of a particular subgroup of a language community.[27] Sturtevant describes both the range and the perpetuity of linguistic innovations:

> There may be a change in the model, that is, in the speech of the person or persons who at the moment set the linguistic fashion. Such innovations are constantly arising in the speech of each one of us. We call some of them mistakes; others, which are more intentional, we call forced uses of words or awkward sentences; still

physico-chemical). Linguistic change should thus in principle be no more predictable than change in art styles ...

See Roger Lass, *On Explaining Language Change* (Cambridge, 1980) 132.
24. Hock, *Principles of Historical Linguistics*, 655 (italics his).
25. *An Introduction to Historical and Comparative Linguistics*, 180.
26. M.L. Samuels, *Linguistic Evolution* (Cambridge, 1972) 1-2 (italics his).
27. E.g., see Otto Jespersen, *Efficiency In Linguistic Change* (Denmark, 1949) 15.

others, which are fully intentional, we call figures of speech or coined words or new phrases.[28]

The procedure by which an innovation may lead to a linguistic change is beautifully stated by Saussure:

> Evolution takes the form of successive and precise innovations that include as many partial facts as could be enumerated, described, and classified according to their nature (phonetic, lexicological, morphological, syntactical, etc.). Each innovation embraces a definite and delimited area. There are two possibilities: either the area of the innovation embraces the whole territory and creates no dialectal differences (the less usual possibility), or the change affects only a part of the territory, each dialectal fact having its special zone (the more common occurrence). We can illustrate with phonetic changes, but other innovations are the same. For instance, while part of a territory may witness the change of 'a' to 'e': it is possible that on the same territory but within other limits, another change, such as 's' to 'z' will occur.[29]

From the semantic realm we may observe linguistic innovations through the examination of written records. In the history of the English language, for example, it is possible to detect semantic shifts in the use of the terms 'meat' and 'flesh'. The following columns illustrate the change in meaning through three separate periods of English usage.[30]

28. E.H. Sturtevant, *Linguistic Change* (Chicago, 1917) 29.
29. Saussure, *Course in General Linguistics*, 200 (italics his).
30. See Bloomfield, *Language*, 430. An illustration of the extent to which a single lexeme might experience semantic change can be see in the German term *Dirne*. Originally this term referred to a 'virgin'; it now is used to designate a 'prostitute'. See Raimo Anttila, *An Introduction to Historical and Comparative Linguistics* (New York, 1972) 149.

meaning:	nourish-ment	edible thing	edible part of animal body	muscular part of animal body
1st stage:	food	meat	flesh	flesh
2nd stage:	food	meat	meat	flesh
3rd stage:	food	food	meat	flesh

External factors constitute the social network in which a language change eventuates. Note for example, the remark of Weinreich, Labov, and Herzog in reference to the role of social factors in phonological change: 'Linguists who wish to avoid the study of social factors will not be able to penetrate very far into this system: there is a social matrix in which the change is embedded as well as a linguistic one'.[31] An earlier comment by Meillet is especially germane:

> Language is an institution with an autonomy of its own; one must therefore determine the general conditions of development from a purely linguistic point of view; ... but since language is [also] a social institution, it follows that linguistics is a social science, and the only variable element to which one may appeal in order to account for a linguistic change is social change, of which language variations are but the consequences—sometimes immediate and direct, and more often mediated and indirect.[32]

The origination and diffusion of linguistic change are thus influenced by social pressures which are constantly bearing upon every language. These social pressures are 'continually operating upon language, not from some remote point in the past, but as an imminent

---

31. Uriel Weinreich, William Labov, and Marvin I. Herzog, 'Empirical Foundations for a Theory of Language Change', in *Directions for Historical Linguistics*, eds. W.P. Lehmann and Yakov Malkiel (Austin, 1968) 175.
32. A. Meillet, *Linguistique historique et linguistique générale* I (Paris, 1926) 17. Cited by Weinreich, Labov, and Herzog, 'Empirical Foundations for a Theory of Language Change', 176.

social force acting in the living present'.[33] Yet, while this social pressure is incessant, it occurs in various degrees of intensity over a given time of duration. As Samuels states:

> Pressures towards change can be strong or weak and for this reason alone, some changes can be expected to take place over a limited period (say, fifty years), whereas others may be more protracted and last for anything up to a millennium.[34]

Some of the more overt forms of pressure result from the interaction between two distinct language communities. Blount and Sanches summarize the various ways interaction between different cultures can result in language change:

> External social forces that may bring about change are numerous and include such phenomena as invasions, conquests, contact, trade, migrations, institutional changes and restructuring, social movements, and revolutions. Essentially any radical change, especially where contact between different cultures is involved, brings about a restructuring of the communication system(s), thereby producing language change.[35]

Historical examples of the type of cultural contact mentioned in the above quote, with the resultant linguistic change could include the Norman conquest of England, the Dutch and English colonization of South Africa, and the Spanish colonization of Mexico. Within a generation, this type of contact can produce a significant amount of linguistic change,[36] particularly in the area of the lexicon.[37]

Another powerful social influence which affects language change is less overt but perhaps equally as effective. This is the social force of prestige. A speaker will favor forms and terms he has heard from other speakers whom he admires. The pressure elicited by prestige also has a considerable impact upon the vocabulary one chooses to use. The French influence on German shortly following the Thirty Years War might be a classic illustration of how languages change because of the prestige of the more powerful nation, in this case

---

33. William Labov, 'The Social Motivation of a Sound Change', *Word* 19 (1963) 275.
34. *Linguistic Evolution*, 154.
35. Ben G. Blount and Mary Sanches, *Sociocultural Dimensions of Language Change* (New York, 1977) 4.
36. Blount and Sanches, *Sociocultural Dimensions of Language Change*, 6.
37. Uriel Weinreich, *Languages In Contact* (New York, 1953) 56.

France.[38] Analogous to the pressure of prestige, but creating the opposite reaction, is the pressure to avoid using forms or terms that will create a social stigma. Forms and words which are considered to be *taboo* by the surrounding culture will be shunned and as a result linguistic change will soon take place.[39] The resultant avoidance of forms and words may effect a rapid linguistic change of the lexical inventory, with a virtual extinction of the unacceptable term/form.[40] An illustration of this type of change from Modern English is the present avoidance of the term 'ass', which earlier was an acceptable synchronic synonym for the term donkey.

The classic example of the impact of social pressures on linguistic change was presented by William Labov in 1963. Labov made an intensive study of speech habits of the native islanders on Martha's Vineyard.[41] He noted a marked difference in the islanders pronunciation of the first element of the diphthongs /ai/ and /au/. Instead of the usual Southeast New England [aI] and [aU], one frequently hears on Martha's Vineyard [ɐi] and [ɐu], or even [əI] and [əU]— a pattern that runs counter to the normal movement of diphthongs over the last two hundred years. As the result of a thorough analysis of the different social groups which inhabited the island, Labov was able to show that the unusual pattern of pronunciation was characteristic of those who planned to remain on the island and who thus had a positive attitude about living on Martha's Vineyard. Those who had this attitude conformed to the distinct pronunciation of these diphthongs which was commonly believed to reflect the pronunciation native to the island. Labov summarizes the significance of his findings:

> Here I would like to suggest that the mixed pattern of uneven phonetic conditioning, shifting frequencies of usage in various age levels, areas, and social groups, as we have observed it on Martha's Vineyard, is the process of linguistic change in the simplest form

38. See Hock, *Principles of Historical Linguistics*, 380. An important offshoot of this, which illustrates on a more individual level the effect of prestige, is the effect of a prestigious language upon a bilingual. 'If one language is endowed with prestige, the bilingual is likely to use what are identifiable loanwords from it as a means of displaying the social status which its knowledge symbolizes'. Weinreich, *Languages In Contact*, 59-60.

39. If massive enough, lexical taboo will require extensive lexical borrowing to replenish the lexical stock. Thus, Hock, *Principles of Historical Linguistics*, 423.

40. Labov, 'The Social Setting of Linguistic Change', 239.

which deserves the name. Below this level, at the point of individual variation, we have events which are sub-linguistic in significance. At the first stage of change, where linguistic changes originate, we may observe many sporadic side-effects of articulatory processes which have no linguistic meaning: no socially determined significance is attached to them, either in the differentiation of morphemes, or in expressive function. Only when social meaning is assigned to such variations will they be imitated and begin to play a role in the language.[42]

Thus, broadly speaking, we can posit two factors of linguistic change—those factors which accompany the natural process of evolution (internal factors), and those factors which are ultimately derived from social influences (external factors). In reality, however, it is extremely difficult to identify causes, and as is often the case, the causes are intricately interwoven.[43] We now turn to the mechanisms of language change which describe for us the processes by which internal and external factors affect language.

Mechanisms for Linguistic Change

As observed in the previous section it may be precarious to adopt hard and fast definitions for the various aspects of language change such as factors, causes, and mechanisms. However, for the sake of a more comprehensive analysis we posit that a mechanism be understood as the *process* by which language change takes place.

The discussion of the processes by which languages change was an important issue for the early historical linguists. Many of their explanations, however, have now been rejected. One mechanism, earlier historical linguistics believed described the *modus operandi* of linguistic change was the process of deterioration or decay.[44] This concept was related to the idea that the earliest language that could

41. William Labov, 'The Social Motivation of a Sound Change', 273-309.
42. Labov, 'The Social Motivation of a Sound Change', 293.
43. Antilla, *Introduction to Historical and Comparative Linguistics*, 380.
44. This is the oldest view, and outside linguistic circles still the most prevalent view of the cause of language change. Thus, Hock, *Principles of Historical Linguistics*, 627. This way of thinking may have contributed to the idea that Mishnaic Hebrew was a decadent variation of biblical Hebrew. See William Chomsky, 'How the Study of Hebrew Grammar Began and Developed', *JQR* 35 (1944-45) 301; and Robert Gordis, 'Studies in the Relationship of Biblical and Rabbinic Hebrew', in *Louis Ginzberg Jubilee Volume* (New York, 1945) 174.

be posited, a proto-language, existed in a pristine form and the subsequent, derived daughter languages were no more than corruptions of the more perfect ancestor. The idea that the earlier form of a language could be described as a 'Golden Age' is derived from this same type of thinking.[45] This concept, however, has now been virtually abandoned in linguistic circles. Hock explains the prevailing attitude among linguists concerning the concept of linguistic decay:

> Most important of all, however, was the neogrammarian insistence that decay (or improvement) are notions inapplicable to linguistic change, that reconstructed languages and their early offshoots are no more perfect than their later descendants, and that all of the linguistic phenomena that are observable in the historical development of attested languages must be considered possible also for the protolanguage and the earliest stages of its descendants.[46]

Moreover, it is impossible to prove that deviations, in the form of deteriorations from an earlier standard, should be cumulative rather than cancelling each other.[47] Put differently, how can something as directionless as a random deviation consistently crop up until it replaces the earlier convention. The moment one deviation arose, the chances are just as great that a competing deviation would arise to challenge the initial deviation's attempt to replace the earlier form.

Another mechanism which earlier linguists constituted as a process by which languages change was the mechanism which might be called the principle of greater ease or comfort. We might cite an explanation by Paul, who was a leading proponent of of this idea:

> Die Ursache, warum die Neigung zur Abweichung nach der einen Seite hin grösser ist als nach der andern, kann kaum anders worin gesucht werden, als dass die Abweichung nach der ersteren den Organen des Sprechenden in irgend welcher Hinsicht bequemer ist.[48]

---

45. The erroneous argument that an older form of a language could be considered the 'Golden Age' with a later stage representing the the 'Silver Age' has been used to describe the linguistic strata of the Hebrew Bible. E.g., see *BDB*, 758. Consonant with this fallacious way of thinking is Driver's frequent assertion that the late writing of the Chronicler was 'uncouth' or 'decadent'. See Driver, *Introduction*, 505, 535.
46. Hock, *Principles of Historical Linguistics*, 630.
47. Hock, *Principles of Historical Linguistics*, 634.
48. Hermann Paul, *Prinzipien der Sprachgeschichte* (Tübingen, 1960) 56. Cited by Weinreich, Labov, and Herzog, 'A Theory of Language Change', 111.

Harmonious with this view is the statement of Samuels: 'The principle of least effort has been amply demonstrated; its most obvious manifestation is that the shorter linguistic forms are preferred to longer ones'.[49] This hypothesis that the pursuit of ease is the principle behind the process of language change does not, however, answer many fundamental questions. For example, as Weinreich, Labov, and Herzog summarize: 'Why do not speakers go about it more quickly, and why do Language Customs split in that some speakers set out on a particular ease-seeking path whereas others retain their less comfortable pattern'?[50] Simply put, the ease of articulation mechanism hypothesis is not able to explain why languages *fail* to change.[51]

A mechanism which does provide a valid description of the process of language change is the analogical mechanism. The analogical mechanism operates upon the existing linguistic system of a given language. As Anttila states: 'Analogy is based on the mechanism of the very rules of grammar. Change results when the rules win over tradition (symbolic aspects)'.[52] The function of analogy is 'to make morphologically, syntactically, and/or semantically related forms more similar to each other in their phonetic (and morphological) structure'.[53] Note the following charts in which the analogic mechanism is behind the phonemic shifts in the Modern English and Modern German verb 'to choose'.[54]

This idea is also maintained by Anttila. See for example, *Introduction to Historical and Comparative Linguistics*, 181.

49. *Linguistic Change*, 10.
50. Weinreich, Labov, and Herzog, 'A Theory of Language Change', 111.
51. Somewhat related to this mechanism is the proposal that languages tend to change toward simpler forms. Thus Robert D. King, *Historical Linguistics and Generative Grammar* (Englewood Cliffs, 1969) 65; and Anttila, *Introduction to Historical and Comparative Linguistics*, 193. This position too, however, is very much open to question. See Hock, *Principles of Historical Linguistics*, 278.
52. *Introduction to Historical and Comparative Linguistics*, 153.
53. Hock, *Principles of Historical Linguistics*, 167.
54. Hock, *Principles of Historical Linguistics*, 168.

	Old English	Modern English
present	ceozan	choose [z]
past singular	ceas	chose [z]
past plural	curon	chose [z]
past participle	(ge-)coren	chosen [z]

	Old High German	Modern German
present	kiusan	küren
past singular	kos	kor
past plural	kuran	koren
past participle	(gi-)koran	gekoren

In both Modern English and Modern German we can see the same principle in operation with the same cognate verb. Both English and German have changed, independently, in an attempt to represent a more uniform morphological pattern in the respective languages.

Another common form of analogy operates on a proportional model. This method of analogy entails the application of an existing pattern of a language to a form in the same language which does not exhibit this pattern. This form of analogy explains the mechanism which was at the source of the shift of the earlier plural of the English *cow*, the term *kine,* to the modern form *cows*. The first proportion, in the following chart, illustrates the formula of the mechanism, while the second formula illustrates the change we have just discussed.[55]

a : á

b : $X = b'$

---

55. Hock, *Principles of Historical Linguistics*, 172.

stone   : stone-s

cow   : X = cow-s

These are some of the important mechanisms which describe the process by which a linguistic change might take place. We now turn to the prominent role played by linguistic variation. According to Blount and Sanches: 'Variation is in fact essential for language change, since it provides the material upon which social processes operate to produce significant social dimensions and categories'.[56] Hence, linguistic variation is believed to be 'the key to the mechanism of language change'.[57]

Variation

As observed from the above quote the concept of linguistic variation is an intrinsic element of the process of linguistic change. Anttila argues that the interdependence of variation and change is true not only for historical linguistics, but is in fact a universal reality:

> Without synchronic variation, change would not have a launching pad. Change is not peculiar to language alone; evolution pervades the whole of 'reality', that is, the inorganic/cosmological, the organic/biological, and the human/psychological. The whole question of variation and change in language has a direct parallel in life, which is complex self-reproducing and self-varying matter.[58]

The phenomenon of linguistic variation, which constitutes an alternative way of expression, occurs continuously in language.[59] In any given language, at any given time, phonological, grammatical, syntactical, and lexical variations are extant which deviate from the practice of the majority of the speech community.[60] Put differently, 'language is characterized by synchronic oscillation in the speech of

56. *Sociocultural Dimensions of Language Change*, 5.
57. Theodora Bynon, *Historical Linguistics* (Cambridge, 1977) 198.
58. *An Introduction to Historical and Comparative Linguistics*, 179.
59. Linguistic variation may often result when two cultures come into contact and one speech community borrows from the other. Anttila, *Introduction to Historical and Comparative Linguistics*, 155.
60. 'Most such variations occur only once and are extinguished as quickly as they arise'. Labov, 'The Social Motivation of a Sound Change', 273.

individuals'.[61] Phoneticians, for example, are able to demonstrate that
no two spoken sounds for the same phoneme of a language, even
from the same speaker, are exactly the same. Anttila comments on
the significance of this truth:

> Linguists always stress the point that no speaker pronounces the
> same sound twice in exactly the same way. If this is true of one
> speaker, there is even more variation between two speakers, and so
> on, until we reach the whole language, or even a language family.
> But in this sea of infinite variability, some variations are rule-gov-
> erned, specifically by socially shared rules. And variation does not
> manifest itself only in sound, but in all areas of language.[62]

Syntax is also characterized by this synchronic variation. As
Birnbaum notes:

> Syntactic synonymy, that is to say, the occurrence and virtual inter-
> changeability of functionally identical or nearly identical formal
> means, in part conditioned and qualified only by stylistic and other
> not strictly grammatical considerations, is thus the norm rather
> than the exception at any given stage in the diachronic variation of a
> linguistic system.[63]

Linguistic structures must thus allow for a certain flexibility which
makes allowances for a considerable amount of linguistic variation.
Bright and Rananujan note:

> It seems probable that no language is as monolithic as our descrip-
> tive grammars sometimes suggest; wherever sufficient data are

---

61. Weinreich, Labov, and Herzog, 'Empirical Foundations for a Theory of
Language Change', 167.
62. *Introduction to Historical and Comparative Linguistics,* 47.
63. Henrik Birnbaum, 'Notes on Syntactic Change: Cooccurrence vs.
Substitution. Stability vs. Permeability', in *Historical Syntax*, ed. Jacek Fisiak
(Berlin, 1984) 28-29. Syntactic variation is in fact more unintermittent than
phonological variation:

> ... while in phonology (except in stylistically conditioned free variations), once a
> gradual shift is completed, one entity perceived as distinctive (a feature, a
> phoneme) fully replaces an earlier one so that on the perceptional (acoustic) level
> an either/or situation obtains, in syntax a both/and situation (syntactic
> synonymy) may prevail for a considerable period of time. In fact, to some degree
> this is the rule, not the exception: language at all times avails itself of a variety of
> formal (structural) means to convey one and the same grammatical meaning
> (separate function or sentential meaning).

Ibid., 40-41.

available, we find diversity within languages on all levels–phonological, grammatical, and lexical.[64]

Bloomfield adds:

> In actual observation, however, no speech-community is ever quite
> uniform. When we describe a language, we may ignore the lack of
> uniformity by confining ourselves to some arbitrarily chosen type of
> speech and leaving the other varieties for later discussion, but in
> studying linguistic change we cannot do this, because all changes
> are sure to appear at first in the shape of variant features.[65]

A variation, which is an alternative way of saying the same thing,
may arise from one speaker and through various processes this feature, which was once a deviation from the norm, becomes the accepted model of the community. As Samuels states: 'Every change is, at
least in its beginnings, present in the variants of the spoken chain; it is
the process of continuous selection that ensures its imitation, spread,
and ultimate acceptance into one or more systems'.[66] Evidence for
linguistic variation may be also be inferred from the different layers
of society which constitute a dialect as well as the range of modes of
expression any given layer will employ. Anttila notes the manifold
nature of linguistic variation in a given speech community:

> But any speech community displays systematic variation on other
> scales—social layer (occupation, ethnic background, and so on), age,
> sex, and social context. The last is known as 'style', or more techni-
> cally as 'register'. Most speech communities have at least three
> varieties: the normal conversational, plus something above it
> (formal) and below it (substandard, slang). All these factors are

64. William Bright and A.K. Ramanujan, 'Sociolinguistic Variation And Language Change', in *Proceedings of the Ninth International Congress of
Linguistics*, ed. Horace G. Lunt (Cambridge, Mass., 1964) 1107. Thus it may be
concluded that the written grammars of a language are no more than
attempts to record the socially accepted standard of a language state at a particular point in time. This thesis was reiterated recently in reference to biblical
Hebrew by Dr. Moshe Goshen-Gottstein at a *Symposium of the Hebrew
Language* at the Hebrew University of Jerusalem on March 16, 1983. Goshen-
Gottstein advocated approaching the linguistic study of Biblical Hebrew in reference to the distinctive quality of each biblical book rather than making gen-
eralizing descriptions about the language as a whole.
65. *Language*, 311-12.
66. *Linguistic Evolution*, 140.

systematically incorporated into the speaker's use of the language, and thus should be spelled out in our grammatical descriptions.[67]

It may be assumed, although not completely empirically verifiable,[68] that a variation from standard usage in a given language takes on significance, and thus constitutes a linguistic change, in the following manner. First, a given speaker creates an innovation which deviates from the accepted speech pattern. This new feature immediately rivals the accepted correspondent. Secondly, this new feature, due to the prestige of the speaker, gains initial acceptance and increases in frequency among a particular subgroup of the community. Sturtevant comments on the role of the linguistic subgroup in effecting language change:

> It is suggested that a linguistic change begins when one of the many features characteristic of speech variation spreads throughout a specific subgroup of the speech community. This linguistic feature then assumes a certain social significance—symbolizing the social values associated with that group.[69]

Finally, the innovation continues to gain social acceptance and reinforcement until it spreads throughout the entire speech community. Labov nicely summarizes the process:

> Most such variations occur only once, and are extinguished as quickly as they arise. However, a few recur, and, in a second stage, they may be imitated more or less widely, and may spread to the point where the new forms are in contrast with the older forms along a wide front. Finally, at some later stage, one or the other of the two forms usually triumphs, and regularity is achieved.[70]

Thus the innovation, which initially was nothing more than a linguistic variation, becomes the newer and accepted element of the grammar or lexicon.

Variations, without which linguistic change would be impossible, result from the mechanisms of language change which were discussed in the previous section. All linguistic changes, whether

---

67. Antilla, *An Introduction to Historical and Comparative Linguistics*, 49 (italics his).
68. 'We can distinguish only in theory between the actual innovation, in which a speaker uses a form he has not heard, and the subsequent rivalry between this new form and some older form'. Bloomfield, *Language*, 408.
69. E.H. Sturtevant, *An Introduction to Linguistics* (New Haven, 1947) 81ff. Cited by Weinreich, Labov, and Herzog, 'A Theory of Language Change', 186.
70. Labov, 'The Social Motivation of a Sound Change', 273.

grammatical, syntactical, or semantic, appear initially as a linguistic variation. What was stated in the beginning of this chapter concerning the universality of language change can equally be said of the occurrence of variation within a language. No language is without variation.[71] For this reason, variation is considered by some to be an intrinsic structural element of language.[72] Thus we acknowledge the role variation plays in language change as variation and change are interdependent.[73]

Conclusion

In this chapter we have discussed some of the important issues relevant to the subject of linguistic change. Specifically, we have examined factors, mechanisms, and the important role of variation in the context of language change. In the next chapter, we restrict our focus to the study of language change in the Hebrew Bible as we examine the history of the diachronic approach to biblical Hebrew.

71. Anttila, *An Introduction to Historical and Comparative Linguistics*, 47.
72. Weinreich, Labov, and Herzog, 'A Theory of Language Change', 185.
73. Weinreich, Labov, and Herzog, 'A Theory of Language Change', 52. Bloomfield maintains that the pervasiveness of variation in language creates a difficulty for the comparative method:

> Since the comparative method does not allow for varieties within the parent language or for common changes in related languages, it will carry us only a certain distance. Suppose, for instance, that within the parent language there was some dialectal difference: this dialectal difference will be reflected as an irreconcilable difference in the related languages.

Bloomfield, *Language*, 314. The diffusion of linguistic variation has not been taken into account by generative grammarians. Weinreich, Labov, and Herzog, 'A Theory of Language Change', 125.

Chapter 2

THE DIACHRONIC STUDY OF THE HEBREW BIBLE

Introduction

As noted from the previous chapter, the *historical-comparative* approach to the study of linguistics emanated from the study of the Indo-European languages. This is not to say that early Jewish and Christian Hebrew studies completely lack any material which might be considered linguistic or philological in nature. Rather, though philological observations can be found (among the Jewish grammarians) at a very early date, historical connections were not made between languages related to Hebrew so that prospective and retrospective historical development might be recognized.

In the early Jewish Rabbinic literature, there is little discussion which might be considered linguistic in nature, apart from a few isolated statements where difficult Hebrew words were explained on the basis of Arabic or Aramaic.[1] This same trend continued in the Middle Ages despite the broader cultural milieu and the heightened interest in BH which resulted from the influence of Arabic philological studies.[2]

Beginning in the sixteenth and seventeenth centuries Christian theologians and orientalists began to compare the language of Hebrew with other Semitic languages. The most notable outcome of these efforts was the production of the Polyglot Bibles which arranged the different Semitic versions in columns as a base for com-

---

1. See for example *b. Roš Haš.* 26b where Arabic is evoked to explain the Hebrew term יְהָבְךָ (Ps 55.23).
2. Most notable in this period were the works of such scholars as Judah ibn Quraysh, Dunash ibn Tamin, Abu al-Faraj, Ibn Janah, Isaac ibn Barun, and Rabbi Jehuda Hayyug. All these scholars observed and commented upon the similarity of Hebrew with either Aramaic or Arabic. See J.H. Hospers, 'A Hundred Years of Semitic Comparative Linguistics', *Studia Biblica et Semitica, Theodora Christiano Vriezen qui munere professoris theologiae per XXV annos functus est, ab amicis, collegis, discipulis dedicata* (Wageningen, 1966) 141; and James Barr, 'Linguistic Literature, Hebrew', *EncJud* 16, 1356-58.

paring these related languages with Hebrew. These studies, however, like earlier and contemporary Jewish efforts, were restricted to making parallels and pointing out the similarities of the cognate languages to BH. Thus, historical questions were not entertained. This limitation arose from the fact that the Hebrew language was considered by many to be a sacred language, as well as the mother language of all languages. Barr explains:[3]

> During the 17th and 18th centuries the study of Hebrew linguistics, in spite of much accurate detailed knowledge was hampered and confused by its entanglement with certain more general cultural problems. It was widely supposed that Hebrew was a language of divine origin, and even that it was the language of the Deity Himself; moreover, even as a human language, it was believed to have been the original tongue of humanity, from which others had been derived.

While these works made a considerable contribution toward establishing parallel features in the cognate languages, they failed to yield any fruit for *historical-comparative* analysis:

> The comparative perspectives of medieval linguistic scholarship, even when accurate observations of similarities and differences were made, and even when certain historical data (like the difference between biblical and Mishnaic Hebrew) were known, did not assume an historical form.[4]

The aim of the 'comparative' studies through the seventeenth century was thus restricted to elucidating the 'sacred language', biblical Hebrew. It was not until the eighteenth century that we can detect any significant departure from this method. For it was at that time that Albert Schultens proposed that Arabic was not a daughter language of Hebrew but indeed should be considered as a related, sister language.[5] He advocated that Hebrew be relegated to the position of one Semitic dialect among others. This innovation, which was later accepted by other scholars, could be seen as constituting a watershed

---

3. 'Linguistic Literature, Hebrew', 1394. Similarly, Walter Baumgartner, 'Was wir heute von der hebräischen Sprache und ihrer Geschichte wissen', *Anthropos* 35-36 (1940-41) 593.
4. James Barr, *Comparative Philology and the Text of the Old Testament*[2] (Winona Lake, 1987) 76.
5. A similar assertion was made about the relation of Hebrew and Aramaic around the beginning of the nineteenth century by Samuel David Luzzatto. Chomsky, 'How the Study of Hebrew Grammar Began and Developed', 300.

in the history of Comparative Semitics.[6] This concept drove a wedge into the older, doctrinal views, and in so doing opened the way for analysis of the Semitic languages along the historical plane. Eventually, late in the nineteenth century scholars such as E. Renan, Justus Olshausen, and Bernard Stade began to analyze the Semitic languages attempting to establish the prehistory of extant Semitic languages and the reconstruction of the Proto-Semitic language.[7]

In the twentieth century, the study of Comparative Semitics has not progressed much beyond the initial observations and reconstructions. Many factors have contributed to this state of affairs. Chief among these are the specialization tendencies among Assyriologists[8] and Arabists, as well as the recent revulsion to comparativism.[9]

By way of summary, it should be noted that while the practice of explaining Hebrew by recourse to other cognate Semitic languages goes well back into the Middle Ages, it was the work of the Indo-European linguists who developed a satisfactory comparative and

---

6. For the significance of Schultens in the history of Comparative Semitics, see Moshe Goshen-Gottstein, 'Comparative Semitics—A Premature Obituary', in *Essays on the Occasion of the Seventieth Anniversary of Dropsie University*, (Philadelphia, 1979) 146, esp. n. 15.

7. See Hospers, 'A Hundred Years of Semitic Comparative Linguistics', 142; and Barr, 'Linguistic Literature, Hebrew', 1397. The earlier outline of Semitic grammar of Canini in the sixteenth century, for example, had Hebrew as its focus and was thus ahistorical. See Goshen-Gottstein, 'Comparative Semitics–A Premature Obituary', 142. For the difficulties inherent in erecting the Proto-Semitic language, see H. Polotsky, 'Semitics', in *The World History of the Jewish People, I, 1: At the Dawn of Civilization*, ed. E.A. Speiser (Tel-Aviv, 1964) 109; Moshe Goshen-Gottstein, 'The History of the Bible–Text and Comparative Semitics—A Methodological Problem', *VT* 7 (1957) 196-97; Joshua Blau, 'Some Difficulties in the Reconstruction of "Proto-Hebrew" and "Proto-Canaanite"' in *In Memoriam Paul Kahle*. BZAW 103, eds. Matthew Black and Georg Fohrer (Berlin, 1968) 29-43; and Barr, *Comparative Philology and the Text of the Old Testament*, 78.

8. The prejudiced interference of Comparative Semitists had in some ways impeded the study of Akkadian. See Polotsky, 'Semitics', 103.

9. See E. Ullendorf, 'Comparative Semitics', *Current Trends in Linguistics*, VI, 3: Afroasiatic Languages, 263; and C. Brockelmann, 'Stand und Aufgaben der Semitistik', in *Beiträge zur Arabistik, Semitistik und Islamwissenschaft* (Leipzig, 1944) 3-4. This negative reaction to comparativism occurred in Indo-European Linguistics as well. The anti-comparativist attitude may be ultimately linked to Saussure with his emphasis on synchronic analysis taking precedence over diachronic analysis. Thus Polotsky, 'Semitics', 103.

historical method. An intrinsic element of this method is the potential projection or reconstruction of a common ancestor or Proto-Language from which the extant languages descended by predictable changes.[10] This methodology established the criterion by which Semitic scholars could examine individual Semitic languages along diachronic lines. Thus, it was not until the establishment of this procedure that the diachronic study of Biblical Hebrew became a viable possibility.

History of the Diachronic Approach to the Hebrew Bible

The same presuppositions which prevented early medieval scholars from going beyond mere parallel studies to *historical-comparative* analysis also prevented these scholars from observing the historical development of the Hebrew language within the Hebrew Bible. The idea of the Hebrew language as the *Philologia Sacra* caused the early Rabbis, and through their influence later Jewish and Christian scholars, to treat all of the Bible as one unit.[11] With regard to the early Christian scholars, Friedman's statement is directly to the point:[12]

> For a great many Christian scholars, Hebrew was a one-dimensional language in which Scripture was written. Because Hebrew was God's language and God never changes, it was easy and perhaps logical to assume that Hebrew had a uniform character and personality and was not subject to either internal or historical development and change.

10. Barr, 'Linguistic Literature, Hebrew', 1396; and *Comparative Philology and the Text of the Old Testament*, 78-79.
11. For this concept among the early Rabbis, see Saul Lieberman, *Hellenism in Jewish Palestine* (New York, 1962) 53; and Kutscher, 'Mishnaic Hebrew', *EncJud* 16, 1592. The Rabbis were aware of the linguistic difference between BH and MH, however. The following quote from *b. Ḥul.* 137b is illustrative: לשון תורה לעצמה ולשון חכמים לעצמה. By contrast, for illustrations of an apparent lack of awareness of the distinction between BH and post-biblical Hebrew on the part of the Rabbis, see Ezra Zion Melammed, *Bible Commentators* 2 vols. (Jerusalem, 1975) 1. 100-103 [In Hebrew].
12. Jerome Friedman, *The Most Ancient Testimony* (Athens, Ohio, 1983) 39. This attitude doubtlessly still exists and is parallel to Hindus of modern times who have a similar veneration for the Veda.

Consequently, as long as this way of thinking remained the prevalent view, any notion of linguistic change or language development within the Hebrew Bible could never be entertained.

The diachronic study of biblical Hebrew may be said to have begun in 1815 with the publication of *Geschichte der hebräischen Sprache und Schrift*[13] by Wilhelm Gesenius. In many regards Gesenius, in light of what was discussed in the previous section, was ahead of his time as he made observations similar to those which would later become fashionable after the Indo-European historical linguists developed the comparative-historical method. Barr discusses Gesenius's contribution in this historical context:[14]

> Gesenius wrote before the unfolding of the comparative-historical linguistics of the 19th century, and his careful attention to Arabic or Syriac still does not produce a developmental framework; though historical in one sense, he had not yet made the systematic projections back into prehistory which were essential to the full comparative method.

Nevertheless, in the above work, Gesenius analyzed the language of the biblical books while frequently drawing attention to late linguistic features. This presentation shows that Gesenius was aware of historical linguistic changes *within* the Hebrew Bible. Furthermore, Gesenius's contribution represents the first attempt toward a diachronic analysis by a Semitic or biblical scholar. But, as mentioned above, the proper conceptions about language change and about the nature of Biblical Hebrew were not yet part of the scholarly consciousness among Semitic scholars.

After Gesenius had made these seminal, diachronic observations, virtually nothing was done to continue this investigation until the beginning of the twentieth century. At that time many of the arguments stemming from the source critical analysis[15] of Graf-Wellhausen were challenging traditional views concerning the authorship and composition of biblical books, particularly the Pentateuch.[16] Many studies were subsequently undertaken to deter-

---

13. (Leipzig).
14. 'Linguistic Literature, Hebrew', 1396.
15. Usually, but perhaps mistakenly, called literary criticism. See Gene M. Tucker, 'Editor's Foreward', in *The Old Testament and the Literary Critic*, by David Robertson (Philadelphia, 1977) viii.
16. Graf-Wellhausen was the impetus to the study of the Hebrew Bible along diachronic lines in the same as Albert Schultens provided the prod for the study of Comparative Semitics along historical/comparative lines. In the same

mine if the conclusions of Graf-Wellhausen could be substantiated along linguistic lines.[17] Particularly noteworthy were the studies by Carlous V. Ryssel, *De Elohistae Pentateuchici Sermone*,[18] Heinrich Holzinger, *Einleitung in den Hexateuch*,[19] J. Estlin Carpenter and George Harford, *The Composition of the Hexateuch*,[20] and Jonathan Kräutlein, *Die sprachlichen Verschiedenheiten in den Hexateuch-quellen.*[21] These studies were the first attempts to analyze Biblical Hebrew against the backdrop of the sweeping conclusions of source critical analysis which were beginning to win the day. At the same time, D.S. Margoliouth, Leo Metmann, and especially S.R. Driver widened the scope of inquiry in observing that Biblical Hebrew contained chronologically distinct linguistic layers. These scholars, in a similar fashion to the work of Gesenius almost a century earlier, observed that books such Chronicles, Ecclesiastes, Esther, Daniel, Ezra, and Nehemiah were linguistically different from earlier books of the Hebrew Bible.[22] Driver, in his *Introduction*, in particular, presented a thorough analysis of the language of each biblical book. Of special interest was his not infrequent manner of describing the language of a late biblical writer as *New Hebrew.*[23]

Though the contributions of these early scholars, particularly Gesenius and Driver, were of great significance, the diachronic study of Hebrew received a greater impetus from Arno Kropat's *Syntax des Autors Chronik* in 1909.[24] Kropat's landmark study was devoted to

way, until the albatross of sacred language was removed the historical study of Biblical Hebrew could not proceed.
17. See M. Tsevat, *A Study of the Language of the Biblical Psalms* (Philadelphia, 1955) 1; and Barr, *Comparative Philology and the Text of the Old Testament*, 76.
18. (Lipsiae, 1878).
19. (Leipzig, 1893).
20. (London, 1902).
21. (Leipzig, 1908).
22. D.S. Margoliouth, 'Language of the Old Testament', in *A Dictionary of the Bible*, vol. 3, ed. James Hastings (Edinburgh, 1900) 31; Leo Metmann, *Die Hebräische Sprache. Ihre Geschichte und lexikalische Entwicklung seit Abschluss des Kanons* (Jerusalem, 1904) 5; S.R. Driver, *Introduction*, 455, 505, 518, 525, 530-31, 535-40; *Hebrew Tenses*, 108, 196; and 'On Some Alleged Linguistic Affinities of the Elohist', *Journal of Philology* 11 (1882) 201-36.
23. The same phrase was also used to described late biblical books by Ewald. See *Lehrbuch* § 3 d, 25. Equally significant was Driver's description of the earlier BH stratum as 'classical'. E.g., see Driver, *Introduction*, 454 n.
24. See bibliography.

analyzing the linguistic features of the Chronicler. His *modus operandi* was contrasting the books of Chronicles with the parallel passages in Samuel/Kings. Presupposing that the Chronicler had as his source a massoretic prototype of Samuel/Kings, Kropat was able to demonstrate the language of the Chronicler through his linguistic adjustments. This work was an extremely important contribution to the diachronic study of Biblical Hebrew as there now existed a systematic presentation of the features of the post-exilic Book of Chronicles in contrast to the earlier language of Samuel/Kings.

In subsequent years many of the Hebrew Grammarians like Bauer and Leander and Joüon were aware of the differences between pre-exilic and post-exilic Hebrew but gave little attention to the specific features which distinguish these two phases of the language.[25] This omission did not mean however that the understanding of Biblical Hebrew was coming to a standstill in the 1920's and 1930's. On the contrary, great contributions were made improving our knowledge of Biblical Hebrew particularly through the discovery and subsequent deciphering of important tablets. Of tremendous importance was the discovery of cuneiform tablets from ancient Ugarit of Syria in 1929. These texts, written in a North-West Semitic dialect, provided an enormous amount of information which greatly enhanced our understanding of biblical literature.[26] The study of Biblical Hebrew was also enhanced as the language of the Hebrew Bible could now be compared with similar material in texts from a cognate language from approximately the fourteenth century BC. The study of Biblical Hebrew had indeed taken on a new dimension. However, little was done to follow up Kropat's investigation of the diachronic study of Biblical Hebrew. Rather, with the discovery of the ancient Ugaritic language, the interest and emphasis in biblical scholarship was naturally on the earlier stages of Hebrew, particularly early Hebrew poetry which seemed to share the same genre and structure of the Ugaritic literature.[27] Thus the influence of Gesenius's and Kropat's

---

25. See H. Bauer and P. Leander, *HG* § 2 q, 26; and P. Joüon, *Grammaire* § 3 a, b, 4-6. The apparent reason for this deficiency was the convenience of presenting the language of Biblical Hebrew as a monolithic unity. See comments in Chapter 1.

26. Ugaritic is generally regarded as a Canaanite dialect. For a differing view, see Albrecht Goetze, 'Is Ugaritic A Canaanite Dialect?' *Language* 17 (1941) 127-38.

27. Chiefly, the studies of W.F. Albright, 'The Old Testament and the Canaanite Language and Literature', *CBQ* 7 (1945) 5-31; *Yahweh and the Gods of*

diachronic studies was negligible as scholars naturally became preoccupied with the great finds at Ras Shamra.

If the first great find of the twentieth century, the discovery of Ugaritic language at Ras Shamra, impeded the diachronic study of the linguistic layers within the Hebrew Bible, the subsequent discovery of the Dead Sea scrolls at Qumran catapulted Gesenius's and Kropat's earlier findings into sharper focus. In particular, after the early publications of the literature from Qumran, Abba Bendavid and E.Y. Kutscher resurrected the diachronic study of the Bible back into scholarly consciousness. *The Biblical Language and the Rabbinic Language*, a two volume study by Abba Bendavid, appeared in 1967 and made full use of the linguistic finds of the Dead Sea scrolls in the discussion of the typologies of Biblical and Mishnaic Hebrew. Kutscher made full use of the finds from Qumran and his vast contribution to this field can be seen in his *The Language and Linguistic Background of the Isaiah Scroll (1QIsa^a)*[28] and in his posthumous work *A History of the Hebrew Language*.[29]

In the 1970s and 1980s the diachronic study of Hebrew has continued to blossom in Israel, particularly through the efforts of Avi Hurvitz, a former student of Kutscher. Since the completion and publication of Hurvitz's Hebrew University doctoral dissertation, *Biblical Hebrew in Transition—A Study in Post-Exilic Hebrew and its Implications for the Dating of Psalms* in 1972, Hurvitz has exclusively directed his efforts to the historical analysis of BH.[30] His contributions to this field have been substantial, but perhaps his greatest donation has been his insistent effort to fashion an objective methodology for the diachronic study of Biblical Hebrew.

Hurvitz's approach to the history of Biblical Hebrew is harmonious with the work of Kropat. He insists, as did Kropat before him, that parallel chapters in the Bible are the most important aids for diachronic research.[31] Like Kropat, he affirms that the differences between the parallel texts in Chronicles and Samuel/Kings are due to

Canaan (London, 1968); Frank Cross and David Freedmen, *Studies in Ancient Yahwistic Poetry* (Missoula, 1975); David Robertson, *Linguistic Evidence in Dating Early Hebrew Poetry* (Missoula, 1972); and Stanley Gevirtz, *Patterns in the Early Poetry of Israel*[2] (Chicago, 1973).

28. (Leiden, 1974).

29. (Jerusalem, 1982). For Kutscher's seminal studies in the diachronic analysis of Hebrew, see bibliography.

30. See bibliography.

31. Hurvitz, *Lashon*, 16 n. 10.

different languages rather than due to stylistic tendencies of different authors. Because Hurvitz believes that lexicographical differences are good indicators in distinguishing pre-exilic from post-exilic Hebrew, he is particularly attentive to Aramaic words that might be found in post-exilic Hebrew.[32]

Apart from the contribution to this field made by these Israeli scholars, Robert Polzin published an important work on the diachronic study of Biblical Hebrew in 1976. In this work, *Late Biblical Hebrew: Toward An Historical Typology Of Biblical Hebrew Prose*,[33] Polzin selectively used Kropat's analysis of the Chronicles to establish nineteen features which he argues are the features of Late Biblical Hebrew. Polzin then analyzed samplings from JE, Dtr, as well as the CH of 2 Samuel/1 Kings in light of these criteria and maintains that he can demonstrate that JE, Dtr, and the CH contain features of Classical or pre-exilic Hebrew, while P (which is divided into Pg and Ps) shows later features and is thus the link between Classical Hebrew and the language of the Chronicles.

Methodologically, Polzin differs from Hurvitz in two major areas. First, in his analysis of the Hebrew of Chronicles he refuses to use synoptic texts which are parallel to Samuel/Kings, believing thereby, that he can get back to the actual language of the Chronicler.[34] He does this to avoid the suspicion that the differences which might exist in the Chronicler's synoptic text might be due to the fact that the Chronicler was using a different source, i.e. not the proto-Massoretic Text of Samuel/Kings.[35] Secondly, Polzin maintains that grammatical-syntactical distinctions provide more objective criteria than lexicographical features and should thus receive more weight in discussions of the typology of Biblical Hebrew. Hurvitz does not make this distinction and in fact the balance of his evidence for post-exilic Hebrew is of a lexicographical nature. A third distinction arising from

---

32. For Hurvitz's methodological procedure in detecting late Aramaisms, see Avi Hurvitz, 'The Chronological Significance of "Aramaisms" in Biblical Hebrew', *IEJ* 18 (1968) 234-40.

33. See bibliography.

34. In this respect he also differs from Kropat as well.

35. Similarly, Werner E. Lemke, 'The Synoptic Problem in the Chronicler's History', *HTR* 58 (1965) 349-63. It is curious, however, that Polzin not infrequently uses the differences in the parallel texts from Chronicles with Samuel/Kings to indicate late language. See *Hebrew*, 41, 46, 53, 58, 62. How Polzin is sure that the non-synoptic portions of Chronicles are not borrowed from a source of unknown date is not stated.

Polzin's work, which is itself non-methodological but has methodological implications, regards Polzin's evaluation of Aramaic influence. As pointed out above, Hurvitz argues that many features of post-exilic Hebrew are due to the influence of Aramaic upon Hebrew. Polzin, on the other hand, minimizes this influence maintaining that the changes which occurred in Biblical Hebrew resulted more from the natural evolution of the language.[36]

Subsequent to the recent work done by both Hurvitz and Polzin, several dissertations emphasizing the diachronic study of Hebrew have been completed. These include the studies of A.R. Guenther, *Diachronic Study*, Ronald Bergey, *Esther*, and Andrew E. Hill, *Malachi*. The influence of both Hurvitz and Polzin, remains perceptible, however. Guenther's and Hill's works are based on Polzin's study, while Bergey worked under Hurvitz's supervision.[37]

With this brief history of the historical approach to the study of the Hebrew Bible as background, we shall now analyze the Book of Ezekiel using the criteria put forth by Polzin as a starting base. Our objective is to determine the relative status of the Book of Ezekiel in the continuum of BH as this work is virtually ignored in Polzin's study. These findings will enable us to determine whether or not

36. Polzin did not, however, establish a framework for linguistic change. See following chapter.

37. It should be noted in this survey of the history of the treatment of the diachronic study of the Hebrew Bible, we have only mentioned those works which exclusively dealt with our topic. Other works could be cited which, while not exclusively devoted to the analysis of the history of Biblical Hebrew, are aware of the development of the Hebrew language within the Hebrew canon. Chiefly among these works are those of *BDB*; Mireille Hadas-Lebel, *Manuel d'histoire de la langue hébraïque* (Paris, 1976) 97-105; Isaac Avinery, 'The Aramaic Influence on Hebrew', *Leshonenu* 3 (1930-31) 273-90, esp. 276 [In Hebrew]; M.B. Schneider, 'The Literary Hebrew Language', *Leshonenu* 6 (1935) 301 [In Hebrew]; H. Torczyner, 'The Influence of Aramaic on Biblical Hebrew', *EM* 1, 593 [In Hebrew]; Baumgartner, 'Was wir heute von der hebräischen Sprache und ihrer Geschichte wissen', 609; Jonas Greenfield, *The Lexical Status of Mishnaic Hebrew* (Ph.D. dissertation, Yale University, 1956) xvi; Mary Ellen Chase, *Life and Language in the Old Testament* (New York, 1955) 145-46; and numerous works by Chaim Rabin including *The Syntax of the Biblical Language*, (Jerusalem, 1967) 1 [In Hebrew]; 'Foreign Words', *EM* 4, 1079 [In Hebrew]; 'Hebrew', *EM* 6, 52, 69 [In Hebrew]; 'Hebrew', in *Current Trends in Linguistics*, ed. Thomas Sebeok (Moulton, 1970) 6. 316; and 'Hebrew and Aramaic in the First Century', in *The Jewish People in the First Century*, 2 vols., eds. S. Safrai and M. Stern (Van Gorcum, 1976) 2. 1014-15.

Ezekiel should be considered as a possible representative of the transitional link between EBH and LBH, a position Polzin claims is best exemplified by the P source.

Chapter 3

EZEKIEL AND THE TYPOLOGY OF BIBLICAL HEBREW

Introduction

The most comprehensive empirical work to date on the history of Biblical Hebrew has to be Polzin's *Hebrew*, published in 1976. In this study Polzin selectively used Kropat's analysis of the Chronicles to establish nineteen features which he argues are the features of LBH. These features are divided between those which are due to natural evolution or change (A), as opposed to those which are attributable to Aramaic influence (B). The following is a comprehensive list of Polzin's LBH characteristics:

A1. Radically reduced use of אֵת with pronominal suffix.

A2. Increased use of אֵת before noun in the nominative case.

A3. Expression of possession by prospective pronominal suffix with a following noun, or לְ + noun, or שֶׁל + noun.

A4. Collectives are construed as plurals.

A5. Preference for plural forms of words and phrases which the earlier language used in the singular.

A6. Less frequent use of the infinitive absolute in immediate connection with a finite verb of the same stem or as a command.

A7. More frequent use of the infinitive construct with בְּ and כְּ not preceded by וַיְהִי (וְהָיָה).

A8. Repetition of a singular word = Latin quivis.

A9. Merging of the third feminine plural suffix with the third masculine plural suffix.

A10. Seldom occurrence of lengthened imperfect or cohortative in first person singular.

A11. וַיְהִי is rare.

A12. Substantive occurs before the numeral and in the plural.

A13. Increased use of the infinitive construct with לְ.

B1. Order of material weighed or measured + its weight or measurement.

B2. ל is often the mark of the accusative.

B3. נ in the preposition מן is often not assimilated before a noun without an article.

B4. Use of ל emphatic before the last element of a list.

B5. רבים used attributively before the substantive.

B6. Use of צד ל.

On the basis of these LBH features Polzin analyzed samplings from JE and Dtr as well as the CH of 2 Samuel/1 Kings. His findings indicated that JE, Dtr, and the CH contain features of Classical or pre-exilic Hebrew, while P (which is divided into Pg and Ps) shows later features and is thus the link between Classical Hebrew and the language of the Chronicles.

A quick survey of Chapter 5 of this study will reveal that not a few of Polzin's LBH descriptions have been adopted as valid illustrations of LBH. Some of the other criteria used by Polzin, however, are open to serious question. For example, Polzin claims that one characteristic of LBH has to do with the way the cardinal numbers occur with the substantive (A12): 'In appositional relationship, the Chronicler prefers to place the substantive before the numeral and most always puts it in the plural. This is contrary to the older general practice of putting the number first'.[1] Whereas Pg follows the EBH practice of putting the number first, Polzin claims that Ps follows the later practice preferring the substantive before the number. Thus Ps would resemble the LBH of the book of Chronicles. While it is true that within the body of material Polzin has labelled Ps there is a strong tendency for the substantive to precede the number, it is also true that close to 90%[2] of his examples comes from the list of Numbers 7. In long lists, irrespective of the stage of BH, it is customary for the substantive to occur first.[3] Another instance in which Polzin has misinterpreted the evidence occurs in B1, again involving his

---

1. *Hebrew*, 58.

2. Moreover, thirty-six of the forty-five attestations can be accounted for in the phrase אילם חמשה עתודים חמשה כבשים בני שנה חמשה.
Num 7.17 = Num 7.23 = Num 7.29 = Num 7.35 = Num 7.41 = Num 7.47 = Num 7.53 = Num 7.59 = Num 7.65 = Num 7.71 = Num 7.77 = Num 7.83.

3. *GKC* § 134 c, 432; Hurvitz, *Linguistic Study*, 167; and Rendsburg, 'Late Biblical Hebrew and the Date of "P" ,' 71. In fairness to Polzin he is aware that substantives normally occur first in lists, such as in Num 7. See *Hebrew*, 59-60. In this acknowledgement he asserts that he will return to this issue but fails to do so.

interpretation of the Pˢ material of Numbers 7. The issue of import in B1 is the position of the material weighed in relation to the actual weight or measurement. As Polzin accurately states: '... the Chronicler often has: material weighed or measured + its weight or measure'⁴—the opposite of what is preferred in EBH. Polzin claims that Pˢ employs the LBH construction in eighteen of the possible twenty chances. What is immediately striking about the list of references from Pˢ is that twelve of these eighteen occurrences not only come from Numbers 7 but occur in the identical phrase:

מזרק אחד כסף שבעים שקל בשקל הקדש

While one can argue about the merits of counting one phrase as twelve distinct illustrations of a phenomenon, what is even more problematic about the use of this example is that the syntax of the phrase has been ignored. Each occurrence of this phrase occurs as a predicate nominative to the nominal subject וקרבנו.⁵ This being the case it becomes impossible for the weight to precede the substantive which is the predicate nominative. Otherwise, the phrase would have to be translated 'And his offering was seventy shekels, after the shekel of the sanctuary'. This is clearly not what the author intended. Simply put, the syntax of these phrases in Numbers 7 demands that the material weighed precede the weight. As a result, Pˢ has six illustrations of the feature, not eighteen.

Another illustration of Polzin's misinterpretation of the data occurs with respect to A3. Only the possessive construction ל + noun occurs in the P material. All thirteen examples in Pᵍ come from the list in Numbers 1 in the phrase פקדיהם למטה, while the three listed examples in Pˢ also occur in a list in the phrase פקדיהם למשפחתם of Numbers 4. The evidence of this feature in both Pᵍ and Pˢ is restricted to the occurrence of a single word פקדיהם in a list context.⁶ Thus this evidence for this late character of P is at least not

---

4. See *Hebrew*, 61.
5. More specifically each occurrence of the phrase is the second predicate nominative succeeding the first predicate nominative in the recurring phrase קערת כסף אחת שלשים ומאה משקלה. It is somewhat curious why Polzin does not use this phrase as evidence as it would illustrate the same phenomenon, as he understands it, just as well.
6. For the problem of using A3 as a characteristic of Pᵍ and Pˢ, see Zevit, 'Converging Lines of Evidence Bearing on the Date of P', 499-500. Moreover, for the possibility that the suffix of פקדיהם is not in fact prospective, see Hurvitz, *Linguistic Study*, 166.

as strong as Polzin suggests, and probably should be disregarded altogether.

Two other characteristics Polzin claims should be considered as a characteristic of LBH should be dismissed outright for lack of evidence. These criteria include (A13) the increased use of the infinitive construct with the preposition ל, and the use of the emphatic ל before the last element of a list. With regard to the increased use of the infinitive construct with the preposition ל, Polzin's own analysis shows that this tendency occurs with the same frequency in EBH.[7] With regard to the use of the emphatic ל before the last element of a list (B4), Polzin acknowledges that this is not a late feature *per se* and that the feature occurs quite frequently in EBH.[8] Furthermore, no linguistic contrast in EBH can be established. There is thus no strong reason for using these phenomena as a basis for analysis in the discussion of the typology of BH.

In addition to these individual problems regarding Polzin's interpretation of the data, other difficulties have recently been raised with respect to his methodology. These include his failing to normalize the length of the text samplings, his method of counting verses of text for statistical analysis, and his failure to explain the chronological distinctions of the data in the terms of linguistic change.[9] The latter deficiency is best illustrated from Polzin's own words: 'It is not altogether clear to me how one is to interpret the nature of these non-Aramaic changes in the late language ...'[10] In addition to these criticisms could be included his abrupt discussion of the avoidance of the features נא and הודו in LBH.[11] What is troublesome about citing these two examples is not that the reluctance to employ these terms is characteristic of LBH, but that they were not included as part of the nineteen features of LBH and hence do not enter into any further lin-

---

7. Polzin, *Hebrew*, 60-61.
8. Polzin, *Hebrew*, 67-68.
9. See Zevit, 'Converging Lines of Evidence Bearing on the Date of P', 496; and especially, Hill, *Malachi*, 39-45. To these criticisms could be added Polzin's disregard for the different types of contexts which might affect language use; particularly as seen in his failure to make an exception for the lists of Numbers 1 and Numbers 7 above. Perhaps even a better illustration is the classification of 1 Chr 1–9 as part of the Chronicler's prose, without any mention that a genealogical list might influence the type of linguistic features which might have occasion to appear.
10. *Hebrew*, 2.
11. See *Hebrew*, 71-72.

guistic discussion. That is, they are not invoked to provide a linguistic contrast with EBH material, neither are they part of subsequent charts which incorporate lists of LBH features and their occurrence or nonoccurrence in biblical sources.[12]

Another problematic technique employed by Polzin is his use of proportion or ratios. Sources which exhibit similar proportional preferences may be typologically linked and thus distinguished from those sources which exhibit different proportions. An example of Polzin's use of this technique may be observed in his discussion of Pg's use of the collective plural (A4):[13]

Corpus	Ratio (singular : plural)
JE	7:2
CH	27:23
Dtr	4:3
Pg	9:10

On the basis of such proportion, Pg is classified as typologically similar to LBH since the plural verb occurs with the collective noun on ten of nineteen possible occasions. Dtr, on the other hand, which uses the plural verb on three of a possible seven occasions, is typologically different and must be classified as EBH. This distinction is too precise and makes such a typological distinction seem artificial.[14]

Despite these deficiencies Polzin has made an immense contribution to the diachronic study of BH as he did attempt to work on a systematic basis and examined a large cross section of BH in his

12. Something similar occurs with regard to feature A10. After Polzin lists this feature as a characteristic feature of LBH, he never again returns to discuss the frequency of this characteristic in the biblical sources he is analyzing.
13. *Hebrew*, 98.
14. Similarly, see Zevit, 'Converging Lines of Evidence Bearing on the Date of P', 500. By criticizing Polzin's use of these ratios in this instance we are not insinuating that the use of proportions or statistics is invalid. They are a legitimate linguistic means of measurement for detecting language change. See Bloomfield, *Language*, 407; and Antilla, *An Introduction to Historical and Comparative Linguistics*, 187.

analysis. He has laid the groundwork for subsequent study, including this work. Hence, we believe it to be legitimate to use his findings as a basis for comparison. In this regard, we will proceed to analyze the language of Ezekiel, using Polzin's proportional method and LBH criteria, apart from the unacceptable features discussed above. But before we begin this task it is imperative that we consider whether or not this is a feasible exercise. Polzin analyzed the linguistic nature of LBH prose; the book of Ezekiel is part of the prophetic genre. In view of subsequent studies which have emphasized, with Polzin, the necessity of restricting diachronic analysis to prose,[15] we must determine if it is a meaningful exercise to compare prophetic literature with the results of studies which have been expressly limited to the study of biblical prose.[16]

While recent scholars in the diachronic study of BH have been quick to point out that the subject of their respective inquiries has been limited to prose as opposed to poetry, the compelling reasons why this is the case have not been equally forthcoming. Certainly the rationale for such a restriction is to avoid including those qualities which are purported to be those which characterize poetry—such features as the avoidance of the use of the definite article, the avoidance of the use of אֲשֶׁר, and the avoidance of the definite object marker אֵת.[17] But is this sufficient basis for making such a sharp generic demarcation?

While the prose/poetry distinction is thought to be universal, the delineation of the actual distinction between the two is problematic.[18] The problem not only entails establishing well-defined criteria to distinguish between the two, but framing acceptable definitions for each genre as well. With regard to prose, for example, Carroll states: 'Literary criticism today does not have any well and sharply defined

15. E.g. Guenther, *Diachronic Study*; Bergey, *Esther*; Hill, *Malachi*.
16. It should be noted, however, that Polzin frequently cites prophetic passages, in his study, without qualification.
17. See David Noel Freedman, 'Pottery, Poetry, and Prophecy: An Essay on Biblical Poetry', *JBL* 96 (1977) 5-26; and Wilfred G.E. Watson, *Classical Hebrew Poetry* (Sheffield, 1984) 54. To these features could possibly be added the distinctive vocabulary that sometimes characterizes poetry.
18. M. O'Conner, *Hebrew Verse Structure* (Winona Lake, 1980) 66; and John Lotz, 'Elements of Versification', in *Versification. Major Language Types*, ed. W.K. Wimsatt (New York, 1972) 1.

set of elements by which a sample of prose may be characterized'.[19] In theory, however, prose is believed to be more nearly representative of the actual speech of a designated people while poetry constitutes a literary, but understandable variation of normative speaking habits.[20] Suggested literary devices which are believed to set poetry apart from prose include such phenomena as alliteration, rhyme, meter, terseness, and parallelism.[21] With regard to biblical literature, however, the distinction between prose and poetry is particularly difficult to maintain as Kugel states: 'The same traits that seem to characterize Hebrew "poetry" also crop up in what is clearly not poetry'.[22] This poetic quality of biblical prose led Eduard Sievers to suggest that most of the Bible was poetry.[23] In view of the distinct nature of the biblical genre Kugel contends that the prose/poetry

19. John B. Carroll, 'Vectors of Prose Style', in *Style In Language*, ed. Thomas Sebeok (New York, 1960) 283.
20. See Michael Riffaterre, 'Describing Poetic Structures: Two Approaches to Baudelaire's *les Chats*', in *Structuralism*, ed. Jacques Ehrmann (New York, 1970) 188; Jan Mukařovsky, 'Standard Language And Poetic Language', in *Linguistics and Literary Style*, trans. Paul L. Garvin, ed. Donald C. Freeman (New York, 1970) 46, 52; Manfred Bierwisch, 'Poetics and Linguistics', in *Linguistics and Literary Style*, 110; Edward Stankiewicz, 'Linguistics and the Study of Poetic Language', in *Style In Language*, ed. Thomas A. Sebeok (New York, 1960) 69-81; and Francis Landy, 'Poetics and Parallelism: Some Comments on James Kugel's " The Idea of Biblical Poetry" ', *JSOT* 28 (1984) 69.
21. See Paul Kiparsky, 'The Role of Linguistics in a Theory of Poetry', in *Language as a Human Problem*, eds. M. Bloomfield and E. Haugen (New York, 1974) 235; Lotz, 'Elements of Versification', 5; Roman Jakobson, 'Linguistics and Poetics', in *Style In Language*, 366. With regards to BH, see Winfred G.E. Watson, 'Verse-Patterns in Ugaritic, Akkadian, and Hebrew Poetry', *UF* 7 (1975) 483-92; *Classical Hebrew Poetry*, 46-47; Raphael Sappan, *The Typical Features of the Syntax of Biblical Poetry in its Classical Period* (Ph.D. dissertation, The Hebrew University, 1974) [In Hebrew]. Since the work of Lowth, parallelism has in particular been singled out as an inherent feature of biblical poetry. James L. Kugel, *The Idea of Biblical Poetry* (New Haven, 1981) 12; and Perry B. Yoder, 'Biblical Hebrew', in *Versification. Major Language Types*, ed. W.K. Wimsatt (New York, 1972) 63. It is also been suggested that parallelism is a regular feature of Semitic poetry. G. Douglas Young, 'Ugaritic Prosody', *JNES* 9 (1950) 133 n. 31.
22. Kugel, *The Idea of Biblical Poetry,* 63. For the blurring of the distinction between prose and poetry in Biblical Hebrew see also Moshe Goshen-Gottstein, *Hebrew and Semitic Languages* (Jerusalem, 1964) 15-16 [In Hebrew]; and Hurvitz, *Lashon*, 56-57.
23. Kugel, *The Idea of Biblical Poetry*, 76.

distinction which has been erected is in fact a Hellenistic imposition upon biblical literature.[24]

In view of the uniqueness of the biblical material, the sharp distinction between poetry and prose should not be maintained in a diachronic study. Even if this distinction is posited there is no apparent reason to treat the two literary genres by separate rules, as it is possible to find linguistic changes in each style.[25] Biblical poetry, for example, does not constitute a different dialect.[26] But even if this prose/poetry distinction is maintained it could still be considered legitimate to compare Polzin's findings on the linguistic nature of LBH prose with the prophetic Book of Ezekiel.

The question of comparing Polzin's conclusions on LBH prose with prophetic material was first broached by Hill in his study of the Book of Malachi. On the basis of Hoftijzer's study of the occurrence of the אֵת syntagmeme,[27] in conjunction with the more recent studies by Andersen and Freedman on the density of the prose particles אֲשֶׁר, אֵת, and the definite article (the morpheme ה only),[28] Hill concluded that Malachi resembled prose rather than poetry. He therefore concluded that comparison with Polzin's results was a valid inquiry. If we apply this same test to the Book of Ezekiel, we find equally compelling reason to consider Ezekiel to be biblical prose. Note Hoftijzer's statement concerning the use of the direct object marker אֵת in Ezekiel: '[In the remaining part of Ezekiel] one comes across a usage of *'t* syntagmemes which *qua* density shows similarity with what we have discovered in narrative and legal material'.[29] According to Andersen and Freedman's theory, prose particles will compose 5% or

24. Kugel, *The Idea of Biblical Poetry*, 85.

25. This is the underlying presupposition of Hurvitz's *Lashon* which is a work dedicated solely to the delineation of late Hebrew features in the Psalms. For a more recent linguistic analysis of LBH in the Psalms, see Elisha Qimron, 'The Language of the Second Temple in the Book of Psalms', *BM* 23 (1978) 139-50 [In Hebrew].

26. Hurvitz, *Lashon*, 56.

27. J. Hoftijzer, 'Remarks Concerning the use of the Particle 'T in Classical Hebrew', *Oud Testamentische Studien* 14 (1965) 1-99.

28. Francis I. Andersen and David Noel Freedman, *Hosea*. Anchor Bible (New York, 1980) 60.

29. Hoftijzer, 'Remarks Concerning the use of the Particle 'T in Classical Hebrew', 69 (italics his). The 'remaining parts' refers to those sections which are not designated as having a poetic genre, and hence unlike Ezek 19; 27; 28.12-19; 32.2-15.

less of a poetic genre and roughly 10-15% of prose texts.[30] Using this criteria, Ezekiel also appears to qualify for prose as the prose particles make up 12.3% of the text of Ezekiel—2,298 prose particles out of a possible 18,722 words.[31] This suggestion is apparently consistent with the view of those scholars who maintain that the style of the later prophets is virtually identical to the earlier prose. Thus Gesenius's statement from many years ago with regard to the later prophets, should be understood as applying to Ezekiel as well:[32]

> The prophets, at least the earlier, in language and rhythm are to be regarded almost entirely as poets, except that with them the sentences are often more extended, and the parallelism is less regular and balanced than is the case with the poets properly so called. The language of the later prophets, on the contrary, approaches nearer to prose.

Similarly, Tucker, approaching this question from a different angle noted: 'Early prophets uttered brief oracles, while later prophets learned to compose longer speeches. What had begun as poetry became prose as prophets developed from ecstatics to preachers and religious thinkers'.[33] The evidence suggests that this is a true description of the Book of Ezekiel.

---

30. Andersen and Freedman, *Hosea*, 60. For the 10% figure see, David Noel Freedman, 'Another Look At Biblical Hebrew Poetry', in *Directions in Biblical Poetry*, ed. Elaine R. Follis (Sheffield, 1987) 14, 15, 17.

31. According to our counting. Andersen and Forbes counted 2,403 prose particles in Ezekiel which would constitute 12.8% of the book. See Francis I. Andersen and A. Dean Forbes, ' "Prose Particle" Counts in the Hebrew Bible', in *The Word of the Lord Shall Go Forth. Essays in Honor of David Noel Freedman*, eds. Carol L. Meyers and M. O'Conner (Winona Lake, 1983) 174-75.

32. *GKC* §2 q, 14. Similarly, see Chaim Rabin, 'Hebrew and Aramaic in the First Century', 1014; Joshua Blau, 'Thoughts on the Tense System in Biblical Literature', in *Festschrift for I.A. Seeligmann, Studies in Bible and the Ancient World*, eds. I. Zakovich and A. Rofe (Jerusalem, 1982) 21 [In Hebrew]; Hurvitz, *Lashon*, 57; and Bergey, *Esther*, 19 n. 2. The change in prophetic literature of BH roughly parallels chronologically the poetic mutation around 600 BC. For reference to the latter, see M. O'Connor, *Hebrew Verse Structure* (Winona Lake, 1980) 164.

33. Gene M. Tucker, *Form Criticism of the Old Testament* (Philadelphia, 1971) 56. With respect to Ezekiel's prose style, see M.H. Segal, *Introduction to the Bible*, 2 vols. (Jerusalem, 1964) 1. 412-13 [In Hebrew]; W.O.E. Oesterley and Theodora H. Robinson, *An Introduction to the Books of the Old Testament* (New York, 1958) 325 n. 1; and Freedman, 'Another Look At Biblical Hebrew Poetry', 14-15.

Thus there is a defensible basis for comparing Polzin's results on the typology of biblical prose with the book of Ezekiel.[34] The results should prove particularly significant as they will enable us to determine how Ezekiel compares typologically with the P, the source which Polzin maintains is the transition link between EBH and LBH.

In the following discussion, Polzin's criteria for LBH, as modified by the above discussion, are listed. Following the LBH characteristics, the results of Polzin's findings for the samplings of JE, CH, Dtr, Pg, Ps, Ezra, N2 are given where they are available. We then compare these with what we have found in the Book of Ezekiel.[35] Explanation of the data or the results may follow the tables where deemed necessary. Particular attention will then be devoted to the results of the findings from Ezekiel with what is found in the P material, in determining which source of material better functions as a transitional source form EBH to LBH.[36]

---

34. While we are maintaining that the bulk of the Book of Ezekiel be considered prose, we still affirm that some of the sections of the book be viewed as poetic, in spite of Kugel's arguments. Poetic passages, including those sections which are introduced as lamentations, include such passages as Ezek 17.1-9; 19; 21; 22.23-31; 26; 27; 28.1-19; 31; 32. See Hoftijzer, 'Remarks Concerning the use of the Particle 'T in Classical Hebrew', 78; Sappan, *The Typical Features of the Syntax of Biblical Poetry in its Classical Period*, esp. 65; and Freedman, 'Another Look At Biblical Hebrew Poetry', 17-18. This concession does not however detract from the possibility of comparing Polzin's results with the Book of Ezekiel as no conclusions on how Ezekiel's language compares with other biblical materials will be determined in the final analysis by any portions of Ezekiel which might be considered poetic. Again, as we have noted the supposed poetic/prose distinction only affects linguistically the relative frequency of the particles אֵת, אֲשֶׁר, and the definite article. Apart from discussions which deal specifically with these particles, there should be no reason why legitimate comparisons cannot be made.

35. Apart from the data on the Book of Ezekiel, the following information can be found in Andrew E. Hill's 'Dating Second Zechariah: A Linguistic Reexamination', *HAR* 6 (1982) 105-34. Following the suggestion of Hill, I am reducing the ratio to the smallest denominator to make the points of comparison more precise. Hill's methodological approach of basing comparison on the basis of occurrence per 1000 verses is used only when the disproportionate sizes of the various sources could possibly distort the results. In a discussion such as A1 where all the ratios are reduced to the denominator of one, this technique no longer becomes necessary. For his methodology see, *ibid*.

36. In this vein, criterion A 10, namely the rare occurrence of the lengthened imperfect or cohortative will not be analyzed as Polzin provides no data for Pg or Ps concerning this feature. Nor does he analyze JE, CH, or Dtr. If this fea-

Ezekiel and Polzin's Typology

A1. *Radically reduced use of* את *with the pronominal suffix*
The comparison expressed in the following ratios is the occurrence of
the verb with a verbal suffix (left number of the ratio) contrasted with
the occurrence of את with the pronominal suffix (right number of
the ratio).

JE	1.81/1	49 vbsf/27 את
CH	2.00/1	50 vbsf/25 את
Dtr	1.63/1	67 vbsf/41 את
Pg	0.46/1	51 vbsf/103 את
Ps	0.25/1	23 vbsf/91 את
Chr	10.07/1	141 vbsf/14 את
Ezra	5.53/1	16 vbsf/3 את
N2	0	23 vbsf/0
N1	4.37/1	35 vbsf/8 את
Ezek	1.53/1	272 vbsf/178 את

These findings indicate that the verbal suffix is generally preferred
over the use of את with the pronominal suffix in BH. We also see that
there is a tendency to use the verbal suffix in later Hebrew in greater
proportion than in EBH. Also significant is the fact that both Ps and
Pg actually prefer the use of the the direct object marker את with
the pronominal suffix. Although this is a distinctive feature of P in
contrast to other portions of BH, this evidence should not be dismissed
as unique. To do so, as Polzin and Hill do, is to ignore evidence which
suggests an association of P with EBH and thus to assume their
conclusion that P is late.

ture where taken into account, Ezekiel's only occurrence of the phenomenon
(26.2) would be harmonious with LBH, given the one occurrence of this feature
in Chronicles.

A2. *Increased use of* אֵת *before noun in the nominative case*

JE	0
CH	0
Dtr	0
Pg	0
Ps	5.19 occurrences per 1000 vss
Chr	5.84 occurrences per 1000 vss
N^2	18.16 occurrences per 1000 vss
Ezek	8.6 occurrences per 1000 vss

Most of the occurrences of this phenomenon occur in the book of Ezekiel. Ezekiel demonstrates this feature more than any other source and to a greater frequency than the Chronicler, but less than N^2.

A4. *Collectives are construed as plurals*

JE	10 out of 47	21.3%
CH	23 out of 50	46%
Dtr	7 out of 16	43.8%
Pg	10 out of 19	52.6%
Ps	14[37] out of 21	66.7%
Ezra	12 out of 13	92.3%
N^2	11 out of 11	100%
Chr	25 out of 27	92.3%
Ezek	9 out of 10[38]	90%

A5. *Preference for plural forms of words and phrases which the earlier language used in the singular*

JE	0

37. Polzin lists fifteen occurrences for P^s but he mistakenly included Num 16.11 which has a double subject.
38. See discussion in Chapter 5.

CH	0
Dtr	0
Pg	0
Ps	0
Chr	28.28 occurrences per 1000 vss
Ezra	4.76 occurrences per 1000 vss
N[2]	22.4 occurrences per 1000 vss
Ezek	20.41 occurrences per 1000 vss[39]

A6. *Less frequent use of the infinitive absolute in immediate connection with a finite verb of the same stem or as a command*

JE	64.83 inf. ab. per 1000 vss
CH	51.36 inf. ab. per 1000 vss
Dtr	18.55 inf. ab.per 1000 vss
Pg	7.35 inf. ab. per 1000 vss
Ps	15.57 inf. ab. per 1000 vss
Ezra	0
Chr	10.71 per 1000 vss
Ezek	26.69 per 1000 vss

A7. *More frequent use of the infinitive construct with בְּ and כְּ not preceded by* (וַיְהִי(ה)

JE	3 out of 7	42.9%
CH	0 out of 5	0%
Dtr	3 out of 7	42.9%
Pg	0 out of 3	0%
Ps	9 out of 9	100%
Ezra	4 out of 4	100%
N[2]	2 out of 2	100%
Chr	21 out of 26	80.8%
Ezek	48 out of 54[40]	88.9%

39. See discussion in Chapter 5.
40. See discussion in Chapter 5.

A8. *Repetition of a singular word=Latin quivis*

JE	0
CH	0
Dtr	0
Pg	0
Ps	0
Ezra	4.76 occurrences per 1000 vss
N²	0
Chr	16.58 occurrences per 1000 vss
Ezek	0[41]

A9. *Merging of the third feminine plural suffix with the third masculine plural suffix*

JE	0 out of 3	0%
CH	0 out of 1	0%
Pg	5 out of 7	71.4%
Ps	6 out of 15	40%
Ezra	1 out of 1	100%
Chr	9 out of 9	100%
Ezek	80 out of 144[42]	56%

A11. ויהי *is rare*

JE	7.03 occurrences per 1000 vss
CH	60.99 occurrences per 1000 vss
Dtr	74.21 occurrences per 1000 vss
Pg	52.92 occurrences per 1000 vss
Ps	12.11 occurrences per 1000 vss
Chr	33.10 occurrences per 1000 vss
Ezra	4.76 occurrences per 1000 vss
N¹	78.96 occurrences per 1000 vss

41. It is tempting to list the occurrence of החלונות והחלונות in Ezek. 41.16 to illustrate this phenomenon, but we agree with the massoretic accentuation which suggests that the second term introduces a new clause.
42. See discussion in Chapter 5.

Ezek   48.67 occurrences per 1000 vss

The use of והיה is as follows:

Dtr   7.42 occurrences per 1000 vss
Pg   23.52 occurrences per 1000 vss
Ps   8.65 occurrences per 1000 vss
Chr   1.95 occurrences per 1000 vss
Ezra   0
N[1]   11.33 occurrences per 1000 vss

Ezek   1.57 occurrences per 1000 vss

A12. *Substantive occurs before the numeral and in the plural*

JE	0 out of 10	0%
CH	0 out of 20	0%
Dtr	1 out of 16	6.3%
Pg	2 out of 152	1.3%
Ps	9 out of 57	15.8%
Ezra	21 out of 22	95.5%
N[1]	3 out of 9	33.3%
Chr	76 out of 120	63.3%
Ezek	9 out of 141[43]	6.4%

---

43. Thus Polzin's repeated assertion that the substantive often precedes the numeral in Ezekiel is not borne out by the facts. See Polzin, *Hebrew*, 58-59.

B1. *Order of material weighed or measured + its weight or measure*[44]

Pg	0 out of 3	0%
Ps	6 out of 18	33.3%
Ezek	9 out of 9[45]	100%

B2. ל *is often the mark of the accusative*

Pg	0
Ps	0
Ezra	28.56 occurrences per 1000 vss
N^2	8.96 occurrences per 1000 vss
Chr	38.93 occurrences per 1000 vss
Ezek	3.14 occurrences per 1000 vss[46]

B3. נ *in the preposition* מן *is often not assimilated before a noun without an article*

---

44. Polzin has no discussion concerning JE, CH, and says that Dtr uses the EBH pattern on two occasions. He does have more discussion about the LBH sources, but only tells us how many times they illustrate the LBH pattern. Hence, we are not able to put the picture into proper prospective. His findings concerning the LBH sources may be demonstrated as follows:

Ezra	19.04 occurrences per 1000 vss
N^1	5.65 occurrences per 1000 vss
N^2	26.88 occurrences per 1000 vss
Chr	9.75 occurrences per 1000 vss

45. This feature as set forth by Polzin resembles the LBH feature discussed in Chapter 5 of this study concerning the position of the measurement dimension in relation to the measurement. The book of Ezekiel often places the measurement dimension before the measurement in accord with LBH practice. Those illustrations which had the measurement as the substantive do not appear to be what Polzin understood in the citing of this characteristic and none of those references have figured into the conclusions concerning the practice of B1 above.

46. See discussion in Chapter 5.

Chr   51 occurrences[47]

B5. רבים *used attributively before the substantive.*[48]

JE	0
CH	0
Dtr	0
Pg	0
Ps	0
Ezra	0
N2	4.48 occurrences per 1000 vss
Chr	0.975 occurrences per 1000 vss[49]

Ezek   0

B6. *Use of* עד ל

JE	0
CH	0
Dtr	0
Pg	0
Ps	0
Ezra	14.28 occurrences per 1000 vss
N1	0
N2	0
Chr	12.68 occurrences per 1000 vss
Ezek	0

47. Polzin does not specify if these are found in the non-parallel texts only so it is not possible to set a ratio as in the other findings.

48. Hill maintains that this feature is 'probably the weakest of all Polzin's diagnostic categories'. See 'Dating Second Zechariah: A Linguistic Reexamination', 127.

49. This feature occurs one other time in BH, in Prov 19.21.

Polzin's LBH Features

LBH Features	JE	CH	Dtr	Pg	Ps	Ezek	Ezra	N^2	Chr
A1							X		X
A2					X	X		X	X
A4						X	X	X	X
A5						X	X	X	X
A6				X			X	X	X
A7					X	X	X	X	X
A8							X	X	X
A9				X		X	X		X
A11					X		X		X
A12							X		X
B1						X			X
B2						X	X	X	X
B3									X
B5								X	X
B6							X		X

Conclusion

By way of summary, several observations should be made particularly in reference to the breakdown of the above table. First of all, it should be noted that all of these features are extant in Chronicles and absent in material considered to be EBH—JE, CH, and Dtr. This reinforces the suggestion that these features are in fact characteristics of LBH. Next, we should notice, that Pg contains two of the fifteen LBH features and Ps contains three late characteristics. Hence, they both demonstrate more of a typological affinity with EBH.[50] This being the

50. It should be remembered, especially in light of Chapter 5 of this work, that these fifteen characteristics of LBH are by no means the exhaustive description

case, the likelihood that P is the best representative of the transitional link between EBH and LBH is diminished. Ezekiel, on the other hand, shares seven of the fifteen LBH characteristics found in Chronicles. Thus, on the basis of Polzin's usable criteria, the Book of Ezekiel, a work virtually ignored in Polzin's *Hebrew*, appears to be a superior model of the transition state between EBH and LBH. These findings appear to be harmonious with the conclusions of Hurvitz's study, *A Linguistic Study of the Relationship between the Priestly Source and the Book of Ezekiel*.[51] In this work, Hurvitz demonstrated conclusively that the morphological and lexical status of the Book of Ezekiel consistently represented language of a later linguistic stratum than language of like content from the source designated as P. As Polzin's and Hurvitz's criteria have preliminarily indicated that Ezekiel is a good candidate to represent the transitional stage between EBH and LBH, it will now be our task to investigate the language of the Book of Ezekiel using broader criteria to ascertain whether Ezekiel is in fact a viable representative for the link between the stages of pre-exilic and post-exilic BH. But before we begin our investigation, we must first consider the methodology to be used in the present study.

of LBH. It is conceivable that another selective arrangement of LBH features might show JE, CH or Dtr as sharing more LBH characteristic features than P, particularly if lexical features could be included in the picture. These fifteen features have been used in this analysis only because they are the features set forth as representative of LBH in Polzin's *Hebrew*.

51. See bibliography.

Chapter 4

METHODOLOGY

Introduction

The methodology used in this study will not differ substantially from the methodologies previously employed in diachronic Biblical Hebrew research.[1] This method, whether stated or implied in the previous studies, involves the execution of two linguistic principles: linguistic contrast, and linguistic distribution.

In order to be able to ascertain the linguistic changes that have occurred in Ezekiel, relative to earlier material, grammatical and lexical features in Ezekiel which differ from linguistic features extant in EBH must be demonstrated. This method involves the principle of linguistic contrast, or linguistic opposition. We may note for example the occurrence of the verb כסם in Ezek 44.20 in the sense of 'shearing' or 'cutting'. This term, which is unique to this passage in BH, is apparently synonymous to the verb גזז which occurs almost exclusively in EBH. Hence, we might feel justified in asserting that כסם is the LBH equivalent for the earlier גזז and that a lexical replacement can be observed based upon this opposition. And yet, as we noticed, the occurrence of כסם is unique to the book of Ezekiel. Thus, since it is not distributed in other portions of literature considered to be LBH, the occurrence of the term in Ezekiel might be due to other factors than those which demonstrate historical change. The occurrence of this term in Ezekiel may be accounted for simply because it was part of Ezekiel's idiolect. Consequently, it is necessary that a second principle, the principle of linguistic distribution, be simultaneously employed. The principle of linguistic distribution must be evoked to rule out the possibility that linguistic differences could be due to stylistic tendencies. On the other hand, linguistic distribution by itself is inefficient as there could be an unequivocal

---

1. For the most detailed treatment of the methodology for diachronic research, see Avi Hurvitz, 'Linguistic Criteria for Dating Problematic Biblical Texts', *Hebrew Abstracts* 14 (1973) 74-79; and 'The Chronological Significance of "Aramaisms" in Biblical Hebrew', *IEJ* 18 (1968) 234-40.

diffusion of a feature in LBH that is absent from EBH and yet, this state of affairs could have resulted from the fact that EBH simply had no occasion to employ this feature. Several lexical examples of this phenomenon in Ezekiel include the occurrence of אבן (9.4; 21.12), אבק[2] (9.4; 24.17; 26.15), and מדינה in Ezek 19.8. All these terms are clearly LBH, but a corresponding EBH equivalent is not extant. It is easy to imagine, particularly in reference to מדינה,[3] how historical realities dictated when this term might be employed. Linguistic distribution involves determining whether the feature which exists in Ezekiel, which differs from what we find in EBH, is distributed among other sources which are known to be linguistically late.[4] These sources include biblical works which are generally recognized to be LBH, such as Esther, Daniel, Ezra, Nehemiah, and Chronicles. The simultaneous employment of these two principles are sufficient controls by which we can determine when linguistic change has occurred in book of Ezekiel. Once this has been demonstrated, the literature from the DSS and Tannaitic sources will be examined to determine if the linguistic change which began in LBH literature continued in later sources.

A classic illustration of the use of these controls for demonstrating a diachronic shift can be seen in the contrast of the occurrence of the terms מלכות/ממלכה, with the meaning 'kingdom'. Our first indication of any possible historical relationship between the terms ממלכה and מלכות may be observed from the Chronicler's preference for מלכות in texts where the parallel text of Samuel employed the term ממלכה. Observe the following examples:[5]

2 Sam 5.12	וכי נשא ממלכתו
1 Chr 14.2	כי נשאת למעלה מלכותו
2 Sam 7.12	והכינתי את ממלכתו
1 Chr 17.11	והכינותי את מלכותו
2 Sam 7.16	וממלכתך עד עולם לפניך
1 Chr 17.14	והמלכותי עד העולם

2. That these first two terms had no EBH equivalent was observed by Hill. See *Malachi*, 111.

3. For a discussion of the historical use of this term, see E.Y. Kutscher, 'Dating the Language of the Genesis Apocryphon', *JBL* 76 (1957) 291-92.

4. For this principle, see Bloomfield, *Language*, 407.

5. For these illustrations, see Hurvitz, *Lashon*, 81; and Bergey, *Esther*, 32.

This preference for מלכות is particularly evident in LBH, especially in Daniel and Esther where only מלכות is used. This trend continued in the DSS where מלכות occurs fourteen times while the earlier term ממלכה occurs only once.[6] In the writings of MH, only מלכות is used.

The distribution of the terms מלכות/ממלכה illustrates the methodology used in this study. The occurrence of these terms in Samuel and Chronicles illustrates not only that the two terms are synonymous but that מלכות appears to be the later linguistic equivalent for ממלכה. This is the principle of linguistic contrast or linguistic opposition. Next, we observed that מלכות which does not occur in EBH, occurs very frequently in LBH literature. This observation takes into account the diffusion of the lexeme—the principle of linguistic distribution. That מלכות is the later LBH equivalent for ממלכה is reinforced by the what is found in post-biblical literature. There we saw an unequivocal preference for מלכות over the earlier ממלכה.

Another premise adopted by modern researchers in diachronic study is the accepted postulate that the Massoretic Text be accepted *in toto* in this kind of linguistic analysis. This is not to affirm that the Massoretic Text is free from corruptions, but to acknowledge both the possibility that difficult readings may be incongruous due to lack of additional information, and our lack of certainty in correctly restoring readings that are corrupt.[7] In essence, it is to affirm that linguists must treat literature as text.[8]

In addition to these broad methodological criteria, other presuppositions bearing on how this study shall be conducted include the following. First, we believe the practice begun by Kropat and adopted by Hurvitz of comparing a text with an earlier text which may be its source, is a solid procedural *modus operandi*. This procedure is especially beneficial in distinguishing late linguistic features used by the Chronicler in contrast to the earlier language reflected in

---

6. See Kuhn, *Konkordanz*, 125; and *DJD* VII, 327.
7. Cf., Barr, *Comparative Philology and the Text of the Old Testament*. See also, S.R. Driver, 'On Some Alleged Linguistic Affinities of the Elohist', 217; Hurvitz, *Lashon*, 67; 'Linguistic Criteria for Dating Problematic Biblical Texts', 74-76; Bergey, *Esther*, 17-19; Hill, *Malachi*, 46-47; and 'Dating Second Zechariah: A Linguistic Reexamination', 113.
8. Thus H.G. Widdowson, *Stylistics and Teaching of Literature* (London, 1975) 6.

Samuel/Kings. By observing the differences in the Chronicler's language with the earlier Samuel/Kings we are in a position to see first hand how the Hebrew language changed.[9] This equally applies to the 'additional' material in Chronicles which reflects late Hebrew.[10] Furthermore, in opposition to Polzin, we believe that a comprehensive analysis of Ezekiel's language is worthy of consideration in determining linguistic developments which have occurred in the book. Polzin has suggested that grammatical-syntactical criteria are a more objective basis for describing language change than lexicographical analysis.[11] This premise is open to question. It should be noted that Polzin gives no rationale why this should be so. Indeed, no such hierarchical bifurcation of criteria exists in linguistic literature. Following Polzin, Hill claims that the recognition of grammatical-syntactical change as a superior measurement of language change to lexicographical change is universal in the field of linguistics.[12] To support this assertion he cites Lehman's *Introduction*.[13] Lehman's discussion, on the page in question, however, is related to the difficulty of tracing *semantic* change of a particular term from a prehistoric stage. This discussion has nothing to do with the unequivocal evidence that exists in BH regarding a lexical replacement of an EBH term by a LBH term. In effect, the citation says nothing about the superiority of grammatical-syntactical analysis over lexical analysis in

9. This procedure has not gone without criticism. Polzin objects to this procedure on the grounds that the *Vorlage* of the Chronicler might not be identical to the proto Massoretic text of Samuel/Kings. But even if we accepted the basis of Polzin's objection—that we cannot be sure the Chronicler was using as his *Vorlage* the proto Massoretic text of Samuel/Kings—comparing these parallel texts still represents the best method for observing how the Hebrew language changed. Unless, of course, one wants to argue that the language of the Chronicler is not after all later Hebrew than what is found in Samuel/Kings. This premise is categorically rejected by Polzin himself who utilizes the language used in the Chronicles as the representative language of LBH.

10. Thus we agree with S.R. Driver's thesis that the additional material in the Chronicles, not contained in Samuel/Kings, is either the Chronicler's own composition or has been borrowed from a contemporary source. See Driver, *Introduction*, 525. For a different view concerning the Chronicler's sources, see H.G.M. Williamson, *1 and 2 Chronicles*. New Century Bible Commentary (London, 1982) 19-21.

11. A premise recently adopted by Fredericks as well. See Daniel C. Fredericks, *Qoheleth's Language: Re-evaluating its Nature and Date* (Lewiston, 1988) 27.

12. Hill, *Malachi*, 45.

13. Lehman, *Historical Linguistics: An Introduction*, 209.

measuring language change, and thus Polzin's and Hill's assumption remains unfounded. Indeed, it is difficult to avoid the suspicion that Polzin relegates lexicographical study to a secondary status because this evidence conflicts with his major argument that P is the mediating source between EBH and LBH. As Polzin admits: 'The number of lexicographic features in P which can be shown to be definitely or probable features of LBH is unusually small'.[14] Since this distinction is without foundation we believe lexicographical change should be recognized as being on equal footing with grammatical-syntactical developments in attempts to describe language change.

Before our study can actually proceed it is first necessary to comment briefly upon a particular aspect of the language of Ezekiel which has methodological implications and could be considered somewhat distinctive. This involves the book's use of earlier sources. This consideration is an issue of vital importance in Kropat's work, but has received little attention in subsequent works on the diachronic study of BH.

Sources in the Book of Ezekiel

As Kropat's study on the language of Chronicles was based in large part on examining the differences in the Chronicler's language with his sources in Samuel/Kings, it is natural to turn to the question of the biblical sources which might have been used in the book of Ezekiel before engaging in linguistic analysis. While many still question the validity of attempts to establish literary dependency in BH,[15] Michael Fishbane's new work, *Biblical Interpretation In Ancient Israel,* has shown in a comprehensive fashion that literary dependency is a widespread phenomenon in biblical literature. In addition, this work has produced models of types of literary dependency which serve as guides in the quest for determining an author's sources. When literary dependency can be demonstrated we have opportunity to see old material embedded in a later literary work. This adds a further dimension to the diachronic study of Hebrew as we are able to examine two chronologically different language strata in the same

---

14. *Hebrew*, 151. See preceding chapter.
15. See for example, Hurvitz, 'Linguistic Criteria For Dating Problematic Biblical Texts', 75; and Kenneth Stanley Freedy, *The Literary Relations of Ezekiel. A Historical Study of Chapters 1–24* (Ph.D. dissertation, University of Toronto, 1969) 404.

literary context. The probability of finding earlier source material in the book of Ezekiel is strong as it has long been recognized that Ezekiel was heir to a rich literary tradition.[16]

The chief difficulty in the endeavor of determining sources is the distinction between the common use of a literary tradition against the actual citation or use of a specific biblical text. The 'Call of Ezekiel' (1.1-3.15),[17] the 'Allegory of Unfaithful Jerusalem' (16),[18] and 'The Two Eagles and the Vine' (17)[19] may qualify for the former whereas Ezekiel 4-5, 22.25-28, and 44.9-16 are some of the texts which apparently made use of other biblical texts.[20]

16. See Y. Kaufmann, *History of the Religion of Israel*4, 4 vols. (Jerusalem, 1937-56) 3. 534-42 [In Hebrew]; M.S. Segal *Introduction to the Bible*, 2. 391, 398 ff.; W. Zimmerli, 'The Special Form- and Traditio-Historical Character of Ezekiel's Prophecy', *VT* 15 (1965) 515-27; Michael Fishbane, 'Famine', *EM* 7, 386 [In Hebrew]; and Millar Burrows, *The Literary Relations of Ezekiel* (Philadelphia, 1925).

17. See N. Habel, 'The Form and Significance of the Call Narratives', *ZAW* 77 (1965) 309-14.

18. See G. Addison Wright, *An Investigation of the Literary Form, Haggadic Midrash, in the Old Testament and Intertestamental Literature* (Ph.D. dissertation, Catholic University of America, 1965) 230-49.

19. Zimmerli, *Ezekiel* I, 360; and Jon D. Levenson, *Theology of the Program of Restoration of Ezekiel 40–48* (Missoula, 1976) 82-84.

20. This list of texts in Ezekiel which reinterpreted earlier biblical texts should not be viewed as exhaustive but rather as representative. Other examples could be cited such as the use of Deut 24.16 in Ezek 18.20; the use of Exod 6.2-9 in Ezek 20.4-11, 33-36; the use of Exod 31.13 in Ezek 20.12; and the use of Gen 49.10 in Ezek 21.32. See Michael Fishbane, 'Torah and Tradition', in *Tradition and Theology in the Old Testament*, ed. Douglas A. Knight (Philadelphia, 1977) 276-77, 79; 'The Sign in the Hebrew Bible', *Annual for the Study of the Bible and the Ancient Near East* 1 (1975) 233-34 [In Hebrew]; Greenberg, *Ezekiel*, 332-33; and William Moran, 'Gen. xlix, 10 and its Use in Ez xxi, 32', *Biblica* 39 (1958) 405-25. To these texts could be added numerous formulaic expressions in the Book of Ezekiel which Ezekiel shares with other literary sources. Some of these expressions include phrases such as נשא עון (Ezek 4.4 = Lev 16.22 ff.), ונבלה וטרפה (Ezek 4.14 = Lev 17.15), ולא תחוס עיני וגם אני לא אחמול (Ezek 5.11 = Deut 13.9), גבעה רמה, ותחת כל עץ רענן (Ezek 6.13 = Deut 12.2), מלאו את הארץ חמס (Ezek 8.17 = Gen 6.13), etc. For further discussion of Ezekiel's use of formulaic expressions, see W. Zimmerli, *I Am Yahweh*, trans. Douglas W. Stott (Atlanta, 1982).

In Ezekiel 4–5 there are numerous terminological connections to the punishments promised for disobedience in Leviticus 26.[21] The affinity of Ezek 4.16-17 to what we find in Lev 26.26,39 is particularly striking. In Ezek 4.16-17, as in Lev 26.26, 39, reference is made to (1) breaking the staff of bread, (2) eating bread by weight, and (3) to the phrase 'pine away in their iniquity'. In chapter 5 of Ezekiel, reference to the covenant curses of Leviticus 26 is continued. Here we see how the covenant curses of Leviticus have become Ezekiel's prophetic dooms. What in the former is a threat contingent upon breach of covenant appears in the latter as certain prediction of accomplished wrongdoing.[22] Taken from the catalogue of curses in Leviticus 26 are (1) the eating of the flesh of offspring (Lev 26.29 = Ezek 5.10), (2) the scattering of the people abroad (Lev 26.33 = Ezek 5.10), (3) the double threat of famine and plague (Lev 26.25-26 = Ezek 5.12), (4) making the land a חרבה 'waste' (Lev 26.31, 33 = Ezek 5.14), (5) the breaking of the staff of bread (Lev 26.26 = Ezek 5.16), (6) the threat of of wild beasts that will deprive the people of their children (Lev 26.22 = Ezek 5.17), and (7) the threat of God's coming sword (Lev 26.33 = Ezek 5.2, 12, 17).[23] What is of particular significance is that in two of these references there is an abrupt grammatical abnormality due to a sudden change of person. In Ezek 5.2 God tells Ezekiel: 'A third part shalt thou burn in the fire in the midst of the city, when the days of the siege are fulfilled; and thou shalt take a third part, and smite it with the sword round about her; and a third part thou shalt scatter to the wind, וחרב אריק אחריהם[24] "and *I* will draw out a sword after them"'. The latter phrase represents an awkward insertion of the referent (God) into the directions for the symbolic act.[25] There is an abrupt shift from the second person, represented by the addressee, to the first person with God acting as the speaker. This change can best

---

21. For discussion of the function of Ezek 4–5 in the wider context of the book, esp. Chapters 4–24, see Michael Fishbane, 'Sin and Judgment in the Prophecies of Ezekiel', *Interpretation* 38 (April 1984) 133-34.
22. Thus, Greenberg, *Ezekiel*, 126.
23. For a fuller discussion of the use of the curses enumerated in Lev 26 in the Book of Ezekiel, see Fishbane, 'Famine', 386.
24. The phrase is repeated in 5.12.
25. For insight on the function of this shift of person in this context, see Michael Fishbane, 'The Qumran Pesher and Traits of Ancient Hermeneutics', in *Proceedings of the Sixth World Congress of Jewish Studies* 1 (Jerusalem, 1977) 109-10.

be explained as due to the fact that the phrase has been lifted almost verbatim from Lev 26.33 in the semantically equivalent phrase והריקתי אחריכם חרב, where God was the speaker in the enumeration of curses. Similarly, in verse six, before the enumeration of curses, Jerusalem's offences are described in third person: 'And she hath rebelled against Mine ordinances in doing wickedness more than the nations, and against My statutes more than the countries that are round about her; for במשפטי מאסו *"they* have rejected my statutes" '. This latter phrase, which again represents an abrupt change of person in Ezekiel 5, is the identical phrase which occurs in Lev 26.43. These two grammatical incongruities have resulted from the fact that the phrases involved are contextually unadjusted citations from Lev 26. 33 and Lev 26.43 respectively. In other words, the incongruity results from the author's lifting material from his source without harmonizing the older material to his text. This same type of incongruity which results from quoting a source occurs also in the historical cuneiform inscriptions of the Assyrian king Adad-Nirari III. In the best preserved stele of this inscription the king is describing his military and architectural achievements in the first person when suddenly the text abruptly changes to the third person *imḫur* 'He received' two thousand talents of silver.[26] A statement has been borrowed from another source and not adapted to the new context. This is analogous to what we see in Ezekiel 5—material, directly borrowed from an existing source, is at variance with the new literary environment.[27] And for our purposes it supports the claim that Ezekiel is applying Leviticus 26, a text which antedates his own situation in the exile, to his contemporaries.

26. Hayyim Tadmor, 'The Historical Inscriptions of Adad-Nirari III', *Iraq* 35 (1973) 141-43. Another possible biblical illustration may be observed in Ezra 5.3-4 which seems to be based on Tattenai's account in Ezra 5.6-10. If this be the case it helps to explain the unusual occurrence of the verb מהרנא. The verb has been lifted from verse nine and not adjusted to its newer context. See H.G.M. Williamson, 'The Composition of Ezra i-vi', *Journal of Theological Studies* 34.1 (1983) 20. The same phenomenon may be observed in the use of sources in the Samaritan Pentateuch. See Jeffrey H. Tigay, 'An Empirical Basis for the Documentary Hypothesis', *JBL* 94 (1975) 334.

27. For a defense of these incongruities on other grounds in biblical literature and in the literature of the ancient Near East, see Moshe Greenberg, 'The Design and Themes of Ezekiel's Program and Restoration', *Interpretation* 38 (April, 1984) 185-89.

Ezekiel 22.25-28 clearly borrows and elaborates upon a Zephanian prototype of Zeph 3.1-4. The shared phraseology and subjects unequivocally suggest that there is a literary dependence involved. The list of officials addressed is almost identical and even the same metaphors are employed to describe their contemptible behavior.[28] Furthermore, the priests are accused in both passages of 'doing violence to the Torah'. Only in these two biblical texts does the verb חמס have תורה as its object. In addition, the literary dependency has caused a semantic shift in the language normally employed in the book of Ezekiel. When an action takes place 'in the midst of' something, Ezekiel consistently uses the preposition בתוך to describe this action.[29] However, in this context he has adopted the Zephanian phrase שר'ה בקרבה.[30] The preposition בקרב is the preposition used for 'in the midst of' in the book of Zephaniah.[31] In Ezekiel the preposition בקרב is used only to mean within an individual (Ezek 11. 19; 36.26, 27). This example of imitating the language of his source may be a further indication that Ezekiel is the borrower in this instance.

Another example of the use of biblical sources in the book of Ezekiel is the re-use of Num 18.1-7, 22-23 in Ezek 44.9-16. This source was probably selected because of the similarity of issues involved in the two passages. Both texts are concerned with a proper establishment of a priestly and levitical hierarchy and both are written in response to a crisis. Numbers 18 was written in response to the Korahite rebellion, while Ezekiel 44 responds to the permission that had been granted to foreigners to enter the Temple. In addition to this similarity in motive, many terminological connections link these two passages together.[32] The key verbs of Numbers 18—קרב, שרת, צבד, and שמר, and נשא in the phrase ישאו עונם, all recur in Ezekiel 44.[33] Furthermore, the Ezekiel passage (v. 6) is introduced by a statement which contains the phrases ב'ת המר'[34] and רב לכם.

---

28. See Fishbane, *BIAI*, 461-63.
29. E.g., see Ezek 1.1, 16; 3.24; 5.2, 5; 9.4; 10.10, etc.
30. This phrase occurs only in these two passages in the Bible.
31. Zeph 3.3, 5, 12, 15, 17.
32. See Fishbane, *BIAI*, 138-43. See pp. 137-38 below.
33. In addition in the wider context of both passages the Levites are described as those who stand before the people to serve them—לשרת םEzek 44.11.
34. Hence I am reading πρὸς τὸν οἶκον τὸν παραπικραίνοντα with the Septuagint. ב'ת המר' is often used for בנ' מר' in Ezekiel, apparently to indicate

Similar phrases function as key elements in the introduction and conclusion of the Korahite incident (Num 16.3,7; 17.25). It is therefore possible that the author of the Ezekiel passage has intentionally selected these expressions which operate as the outer frame to the Korahite rebellion to introduce his reworking of the passage in his own day. These three examples of the use of sources in the book of Ezekiel are illustrations of the ways the author incorporated his source material. The implications of this for our study are threefold. First, it confirms the opinion of numerous scholars who maintain that the book of Ezekiel made wide use of earlier biblical material. Secondly, with regard to the diachronic study of Biblical Hebrew, we note that since Ezekiel stands chronologically later than his source material the possibility exists that any variations in his language may be due to changes that have taken place in the Hebrew Language.[35] Thirdly, any material which the book of Ezekiel has directly borrowed from another source without adjustment is not the intrinsic language of the book. Thus, not all the language of the book of Ezekiel should be viewed as characteristic of the exilic period, since to some extent the book preserves earlier source language.[36]

We now turn to the text of the book of Ezekiel to determine its linguistic status within the Hebrew Bible. We will first examine the grammar of the book, and then turn to the vocabulary to discover the extent to which Ezekiel may be distinguished from the classical Hebrew of the pre-exilic period and function as a transitional work between the two linguistic strata, EBH and LBH.

that Judah's rebellion had taken on a dynastic quality. See 2.5, 6, 8; 3.9, 26, 27; 12.2, 3, 9, 25; 17.12; 24.3.

35. For a classic example compare the language of Lev 10.10 and Ezek 22.26 on p. 117 below.

36. Thus the prophetic literature which borrows and makes use of earlier material may illustrate late language in much the same way that late poetic texts, which by nature of being poetic have a propensity of being archaistic, demonstrate later linguistic qualities. In late poetic texts, as well in late prophetic texts, it is possible to observe later linguistic features reflecting the author's historical situation embedded in material which copies or emulates earlier style. For discussion of this phenomenon in reference to poetic and prophetic texts, see Hurvitz, *Lashon*, 56-58; and Watson, *Classical Hebrew Poetry*, 36.

Chapter 5

LATE GRAMMATICAL FEATURES IN THE BOOK OF EZEKIEL

As was indicated in the previous chapter, this study, not unlike previous studies of the diachronic analysis of BH, operates on the basis of the linguistic principles of contrast and distribution. We have no basis to assume that a linguistic development has taken place in the book of Ezekiel unless we first isolate earlier features from which a feature in Ezekiel is now distinct. In a similar manner, we cannot assume that the diverse characteristic of Ezekiel illustrates linguistic evolution until we observe the same phenomenon prevalent in other texts known to be late.

In this chapter we begin our investigation of the language of the book of Ezekiel by examining grammatical traits of Ezekiel which depart from the conventional practice observable in classical or early BH. In so doing we will be in a position to observe linguistic change first-hand. We will consider changes in the book of Ezekiel from the EBH conventions in the areas of orthography, morphology, and syntax. In the linguistic shifts we will be particularly attentive to any resultant similarity to Aramaic, as we noted in Chapter 1 that language contact is a primary mechanism of language change.

The two columns below provide a summary for the detailed discussion of the grammatical developments which are treated in this chapter. The right column represents a LBH feature which occurs in the Book of Ezekiel. The left column represents the corresponding trait extant in EBH. It has been attempted in each case to contrast the grammatical development in Ezekiel with the closest possible illustration of the complementary feature which is indicative of the EBH practice. Where this was not possible the grammatical feature characteristic of EBH was reconstructed. These forms are indicated by the symbol *. There is, however, no doubt that these reconstructions accurately reflect EBH phenomena. The arrangement of the columns, and the treatment of the grammatical features in the chapter, proceed from nominal, to verbal, to clausal categories. In the actual discussion of these features in this chapter the LBH example given below is often preceded by a concrete description of the LBH feature under discussion.

It should be noted that evidence of a LBH feature in Ezekiel does not necessarily imply that Ezekiel only employs the LBH phenomenon to the exclusion of the corresponding EBH feature. On the contrary, in each of the LBH features listed in the right column, we may find, in varying degrees, evidence of the EBH trait in Ezekiel. It should be kept in mind that this situation is not unique to Ezekiel but is true of other late books of the Bible as well. This fact should not be surprising as we are attempting to isolate language change within a generally short span of time. The import of the examples of LBH in Ezekiel is thus, necessarily, cumulative.

Orthography

EBH feature	LBH feature
דוד	דויד

Morphology

EBH feature	LBH feature
אנכי	אני
ארץ	ארצות
הן	הם
חי	חיה
הקים	קים
* חללו אתו	חללוהו

Syntax

EBH feature	LBH feature
* הנשיא ישב	את הנשיא ... ישב
בבא משה	בבאו האיש
ויגוע כל בשר	וראו כל בשר
כפר את	כפר ל
ויולד בן	והוליד בן
ויהי בצאת	בצאת
יומו יבוא	לבוא עתה

עמדים אצל	היה עמד אצלי
ידע בי	ידע אשר
וחמש אמות	ורחב חמש
רחב	אמות
על... ועל	על... ו
בין ... בין	בין ... ל
ואם ... והמחתני	כי... ימות

Orthography

דויד

It has long been recognized that one characteristic feature of the orthography of the Chronicler, in contrast to the orthography of Samuel/Kings, is the Chronicler's insistence in writing דויד with the plene spelling.[1] The plene spelling is completely absent from Samuel, and occurs in Kings only in 1 Kgs 3.14; 11.4, 36.[2] Thus of the 671 cases of the occurrence of the name David in Samuel/Kings, only three are written plene while the remainder are defective. By contrast, in Ezra, Nehemiah, and Chronicles, the name 'David' occurs 271 times, all of which have the plene spelling. Just a few illustrations are sufficient to indicate the diachronic nature of this orthographic shift:[3]

2 Sam 6.16	ארון ה׳ בא עיר דוד
1 Chr 15.29	ארון ברית ה׳ בא עד עיר דויד
1 Kgs 12.19	ויפשעו ישראל בבית דוד
2 Chr 10.19	ויפשעו ישראל בבית דויד

Other biblical books such as Isaiah[4] and Jeremiah use only the defective spelling, like Samuel/Kings, while the Psalms have the defective spelling in eighty-seven of a possible eighty-eight cases.[5] The Minor Prophets, on the other hand, consistently use the fuller spelling.[6]

1. For the full discussion, see David N. Freedman, 'The Spelling of the Name "David" in the Hebrew Bible', *HAR* 7 (1983) 89-102; and Francis I. Andersen and A. Dean Forbes, *Spelling in the Hebrew Bible* (Rome, 1986) 4-9.
2. Passages which Anderson and Forbes suggest were subject to editorial activity. *Spelling in the Hebrew Bible*, 5.
3. See also, 2 Sam 7.26 = 1 Chr 17.24; 1 Kgs 7.51 = 2 Chr 5.1.
4. Freedman suggests that the consistent use of the defective form in Isaiah is due to an attempt to normalize the spelling in individual books. See Freedman, 'The Spelling of the Name "David" in the Hebrew Bible', 94.
5. The large number of defective/early spellings in the Psalms may be due to the fact that most of the occurrences of the name occurs in titles or headings, where one might expect a more archaic form. Thus Freedman, 'The Spelling of the Name "David" in the Hebrew Bible', 94, 101.
6. In the Minor Prophets we must assume that the occurrences of דויד in Amos and Hosea indicate normalization toward the later spelling. Freedman,

In the Book of Ezekiel, while the name דוד occurs only four times, it is significant that one of these spellings is plene, identical to the pattern in the post-exilic works (34.23). Ezekiel thus would appear to occupy an intermediate or transitional status in the דויד > דוד shift.[7]

The same trend of LBH toward the plene spelling of the personal name דויד is evident in the DSS. As Freedman states:[8]

> It is important to point out that at Qumran the later spelling predominates not only in the books of the Bible where the long spelling occurs but in non-biblical documents, showing that the long spelling was the standard spelling of that period. Furthermore many of the books of the Bible in which the short spelling predominates in MT have the long spelling at Qumran.

This tendency can best be demonstrated by looking at occurrences of דויד in 1QIsaᵃ, which is always plene, against the corresponding passages from the MT:[9]

Isa 29.1	קרית חנה דוד
1QIsaᵃ 29.1	קרית חנה דויד
Isa 37.35	ולמען דוד עבדי
1QIsaᵃ 37.35	ולמען דויד עבדי

As noted above, the spelling of David in MT Samuel is always defective. This situation is completely different from the later spelling of 4QSamᵃ which is always plene. The following are just two of the many plene spellings of David in 4QSamᵃ which demonstrate the orthographic shift:[10]

'The Spelling of the Name "David" in the Hebrew Bible', 95. This illustration of leveling reinforces the view that the Minor Prophets were treated as one unit.

7. Thus Freedman, 'The Spelling of the Name "David" in the Hebrew Bible', 92 n. 7, 95, 96, 99, 102.

8. Freedman, 'The Spelling of the Name "David" in the Hebrew Bible', 96-97.

9. For these and other examples, see Kutscher, *Isaiah*, 99.

10. For these readings see Emmanuel Tov, 'Determining the Relationship between the Qumran Scrolls and the LXX: Some Methodological Problems', in *The Hebrew and Greek Texts of Samuel,* ed. Emmanuel Tov (Jerusalem, 1980) 55; and Eugene Charles Ulrich, *The Qumran Text of Samuel and Josephus* (Missoula, 1978) 45, 83, 138, 143. For additional plene spellings of דויד in 4QSamᵃ, see Ulrich, *ibid.,* 45, 56, 82, 86, 88, 196, 197.

2 Sam 3.1	ודוד
4QSam[a] 3.1	ודויד

2 Sam 12.15	לדוד ויאנש
4QSam[a] 12.15	לדויד

That this practice was neither stylistic nor unique to the writers of
1QIsa[a] and 4QSam[a] is borne out by the additional examples below:[11]

4Q161.17	דויד העומד
4Q174.7	ואשר אמר לדויד
11QPs[a] 27.2[12]	ויהי דויד בן ישי חכם

In the Mishnah we find the plene spelling in the following two
passages:[13]

m. Sanh. 2.3(2)	שכן מצינו בדויד שנשא
m. Sanh. 2.4(3)	שכן מצינו בדויד שיצא

In conclusion, it is clear from the observations of the spelling of the
name 'David' in Samuel/Kings in comparison to Chronicles, that by
the Second Temple period the דויד > דוד orthographic shift had
occurred. This shift is fully realized in the late books of Chronicles,
Ezra, and Nehemiah. Substantiating evidence for this shift is provided by the DSS where the spelling of David in the plene was the
prevailing practice. Ezek 34.23 provides an early attestation to this
trend, and we may conclude that this trend to write the name of דויד
as plene was beginning to increase in frequency in the exilic period. As
Freedman states:[14]

> The viewpoint propounded here is that the books of the Hebrew Bible
> which contain the name of David reflect, in the predominant
> spelling of each book, the period during which they were compiled
> and formally published. Thus the books containing the three letter

11. For transcriptions of these examples and other illustrations of the plene
spelling of David in the DSS, see *DJD* V, 14, 53, 69; *DJD* IV, 54, 60, 92.
12. As in the case of 4QSam[a] and MT Samuel, the spelling of David in the
Psalms Scroll from Cave 11 is consistently plene in contrast to MT Psalms.
13. The defective spelling occurs two times as well, in *m.'Abot* 3.8(7) and
m.Ta'an. 4.6(5). In the Tosefta, on the other hand, only the shorter, defective
term is used.
14. 'The Spelling of the Name "David" in the Hebrew Bible', 99.

spelling should be assigned to the First Temple period, the books with the four letter spelling to the Second Temple period, and those with mixed spelling to the transitional period between the two others.

Freedman adds that the manner in which David is written in Ezekiel supports the traditional viewpoint regarding the composition of this work:[15]

> The Book of Ezekiel, as alredy [sic] noted, exhibits the mixed orthography that should be characteristic of the middle exilic period. The proposed date of publication of Ezekiel (c. 570-567 BCE, on the basis of the content and dates in the book itself) would fit well with the mixed picture of spelling: even the ratio of three to one in favor of the older spelling would reflect the period before the return from Exile.

Furthermore, this use of the plene spelling of דויד in Ezekiel and LBH is but one example in the larger issue of the historical significance of the use of plene spelling in the Hebrew Bible. Although many maintain that the orthography of the Hebrew Bible as a whole reflects the spelling system of the post-exilic period, it is still true that EBH, i.e. Genesis—Kings, reflects a more conservative, or defective spelling. Ezekiel, on the other hand, which to a limited degree displays a fuller orthography 'already exhibits the new style that would come increasingly to the fore in the exiled community in Babylon and would continue to do so in post-exilic times'.[16]

---

15. 'The Spelling of the Name "David" in the Hebrew Bible', 100.
16. Andersen and Forbes, *Spelling in the Hebrew Bible*, 315. See also in this work, x, 312-15. Thus the study of orthography may provide results useful for diachronic analysis. We do not believe it justified, however, to limit the uncovering of linguistic strata to the study of orthography. The latter view is advocated by Lambert. See Mayer Lambert, *Traité de Grammaire Hébraïque* (Hildesheim, 1972) § 7, 4.

Morphology

אֲנִי > אָנֹכִי

It has long been recognized that the independent personal pronoun
אָנֹכִי is more ancient than the equivalent, shorter form אֲנִי: 'אֲנִי
gehört auch offenbar der jüngeren Schicht an, während אָנֹכִי das
altkanannaisch Wort für 'ich' darstellt'.[17] The lengthened form of the
personal pronoun with the *kaph* corresponds to the first person
personal pronoun in Egyptian, Akkadian, Phoenician and Moabite.[18]
In Biblical Hebrew as well, the longer term אָנֹכִי was preferred in
EBH as well as in poetic texts.[19] In the literature designated as JE, for
example, אָנֹכִי is used in preference to אֲנִי by the ratio of 81: 48. In
later Hebrew, on the other hand, we can detect an increasing preference for אֲנִי. This may be observed in the book of Jeremiah, where
אֲנִי is preferred over אָנֹכִי by a ratio of 54: 37.[20] This change is even
more marked after the advent of the Babylonian Exile. In the texts of
LBH, the shorter form of the first person singular pronoun אֲנִי, is
used almost to the exclusion of the longer אָנֹכִי.[21] אָנֹכִי does not
occur at all in Haggai, Zechariah 1–8, Ecclesiastes, Lamentations,

---

17. Bauer-Leander, *HG* § 28 k, 249. See also, Wagner, *Aramäismen*, 130.
18. See Sir Alan Gardiner, *Egyptian Grammar* (Oxford, 1927) § 64, 53;
Friedrich-Röllig, *PPG* § 110, 45; and Donner-Röllig, *KAI* I, 33. The shorter
form has an early attestation in Ugaritic literature. See Cyrus Gordon,
Ugaritic Textbook (Rome, 1967) § 6.1, 35; and Stanislav Segert, *A Basic
Grammar of the Ugaritic Language* (Los Angeles, 1984) § 51.11, 47.
19. See Kutscher, *History*, 30; J. Blau, *EncJud* 16, s.v. 'Hebrew Language,
Biblical Hebrew', 1572; and J. Blau, 'The Historical Periods of the Hebrew
Language', in *Jewish Languages: Themes and Variations*, ed. Herbert H.
Paper (Cambridge, Mass., 1978) 2. אֲנִי is preferred in the Psalms, however,
occurring seventy times in contrast to only thirteen occurrences of the longer
form אָנֹכִי. See F. Giesebrecht, 'Zur Hexateuchkritik. Der Sprachgebrauch
des Hexateuchischen Elohisten', *ZAW* 1 (1881) 251-52. Similarly, in the Psalms
Scroll from Cave 11, אֲנִי occurs in five of a possible six occasions. See *DJD* IV,
55, 60, 77, 80, 86.
20. See *BDB*, 59. The shift was already under way earlier in Samuel where
each of the variant forms of the personal pronoun occurs fifty times. F.
Giesebrecht, 'Zur Hexateuchkritik. Der Sprachgebrauch des Hexateuchischen
Elohisten', 253. This state of affairs should be contrasted with Amos where the
earlier form אָנֹכִי occurs on eight of a possible nine occasions.
21. Noted also by Harris. See Zellig S. Harris, *Development of the Canaanite
Dialects* (New Haven, 1939) 74.

Ezra, or Esther and only one time in Ezekiel, Malachi, Daniel, Nehemiah, and Chronicles.[22] This historical shift can be demonstrated by examining the following parallel texts:[23]

2 Sam 24.17	אָנֹכִי חטאתי
1 Chr 21.17	וַאֲנִי הוא אשר חטאתי

2 Kgs 22.19	וגם אָנֹכִי שמעתי
2 Chr 34.27	וגם אֲנִי שמעתי

Ezekiel, as noted above, sides with LBH in the use of the independent first personal pronoun as the shorter form אֲנִי occurs 138 times in the book, while the older form אָנֹכִי occurs only in one text, Ezek 36.28.[24]

This trend to prefer the shorter form אֲנִי over the longer more ancient form אָנֹכִי, continued in post-biblical literature. In the DSS, אֲנִי is the customary form for the first person personal pronoun, while the longer form אָנֹכִי occurs less frequently and always with reference to God.[25] The following parallel texts illustrate the preference of the shorter from אֲנִי in the DSS:

1 Sam 2.23	תעשון כדברים האלה אשר אָנֹכִי שמע
4QSam^a 2.23[26]	תעשו[ן כדברים האל]ה א[ש]ר אֲנִי [שו]מ[ע]

Isa 46.9[27]	כי אָנֹכִי אל ואין עוד
1QIsa^a 46.9	כיא אֲנִי אל ואין עוד

---

22. See *BDB*, 59. אָנֹכִי is rather common in Zech 9–14 however. See Hill, *Malachi*, 87-88.

23. See also 2 Sam 7.18 = 1 Chr 17.16 and 2 Sam 24.12 = 1 Chr 21.10.

24. According to Polzin's counting. See Polzin, *Hebrew*, 127. Zimmerli postulates that the lone occurrence of the longer form in 36.28 should be credited to a later hand. See Zimmerli, *Ezekiel* II, 249.

25. Qimron, *DSS Hebrew*, 57.

26. For reading and reconstruction see Ulrich, *The Qumran Text of Samuel and Josephus*, 41.

27. See Kutscher, *Isaiah*, 219. It should be noted, however, that the reverse is true in Isa 46.4 and 56.3, where God is the speaker. See note 25 above.

This same preference for אֲנִי can be observed in the Mishnah as the longer form אָנֹכִי is used only in biblical citations or direct biblical allusions.[28]

In conclusion, it should be apparent that in the history of BH there occurred a shift in the use of the first person personal pronoun illustrated in the formula אֲנִי > אָנֹכִי. This preference to favor the shorter אֲנִי over אָנֹכִי continued in a unilateral fashion in the post-biblical literature as attested in the DSS and in the Mishnah.[29] The change is analogous to the English thou > you shift. It should also be clear that in the use of the independent personal pronoun אֲנִי, Ezekiel is aligned unequivocally with LBH.

28. Segal, *MHG*, 39. This practice by writers of MH to use the longer form אָנֹכִי when biblical passages are in view may provide the clue for the single occurrence of אָנֹכִי in Ezek 36.28. Is it not possible that the writer of the phrase וְאָנֹכִי אֶהְיֶה לָכֶם לֵאלֹהִים in Ezekiel may have had in mind the ancient expression וְאָנֹכִי לֹא אֶהְיֶה לָכֶם (Hos 1.9)? In referring to an ancient allusion it is apparent that the writer consciously or unconsciously resorts to more archaic language in the same manner as the writers of MH.

29. The frequency and distribution of these personal pronouns in Hebrew literature clearly appears to be historically conditioned. Thus we are unable to accept Rendsburg's hypothesis that the distinction between these two forms of the personal pronoun is due to the fact that אָנֹכִי is the literary form while אֲנִי represents the spoken language. Because of the difficulty involved in proving such a hypothesis, we believe that understanding אֲנִי as a later substitute for the earlier אָנֹכִי reflects a more logical deduction from the available data. For Rendsburg's discussion, see Gary Rendsburg, *Evidence for a Spoken Hebrew in Biblical Times* (Ph.D. dissertation, New York University, 1980) 28-30.

Pluralizing Tendency

ארצות > ארץ

There was a growing tendency for the writers of LBH to use plural forms for forms normally construed in the singular in EBH.[30] This inclination can be observed not only in the tendency to assimilate a singular *nomen rectum* to a plural *nomen regens* in LBH texts, but also in the tendency for post-exilic writers to substitute a plural term for a term which customarily occurs in the singular in EBH.

Particularly significant are the parallel passages of late biblical books which contain a plural *nomen regens*. Notice how the *nomen rectum* of LBH texts readily assimilate to a plural *nomen regens*:[31]

Gen 6.4	אנשי <u>השם</u>
1 Chr 5.24	אנשי <u>שמות</u>
2 Sam 5.11	וחרשי <u>עץ</u>
1 Chr 14.1	וחרשי <u>עצים</u>

This same proclivity can be observed in the DSS.[32]

1QS 10.6	ראשי <u>שנים</u>
11QTemple 43.15	בימי <u>המועדים</u>

The pluralizing tendency with reference to individual terms in LBH, can be best demonstrated by comparing parallel texts from a different chronological periods:[33]

Josh 21.9	אשר יקרא אתהן <u>בשם</u>
1 Chr 6.50	אשר יקראו אתהם <u>בשמות</u>
2 Kgs 8.27	וילך <u>בדרך</u> בית אחאב
2 Chr 22.3	הוא הלך <u>בדרכי</u> בית אחאב

---

30. See Kropat, *Syntax*, 8-11; Hurvitz, *Lashon*, 37-38; and Polzin, *Hebrew*, 42-43.
31. See also, 2 Kgs 15.20 = 1 Chr 7.5; 2 Kgs 25.18 = 1 Chr 9.19. Hadas-Lebel observed that this was a feature of post-exilic syntax. See Mireille Hadas-Lebel, *Manuel d'histoire de la langue hébraïque* (Paris, 1976) 98.
32. For additional examples see Qimron, *DSS Hebrew*, 74-75.
33. See also, 2 Kgs 11.10 = 2 Chr 23.9; 1 Kgs 10.22 = 2 Chr 9.21.

Again a similar phenomenon can be perceived in the DSS by high-lighting the difference of the following form in 1QIsaᵃ with the earlier text of the MT:[34]

Isa 11.8	וְעַל מְאוּרַת צִפְעוֹנִי גָּמוּל
1QIsaᵃ 11.8	וְעַל מְאוּרוֹת צִפְעוֹנִים גָּמוּל

Ezekiel apparently reflects this same tendency exhibited in LBH. For example, the plural of אֶרֶץ which occurs predominantly in LBH and only infrequently in EBH[35] is used profusely in Ezekiel (twenty times). By contrast, אֲרָצוֹת occurs but fourteen times in both 1 and 2 Chronicles. Polzin's remark concerning the occurrence of the plural of this term is instructive: '... the frequent use of *'arāṣôt* in Chr and the other late books of the OT is a chronologically significant feature of LBH'.[36]

The occurrence of אֲרָצוֹת in Ezekiel is not the only example of this pluralizing tendency in the book. Another example of this trend may be observed in the occurrence of the term גְּזֵלוֹת in Ezek 18.12 for the singular גְּזֵלָה.[37] This is the only occurrence of this term in the plural in the Bible. The plural does occur in post-biblical literature, however, as can be seen from the following examples from MH:

m. Sanh. 1.1	גְּזֵלוֹת וַחֲבָלוֹת בִּשְׁלֹשָׁה
m. Zebaḥ. 5.5	אָשָׁם גְּזֵלוֹת אָשָׁם מְעִילוֹת

---

34. Cited by Hurvitz. *Lashon*, 37.

35. It occurs fifty-four times from Jeremiah on and in only thirteen EBH passages. Polzin, *Hebrew*, 127.

36. Polzin, *Hebrew*, 127. In light of this statement, the occurrence of the plural term in Ezekiel is even more impressive when one considers that this plural form does not occur in the post-exilic prophets. See Hill, *Malachi*, 88.

37. See Hurvitz, *Linguistic Study*, 43-46. It should not be overlooked, however, that in this same context we find the singular terms גֵּזֶל (18.12) and גְּזֵלָה (18.16). This indicates that while Ezekiel demonstrates the pluralizing tendency as do other works of LBH, by no means does this late feature occur profusely throughout the book.

Similarly, נָאֳקֹת (30.24) and לְצָמֹת (45.7)[38] are the only respective plural forms of נָאֳקָה and לְצָמָת in the Bible. Additional examples of this pluralizing inclination of LBH occurs with the plurals עִתִּים[39] in Ezek 12.27 and נֹאֲצֹות in Ezek 35.12. The plural of עֵת occurs almost exclusively in LBH,[40] while the plural of נֶאָצָה occurs in the Bible elsewhere only in the late book of Nehemiah (9.18, 26). Other possible illustrations of this phenomena from the book of Ezekiel include לְמִשְׁלִים (14.8),[41] the occurrence of וַשֻׁפַּבַת דָּם (16.38) for שָׁפֵךְ דַּם of Gen 9.6, שְׁמָמֹות (35.9), which occurs in the plural elsewhere only in Jer 51.26, 62; 25.12, and פְּקֻדֹות (9.1; 44.11) which occurs elsewhere in the plural only in 2 Kgs 11.18; Jer 52.11; 2 Chr 23.18. Both of these latter illustrations occur numerous times in the singular. Strikingly, פְּקֻדֹות occurs in the singular in Jeremiah (8.12; 10.15; 11.23; 23.12; 46.21; 48.44; 50.27; 51.18) and Chronicles (1 Chr 24.3, 19; 26.30; 2 Chr 17.14; 24.11; 26.11), but not in Ezekiel.

Thus Ezekiel, through the use of various terms, clearly demonstrates the pluralizing tendency that is found in LBH as well as in the Hebrew of the DSS and the Mishnah. In this characteristic we may thus detect a deviation from the practice common among the earlier writers of EBH.

38. We recognize that this term might be understood as a preposition, but, even if that be the case, it still illustrates the pluralizing tendency under discussion.
39. Polzin acknowledges the prevalence of this plural form in LBH. See, *Hebrew*, 42.
40. Isa 33.6; Job 24.1; Est 1.13; Dan 9.25; 11.6, 13, 14; Ezra 10.14; Neh 9.28; 13.31; 10.35; 1 Chr 12.33; 29.30; 2 Chr 15.5. See Polzin, *Hebrew*, 75. This plural form also occurs in MH in *Tamid* 1.2.
41. Dietrich maintains that this plural represents an abstract idea. See F.E.C. Dietrich, *Abhandlungen zur hebräische Grammatik* (Leipzig, 1846) 28. He sees the pluralizing tendency elsewhere in Ezekiel in 27.36 and 28.19 in the phrase בַּלָּהֹות הָיִית, as well as in 30.12 with the term יְאֹרִים. *Ibid.*, 17-18, 23.

Masculine Plural Suffix For Feminine

$$-(ה)ם > -(ה)ן$$

In LBH there is a tendency to avoid using the third feminine plural
pronominal suffix and to use instead the third masculine plural suffix
to refer to both masculine and feminine antecedents. This practice is
most notably evident in the Chronicles:[42]

1 Chr 23.22	כי אם בנות וישאום בני קיש אחיהם
1 Chr 28. 15	ומשקל למנרות הזהב ונרתיהם זהב
2 Chr 11.11	ויחזק את המצרות ויתן בהם

This feature is prevalent in other late books as well. For example,
observe the appearances of this trait in both Ezra and Nehemiah:

| Ezra 10.3 | כל נשים והנולד מהם |
| Neh 1.9 | ושמרתם מצותי ועשיתם אתם |

By comparing 1 Chr 10.7 with the parallel text in 1 Sam 31.7 we
see this change from a diachronic perspective:

| 1 Sam 31.7 | וישבו בהן |
| 1 Chr 10.7 | וישבו בהם |

A chronological distinction may also be seen in the following parall-
lel texts as well:

| Josh 21.3 | את הערים האלה ואת מגרשיהן |
| 1 Chr 6.49 | את הערים ואת מגרשיהם |

| Josh 21.9 | הערים האלה אשר יקרא אתהן בשם |
| 1 Chr 6.50 | הערים האלה אשר יקראו אתהם בשמות |

The beginnings of the this tendency to substitute the masculine plural suffix for the the feminine plural suffix is heralded by the book of

---

42. Kropat, *Syntax*, 61-62. For a different interpretation of this phenomena see,
Hurvitz, *Linguistic Study*, 168-69; and Gary Rendsberg, 'Late Biblical Hebrew
and the Date of "P"', *JANES* 12 (1980) 69-70.

Ezekiel. Kropat acknowledged Ezekiel's pivotal role in this diachronic shift:

> Das Nebeneinander von maskulinem und femininem Suffix in den älteren Schriften bis Ezechiel, das vollständige Fehlen des femininen Suffixes 3. pers. plur. in den jüngeren Schriften zeigt deutlich, dass dieses schon in der Zeit nach Ezechiel nicht mehr gebraucht wurde.[43]

Our investigation indicates great inconsistency of the use of the third feminine plural suffix in the book of Ezekiel. Whereas the feminine plural antecedent has a feminine plural suffix in sixty-four cases, the masculine plural suffix is used for the feminine plural in eighty cases. Thus the LBH practice is preferred in Ezekiel by a ratio of 5: 4. A few examples of the LBH phenomena are listed below:[44]

Ezek 1.5-6	דמות ארבע חיות ... וארבע כנפים לאחת ל<u>הם</u>
Ezek 3.13	וקול כנפי החיות משיקות... וקול האופנים לעמת<u>ם</u>
Ezek 23.47	ורגמו עליהן אבן קהל ובָרא אותהן בחרבותם בני<u>הם</u> ובנותי<u>הם</u> יהרגו

This practice in Ezekiel is by no means uniform, however, as different preferences are reflected in different sections of the book.[45] What is perhaps more indicative of the state of confusion in the use of these suffixes in the book of Ezekiel is the occurrence of the feminine plural suffix for a masculine plural suffix! This occurs about seven times in the book.[46]

---

43. Kropat, *Syntax*, 62.
44. The other occurrences of this LBH feature in Ezekiel include: 1.7, 8, 9, 10, 11, 13, 19, 20, 21, 22, 23, 24, 25, 26; 13.20; 18.26; 23.37, 39, 45; 34.11, 12, 13, 14, 15, 18, 19, 21, 23, 25, 26, 27, 27, 28, 30, 31, 37.2, 4, 8, 10; 42.4, 11; 46.19, 22, 23.
45. See Zimmerli, *Ezekiel* I, 102; and *Ezekiel* II, 209.
46. See 1.16, 17, 18; 30.17; 42.14. The occurrence of the feminine suffixes in chapter one has led Höhne to suggest that the masculine suffixes in the chapter were in fact feminine also but were later altered. Ernst Höhne, *Die Thronwagenvision Hesekiels. Echtheit und Herkunft der Vision Hes. 1, 4-28 und ihrer einzelnen Züge* (Ph.D. dissertation, Friedrich-Alexander Universität, 1953) 80-84.

In the Hebrew of the DSS the LBH convention of using the masculine plural suffix for the feminine plural antecedent was practised. The following are some examples of this phenomena at Qumran:[47]

1QS 1. 8-9	כול הנגלות למועדי תעודותם
11QTemple 48.16	ולנשים בהיותמה בנדת ...
	טמאתמה ובללדתמה

The use of the masculine plural suffix for the feminine plural becomes somewhat more complicated when we examine MH. In MH the third masculine plural is often written as ן!‏[48] However, there still are cases where the masculine suffix ם is used for the feminine plural antecedent. Note the following examples:

| *m. Ḥal.* 1.7 | נשים שנתנו לנחתום לעשות להם |
| *m. Ter.* 8.12 | וכן נשים שאמרו להם גויים |

It is not easy to ascertain the cause for this diachronic shift. We do know as noted above, that ם and ן as the only nasal consonants in Hebrew, were often interchanged. This was the case in both Hebrew and Aramaic after the Babylonian Exile.[49] Polzin is correct in arguing that the influence behind this change in BH did not come from Aramaic as the Aramaic influence would be in the opposite direction: ם > ן. He speculates that Hebrew purists may have attempted to resist the Aramaic influence and changed *mem* endings in texts that had originally *nun*.[50] Dahood has suggested that the primary influence for this change may have come from Phoenician. He infers that the lack of a third feminine plural suffix in Phoenician may have given rise to the use of the masculine plural suffix for the feminine plural suffix. This practice, he points out is especially prevalent in

---

47. See Qimron, *DSS Hebrew*, 62-63; and T. Leahy, *A Study of the Language of the Essene Manual of Discipline* (Ph.D. dissertation, The John Hopkins University, 1958) 79. Normally in 1QS, however, the earlier practice of using the third person feminine plural suffix is preferred. See Leahy, *ibid*.

48. Segal, *MHG*, 41. This is analogous to what we found in Ezekiel above.

49. Cf. E.Y. Kutscher, *Studies In Galilean Aramaic* (Jerusalem, 1976) 58-67. For the use of the masculine suffix for the feminine plural in Galilean Aramaic, see Gustaf Dalman, *Grammatik des Jüdisch-Palästinischen Aramäisch* (Leipzig, 1905) 202.

50. Polzin, *Hebrew*, 53.

Ecclesiastes.[51] This trend did not continue everywhere, as noted above, as for example in 1QS where the feminine plural suffix with *nun* was predominantly used.[52]

However difficult it may be to determine the cause for the diminishing use of the third person feminine plural suffix in BH and its complete absence in BA, it is clear that its repercussions were being felt as early as the Book of Ezekiel. Ezekiel often avoids the feminine plural suffix, substituting the masculine plural suffix in its place. In so doing he functions as a precursor of the writers of LBH.[53]

51. See M. Dahood, 'Canaanite-Phoenician Influence in Qoheleth', *Biblica* 33 (1952) 79.

52. T. Leahy, 'Studies in the Syntax of 1QS', *Biblica* 41 (1960) 156. However it is possible that this resulted from a conscious imitation of EBH style. When the writers of the DSS attempted to imitate BH they would usually write in the earlier, classical style of EBH rather than the later style of the LBH writers. See Polzin, *Hebrew*, 7.

53. The merging of masculine and feminine is not unique to LBH. In Egyptian, for example, we see the feminine genitival adjective merging with the masculine genitival adjective. See Sir Alan Gardiner, *Egyptian Grammar* (Oxford, 1978) § 86, 66. Hittite and Hurrian did not distinguish between the masculine and feminine third person pronoun. See Gary Rendsburg, 'A New Look At Pentateuchal HW', *Biblica* 63 (1982) 351-69. In addition, in Modern Dutch we find the complete coalescence of the masculine and feminine categories. See Arlotto, *Introduction to Historical Linguistics*, 163.

חיה > חי

The verb חֵי 'to live', occurs very frequently in BH in both early and late texts. The lengthened חיה is by contrast rare in the Bible, occurring in only five passages.[54] Two of these occurrences are in Ezekiel (18.23; 33.11) while the other three occurrences are in Eccl 6.6; Est 4.11; and Neh 9.29. The form is thus virtually restricted to exilic and post-exilic literature in BH.[55] The diachronic difference can be viewed by observing the following parallel texts:

Lev 18.5[56]	יעשה אתם האדם וָחַי בהם
Neh 9.29	יעשה אדם וְחָיָה בהם

In post-biblical sources, the lengthened form חיה is also rare. The form is extant on one occasion in the DSS in the Damascus Covenant.[57] Note the similarity of the phrase in the Damascus Covenant to the verses cited above:

CD 3. 15-16	יעשה האדם וְחָיָה בהם

The phrase in the Damascus Covenant is virtually identical to LBH Neh 9.29 and thus differs from the similar, but earlier phrase of Lev 18.5.

The lengthened verbal form חָיָה is absent from the Mishnah but does occur in the Tosephta in *t. Šabb.* 15.8; *t. Ohol.* 2.6; and *t. Ṭohar.* 7.1.[58]

In conclusion, it should be acknowledged that though the occurrence of the form חיה is rare in BH, its restriction to later writings does establish a certain diachronic value. Ezekiel thus occupies a critical place in this development, and by its employment of this form should be considered a forerunner of LBH.

---

54. The form does also occur in the Qere in two additional places, Jer 21.9 and 38.2.

55. Only the shortened, earlier form חי occurs in the Lachish letters. See III.9; VI.12; and XII.8. Torczyner, *Lachish Letters*, 50, 104, 152-53.

56. In view of the fact that Ezekiel employs the lengthened form, the repetition of the above phrase from Lev 18.5 in Ezek 20.11, 13, 21 makes us suspect that Ezekiel was citing an older text in these instances.

57. See Rabin, *The Zadokite Documents*, 13.

58. See Hurvitz, *Linguistic Study*, 47 n. 70; and Bergey, *Esther*, 36 n. 1.

קִים > הֵקִים

A linguistic phenomenon which began shortly after the destruction of the first temple was the increased use of the Piel stem.[59] This phenomenon was accompanied by an incremental tendency to consonantalize the middle radical of hollow verbs.[60] These latter forms should be deemed as secondary developments from EBH.[61] One example of this phenomenon can be illustrated in the distribution of the Piel stem of the root קוֹם in BH. The root קוֹם which occurs in the Hiphil stem in most of the Bible and exclusively in EBH, occurs in the Piel stem on only eleven occasions—all LBH. As Hurvitz states:

> There is no doubt, then, that *hēqîm* is a common term in standard BH as a whole—regardless of the subject matter or the literary genre of the composition in which the word may happen to appear. The fact that *hēqîm* = 'confirm, maintain, fulfill' is found in ancient biblical compositions further justifies our classification of this usage as classical. In post-classical works, on the other hand, *hēqîm* begins to be superseded by the rival form *qiyyēm*.[62]

The following examples exemplify the LBH usage:[63]

Ruth 4.7	וְזֹאת לְפָנִים בְּיִשְׂרָאֵל ... לְקַיֵּם כָּל דָּבָר
Est 9.20-21	וַיִּשְׁלַח ... לְקַיֵּם עֲלֵיהֶם

The clear diachronic shift between the use of the Hiphil stem in EBH, and the Piel stem in the later texts can be graphically illustrated by the parallel usages which follow:[64]

Gen 26.3	וַהֲקִמֹתִי ... נִשְׁבַּעְתִּי
Ps 119.106	נִשְׁבַּעְתִּי וָאֲקַיֵּמָה
2 Kgs 23.24	לְמַעַן הָקִים אֶת דִּבְרֵי ... עַל הַסֵּפֶר

---

59. William James Adams, Jr and L. La Mar Adams, 'Language Drift and the Dating of Biblical Passages', *Hebrew Studies* 18 (1977) 162. For this tendency in MH and in the Samaritan tradition, see Z. Ben-Hayyim, 'The Samaritan Tradition and its Relation to the Tradition of the Language of the Dead Sea Scrolls and Rabbinic Literature', *Leshonenu* 22 (1958) 236-37 [In Hebrew].
60. *GKC* § 72 m, 197; cf. Bendavid, *Leshon* II, 481, 485.
61. *GKC* § 72 a, n. 1, 194. *BDB* asserts that the Piel of קוֹם is 'late'. *BDB*, 878.
62. *Linguistic Study*, 33.
63. See also, Ps 119.28; Est 9.27, 29, 31, 32.
64. See Hurvitz, *Lashon*, 142; and Bergey, *Esther*, 41.

Est 9.32   ומאמר אסתר קִיַּם דברי ... ונכתב בספר

1 Kgs 2.4   למען יָקִים ה׳ את דברו
Ezek 13.6   ויחלו לְקַיֵּם דבר

In post-biblical literature the increased tendency to favor the Piel of
קום continued as illustrated by the following passages:

CD 20.11-12[65]   קִיֵּם בארץ דמשק
m. Šebu. 3.6   לְקַיֵּם את המצוה ולא קִיֵּם פטור
Num. Rab. 36b[66]   יכופו אותו כדי לְקַיֵּם דבריו

The Piel stem of קום is especially prominent in the Aramaic
Targum where it was expanded to translate several different Hebrew
verbs. With specific regard to the הקים > קים shift, the following
translations are explicit:[67]

Gen 26.3   והֲקִמֹתִי את השבעה אשר נשבעתי
Tg. Onq.   וַאֲקַיֵּים ית קימא דקיימית

Deut 27.26   אשר לא יָקִים את דברי
Tg. Onq.   דלא יְקַיֵּים ית פתגמי

The above discussion makes it abundantly clear that within the
history of BH the tendency to employ the Piel stem of the root קום
increased at the expense of the Hiphil stem. This trend continued in
post-biblical literature, so that by the time of the Mishnah, the occurrence of קום was all but restricted to the Piel stem.[68] In the phrase
קים דבר Ezekiel, again, portrays an affinity with LBH and the
post-biblical literature of the Second Temple period. Ezekiel 13:6 in

---

65. For a reading, see Rabin, *Zadokite Documents*, 39. Another possible illustration of the Piel use may occur in CD 15.5-6. See Rabin, *Zadokite Documents*,
73 n. 62.
66. Observe how this late Midrash uses the Piel of קום in this phrase
identically to Ezek 13.6, and thus in contrast to the Hiphil stem of the earlier 1
Kgs 2.4. The late phrase is also found in the Mishnah in *m. Ḥag.* 2.4; *m.
Yebam.* 4.13; 8.4; *m. Neg.* 9.3; 11.17. For the voluminous number of passages
in the Mishnah and the Midrashim which use the Piel of קום, see Ben
Yehuda, *Thesaurus* VII, 5910-15.
67. This shift may also be observed in *Tg. Onq.* Num 30.15.
68. See Bendavid, *Leshon* II § 115, 481; and Bergey, *Esther*, 41.

fact, is not only the first recorded occurrence of the Piel stem of this root in the Bible,[69] but constitutes the earliest attestation of the consonantalization of hollow roots in Hebrew.[70] This increased tendency to use the Piel stem of קום as well as to consonantalize the middle radical root of hollow verbs is probably due to Aramaic influence.[71]

69. See Cooke, *Ezekiel*, 143; Ehrlich, *Ezekiel*, 307; Paul Joüon, 'Notes Philologiques sur le Texte Hébreu d'Ezéchiel', *Biblica* 10 (1929) 304; and Greenberg, *Ezekiel*, 236.
70. Wagner, *Aramaismen*, 138; and Selle, *Aramaismis*, 28-29.
71. Thus Bauer-Leander, *HG* § 56 l', 394-95; Wagner, *Aramaismen*, 138; Zimmerli, *Ezekiel* I, 293; and the Targumic examples cited above. For illustrations of the Piel of קום in Nabataean, see Cooke, *NSI*, 217, 235.

Plural Verb With Masculine Suffix

חללוהו

In his study of the masculine plural verb ending in ו (plene or defective), Guenther found that EBH tended to avoid the masculine singular suffix הו and uses in its place the direct object marker את with the pronominal suffix. LBH, on the contrary, often adds the suffix directly to the verb after the ו ending.[72] Using Polzin's samplings Guenther found that the Pentateuch and other EBH writings preferred the use of the direct object marker with the masculine suffix by a ratio of 3: 1, while LBH writings[73] preferred that the suffix be attached directly to the verb by a 14: 1 ratio. Note the following examples from parallel texts which illustrate the diachronic nature of this linguistic phenomenon:[74]

2 Kgs 9.28	<u>ויקברו אתו</u>
2 Chr 22.9	<u>ויקברהו</u>
2 Kgs 14.20	<u>וישאו אתו</u>
2 Chr 25.28	<u>וישאהו</u>

Certainly related to this linguistic change, or at least to the tendency of the Chronicler to add the masculine singular suffix directly to the plural verb, is the frequent substitution of the form ויקברהו for the Niphal ויקבר in the parallel texts of Kings:

<u>ויקבר</u>	<u>יקברהו</u>
1 Kgs 15.24	2 Chr 16.14
2 Kgs 8.24	2 Chr 21.20
2 Kgs 11.43	2 Chr 9.31
2 Kgs 16.20	2 Chr 28.27
2 Kgs 21.18	2 Chr 33.20

---

72. Guenther, *Diachronic Study*, 199, 217-18.
73. These include Esther, Daniel, Ezra, Nehemiah, Ezra and Chronicles. *Diachronic Study*, 198.
74. See also, 2 Kgs 21.23 = 2 Chr 33.24; 2 Kgs 23.30 = 2 Chr 36.1.

The LBH practice of attaching the third masculine singular suffix directly to the verb ending with ו (plene or defective) occurs quite frequently in the Book of Ezekiel. Note the following examples:

Ezek 31.12	ויברתהו ... ויטשהו
Ezek 31.12	ויטשהו
Ezek 36.21	חללוהו
Ezek 44.24	ושפטהו
Ezek 48.19	יעבדוהו

Similarly, we find the feminine singular suffix suffixed to a verb ending in ו in the form טמאוה (Ezek 36.18).[75]

This practice was continued in post-biblical times as may be demonstrated by the following examples from DSS Hebrew and MH:

11QTemple 57.6	יעוובוהו
m. Yoma 8.7	יניחוהו

In conclusion, we observe in Ezekiel's frequent use of the masculine singular suffix suffixed directly to the verb, a departure from the classical style of EBH and the employment of a feature of the later style of LBH and post-biblical Hebrew.

75. The forms יבאהו (19. 9), ויבאהו, ויבאהו, ויחנהו (19.4), ויבאהו (7.22), וחללוה (31.4), גדלוהו (31.8), צממהו (31.9), ויקנאהו, and וקוננוהו (32.16) exhibit the same phenomenon but are not included in the discussion as they occur in poetic contexts which prefer the non-use of the particle את.

Syntax

את הנשיא ... ישב

One often cited characteristic trait of LBH is the use of the particle את before a noun in the nominative case.[76] This characteristic is not completely lacking in EBH but appears to occur to a greater degree in the post-exilic period.[77] A few examples from late biblical texts demonstrate this usage:[78]

Hag 2.17	ואין אתכם אלי
Zech 7.7	הלוא את הדברים
Neh 9.32	את כל התלאה
2 Chr 31.17	ואת התיחש הכהנים

In the Book of Ezekiel את occurs before the nominative on at least eleven occasions. The following is a representative list:

Ezek 10.22[79]	המה הפנים ... מראיהם ואותם

76. *GKG* § 117 i, 365; and *BDB*, 85. For fuller discussion see Kropat, *Syntax*, 2-3; König, *LHS* III, 220-23; Polzin, *Hebrew*, 32-37; and Ziony Zevit, 'Converging Lines of Evidence Bearing on the Date of P', *ZAW* 94 (1982) 496, 499. For a different evaluation of the diachronic nature of this feature, see Rendsburg, 'Late Biblical Hebrew and the Date of "P" ', 66. For a different interpretation of this phenomenon, see Joshua Blau, 'Zum Angeblichen Gebruch von את vor dem Nominativ', *VT* 4 (1954) 7-19.
77. את with the nominative can be observed in the following texts: Num 3.26,46; 5.10; 35. 6; and thirteen times in the so-called Deuteronomistic literature: Deut 14.13-17; 22.24; Josh 17.11,22.17; Judg 20.44, 46; 1 Sam 17.34; 20.13; 2 Sam 11.25; 2 Kgs 6.5; 9.25; 10.15. See Kropat, *Syntax*, 2; König, *LHS* III, 220, 222; *GKC* § 117 m, 366; and Polzin, *Hebrew*, 35. Polzin believes these Deuteronomistic texts should be regarded as later insertions. *Ibid.*
78. See also, Jer 45.4; Dan 9.13; Neh 9.19 (x2), 34; 1 Chr 16.39; 2 Chr 31.10.
79. Saydon asserts that ואותם can have no other interpretation here than that of an emphatic nominative. P.P. Saydon, 'Meanings and Uses of the Particle את',*VT* 14 (1964) 202. Also taken as nominative by Kimchi, G.R. Driver, and Brownlee. Driver and Brownlee maintain that ואותם should be understood as the subject of the following verb ילבו, however. G.R. Driver, 'Ezekiel: Linguistic And Textual Problems', *Biblica* 35 (1954) 150; and Brownlee, *Ezekiel*, 148.

Ezek 16.4[80]   ביום הולדת אתך
Ezek 17.21[81]   ואת כל מברחו ... יפלו
Ezek 20.16[82]   ואת חקותי לא הלכו בהם
Ezek 29.4[83]   ואת כל דגת יאריך בקשקשתיך תדבק
Ezek 35.10[84]   את שני הגוים ואת שתי הארצות
לי תהיינה
Ezek 44.3[85]   את הנשיא נשיא הוא ישב בו

This use of את before the nominative in Ezekiel and LBH did not subsequentially continue unilaterally. This construction is notably absent in the Hebrew of the DSS which almost exclusively uses the particle before the definite direct object. The apparent reason for this absence is the successful archaizing proclivities of the Scrolls.[86] The

80. Thus J. Hoftijzer, 'Remarks concerning the Use of the Particle 'T in Classical Hebrew', 70.
81. See *GKC* § 117 m, 366; Kraetzschmar, *Ezechiel,* 160; Saydon, 'Meanings and Uses of the Particle את', 195; Hoftijzer, 'Remarks concerning the Use of the Particle 'T in Classical Hebrew', 69; and Brownlee, *Ezekiel,* 259. For a slightly different nuance see Ewald, *Lehrbuch* § 277 d 2, 691; and Smend, *Ezechiel,* 112.
82. See Smend, *Ezechiel,* 131; Kraetzschmar, *Ezechiel,* 172; and Cooke, *Ezekiel,* 224.
83. For the use of את with the nominative here, again, see Saydon, 'Meanings and Uses of the Particle את', 195; and Hoftijzer, 'Remarks concerning the Use of the Particle 'T in Classical Hebrew', 69.
84. Smend, *Ezechiel,* 279; Kraetzschmar, *Ezechiel,* 246; Cooke, *Ezekiel,* 384-85; Brockelmann, *Hebräische Syntax* § 31 b, 28; Saydon, 'Meanings and Uses of the Particle את', 196; and Hoftijzer, 'Remarks concerning the Use of the Particle 'T in Classical Hebrew', 69. Segal cites this example as an illustration of the use of the Mishnaic את. 'Mišnaic Hebrew and its Relation to Biblical Hebrew and to Aramaic', *JQR* 20 (1908) 659.
85. Kimchi; Smend, *Ezechiel,* 359; Kraetzschmar, *Ezechiel,* 282; G.R. Driver, 'Ezekiel: Linguistic And Textual Problems', *Biblica* 35 (1954) 308-309; and Hoftijzer, 'Remarks concerning the Use of the Particle 'T in Classical Hebrew', 71. Other examples include Ezek 16.5; 44.7; and possibly 34.23; 47.17; 47.18; and 47.19. The last three examples from Ezek 48 might be textual corruptions as ראת was misread as ואת. It is, however, difficult to believe that the same error occurred three consecutive times. Zimmerli *Ezekiel* II, 519; and Cooke, *Ezekiel,* 530-31.
86. That the writers of DSS Hebrew were in effect *bound* to the earlier biblical tradition has been noted most recently by Morag. See Shelomo Morag, 'Qumran Hebrew: Some Typological Observations', *VT* 38 (1988) 150.

use of אֵת before the noun in the nominative case has been found in only four texts:[87]

CD 15.9[88]	אֶת הברית לֽ[שוב א]ל תורת משה
1QWM 1.4-5[89]	אֶת הכול היט[ניב]

By contrast, in MH, the LBH practice continued to be used and in fact became more widespread:

> אֵת steht schon im AT häufig nur zur Hervorhebung eines Nomens, also auch vor dem Nominativ ... Dieser Gebrauch ist in der Mišna noch weiter fortgeschritten: אוֹתְךָ אוֹתָהּ אוֹתוֹ sind geradezu zu einem neuen Pronomen in Sinne von 'derselbe, ebenjener' geworden, zB 'AZ 1.3 אֵינוֹ אָסוּר אֶלָּא אוֹתוֹ הַיּוֹם וְאוֹתוֹ הָאִישׁ Nur dieser Tag und dieser Mann sind verboten...[90]

A few examples will be sufficient to illustrate the wide use of אֵת before the nominative in MH:[91]

m. Ber. 3.1	אֵת שלפני המטה ואת שלאחר המטה
m. Menaḥ. 2.2	אוֹתָהּ החלה וְאוֹתוֹ הסדר

In summary, it is apparent that the use of אֵת with the nominative, a characteristic feature of LBH, is in wide use in the book of Ezekiel. Though this feature was not unknown in the pre-exilic period, it must be concluded that Ezekiel signals its more widespread use in LBH which lead to its further development in MH.

87. See also, 1QM 2.1, 6.
88. For restoration, see Rabin, *Zadokite Documents*, 73.
89. Cited by Polzin, *Hebrew*, 37 n. 12 (78).
90. K. Albrecht, *Neuhebräische Grammatik auf Grund der Mishna* (München, 1913) § 30f, 53.
91. See Segal, *MHG*, 42.

Proleptic Pronominal Suffix

בבאו האיש

The use of the proleptic pronominal suffix increased in frequency in the history of BH and can be seen as a characteristic feature of LBH.[92] This construction, however, was not a late development in the Semitic languages generally, as this feature is attested in early Phoenician and in Akkadian.[93] The use of the proleptic suffix is somewhat common in Old Phoenician occurring especially with the infinitive construct, as for example in the phrase לשבתנם דננים 'that the Danunians may dwell'.[94] It has been suggested that an early Hebrew example of this feature may be the occurrence of the recurring phrase ירחו in the Gezer inscription,[95] but this is not certain.

In spite of this early attestation of the use of the proleptic pronominal suffix outside of BH, the appearance of this feature within BH is largely restricted to passages which are considered to be late. A few examples from LBH illustrate the use of this phenomenon in BH:[96]

Neh 7.64	אלה בקשו כתבם המתיחשים
2 Chr 31.18	ולהתיחש בכל טפם נשיהם ובניהם
	ובנותיהם לכל קהל

In addition to the occurrence of this phenomenon in LBH, this feature is also extant in the book of Ezekiel. In the book of Ezekiel this late feature occurs on three occasions:[97]

---

92. See Polzin, *Hebrew*, 38; and Zevit, 'Converging Lines of Evidence Bearing on the Date of P', 496.

93. For the occurrence of this construction in Akkadian see Stephen A. Kaufman, *The Akkadian Influences On Aramaic* (Chicago, 1974) 131-32.

94. See Donner-Röllig, *KAI* I, 26 A, I. 17-18; and Cyrus Gordon, 'Azitwadd's Phoenician Inscription', *JNES* 8 (1949) 110, 113-14. For other examples, see W. Randall Garr, *Dialect Geography of Syria-Palestine, 1000-586* (Philadelphia, 1985) 167; and Friedrich-Röllig, *PPG* § 287 c, 147.

95. So Skehan in Frank M. Cross and David N. Freedman, *Early Hebrew Orthography* (New Haven, 1952) 47 n. 11; and Polzin, *Hebrew*, 39. This interpretation of ירחו is open to question, however. E.g. see Garr, *Dialect Geography of Syria-Palestine, 1000-586*, 168.

96. In addition, see Ezra 9.1.

97. Smend, Cooke, Gesenius-Kautzsch, Bauer-Leander, Brockelmann, and Zevit acknowledge the use of the proleptic pronominal suffix in Ezek 10.3 and 42.14. Smend, *Ezechiel*, 25, 59, 349 (note his translation of 42.14); Cooke,

Ezek 10.3	בבאן האיש
Ezek 31.14	לא יגבהו בקומתם כל עצי מים
Ezek 42.14	בבאם הכהנים

In addition to the occurrence this feature in LBH, there is evidence for the existence of this construction in BA, especially accompanied by the use of the particle די, as the following examples demonstrate:

Dan 2.20	שמה די אלהא
Dan 2.44	וביומיהן די מלכיא
Dan 3.26	עבדוהי די אלהא

This use of the proleptic suffix continued in a similar fashion in Hebrew and Aramaic post-biblical texts as illustrated by the following representative phrases:

| CD 2.9-10[98] | קציהם לכל הוי עולמים |
| *m. 'Abot* 1.9(12) | תלמידין שלאהרן |

Thus the use of the proleptic pronominal suffix, while prevalent in some early Semitic languages, particularly Phoenician and Akkadian, did not become more widespread in BH until after the First Temple period.[99] This construction continued to be employed by

---

Ezekiel, 119; *GKC* § 131 n, 425; Bauer-Leander, *HG* § 65 i, 525; Brockelmann, *Hebräische Syntax* § 68 b, 64; and Zevit, 'Converging Lines of Evidence Bearing on the Date of P', 499. In addition, Kimchi observes the occurrence of the pronominal suffix in Ezek 10.3. Smend adds Ezek 41.25 as another example of this phenomenon in the book of Ezekiel. *Ezechiel*, 25.

98. Cited by Polzin, *Hebrew*, 78 n. 18. See also, *m. Kil.* 7.4; *m. Šabb.* 1.2(1); *m. Yebam.* 7.3; 1QapGen 22.22-23. For the latter reference, see Polzin, *Hebrew*, 40.

99. The early attestation of a feature and its subsequent disappearance, only to reappear again, should not alarm us. This phenomenon can be illustrated on numerous occasions in post-biblical literature which preserves archaic Semitic features not extant in BH. See Jonas Greenfield, *The Lexical Status of Mishnaic Hebrew*; Baruch Levine, *Survivals of Ancient Canaanite in the Mishnah* (Ph.D. dissertation, Brandeis University, 1962); 'MELŪGU/MELŬG: The Origins of a Talmudic Legal Institution', *JAOS* 88 (1968) 271-85; and Ariella Goldberg, *Northern-Type-Names in the Post-Exilic Jewish Onomasticon* (Ph.D. dissertation, Brandeis University, 1972). See also, Cyrus Gordon, 'Northern Israelite Influence on Post-Exilic Hebrew', *Eretz-Israel* 3

post-biblical writers until this feature became a characteristic trait of MH.[100] The employment of this feature in the Book of Ezekiel is thus another example of the distinct affinity of the language of Ezekiel with LBH.

(1954) 104-105 [In Hebrew]; and in English, 'North Israelite Influence on Postexilic Hebrew', *IEJ* 5 (1955) 85-88.
100. Thus Segal, *MHG*, 192.

Collective With Plural

 וראו כל בשר

Collective nouns are usually construed as plurals in LBH. This differs from the earlier practice in EBH where the option was exercised to use either the singular or the plural verb with collective nouns.[101] The following LBH texts illustrate this feature:

Est 1.5	לכל העם הנמצאים
2 Chr 29. 31	ויביאו הקהל זבחים

Particularly significant are parallel passages where the Chronicler employs a plural verb with the collective, whereas in Samuel and Kings a singular verb was used:[102]

2 Sam 23.11	והעם נס
1 Chr 11. 13	והעם נסו
2 Kgs 23.30	ויקח עם הארץ
2 Chr 36.1	ויקחו עם הארץ

This same tendency to construct collective nouns as plurals is a dominant feature of the Book of Ezekiel. In the ten cases where a collective noun occurs with a predicate, the verb occurs in the plural in nine of these cases.[103] A few examples will demonstrate this phenomenon in Ezekiel:

Ezek 21.4[104]	וראו כל בשר

---

101. Joüon, *Grammaire* § 150 e, 459. For illustrations of the optional use of the plural and singular verb with the collective in 2 Kings 17, see Marc Brettler, 'Ideology, History, and Theology in 2 Kings XVII', *VT* (forthcoming). See also Polzin, *Hebrew*, 40-42; and Zevit, 'Converging Lines of Evidence Bearing on the Date of P', 496, 500. Rendsburg, on the other hand, does not view this phenomenon as diachronically significant. See 'Late Biblical Hebrew and the Date of "P"', 67.

102. See Kropat, *Syntax*, 28.

103. The phrase והעם לא נזהר in Ezek 33.6 is the lone exception.

104. The same phrase occurs in Isa 40.5. It might be argued that occurrences of the collective preceded by כל be considered exceptional, although in those cases where כל occurs the *nomen rectum* is determinative for the the number

Ezek 22.29
Ezek 23.47[105]

עם הארץ <u>עשקו</u>
<u>ורגמו</u> עליהן אבן קהל

If the terms בית ישראל and בית המרי are to be included in this discussion, then we could conclude that this phenomenon occurs twenty-six out of twenty-seven times in the book of Ezekiel. We have not included these terms however, because these terms are normally construed as plural in both EBH and LBH. In addition we have only considered those cases where the collective occurs in the immediate vicinity of the predicate. If those cases are included where the collective noun is the understood subject of the plural predicate then this phenomenon occurs at least 215 times in Ezekiel.[106] Moreover, the assertion that Ezekiel construes the collective as plural, is reinforced by the fact that a plural suffix has a collective noun as its antecedent on at least 312 occasions in the book.[107]

This LBH practice of preferring the plural verb with the collective noun was practiced by the writers of the DSS, as the following examples demonstrate:

1QM 1.13
1QS 2.21[108]

<u>יתאזרו</u> חיל בליעל
וכול העם <u>יעבורו</u>

Particularly noteworthy are those cases where the writers of the DSS use the plural verb with the collective noun, whereas the parallel passage in the MT has the singular verb:[109]

---

of the predicate. See *GKC* § 146 c, 467. Yet, even if we remove from the discussion those few occurrences of the collective with ל כ, our contention that Ezekiel prefers the plural predicate with the collective noun is in no way diminished.

105. The other occurrences of this phenomenon occur in 21.10; 24.19; 31.17; 33.2; 39.13; 46.3, 18.

106. See for example, Ezek 3.7, 8, 25; 5.6, 7, 12, 13; 8.17, 18; 11.6, 7, 10, 12, 15; 12.2, 15; 14.5, 6, 10, 11; 18.30; 20.7, 8, 39; 21.12, 29; 24.21, 24; 25.12, 14; 28.26; 30.26; 32.9; 33.10; 34.6, 21; 35.9, 13; 36.19, 22, 30; 37.13; 39.23, 28; 43.7, 8; 44.10, 30; 46.9, 10 passim. Most of these cases would occur with the most frequent collective noun in the book, בית ישראל.

107. See Ezek 3.7, 15; 4.4, 5; 5.7, 12; 8.17, 18; 11.5, 6; 12.2, 3; 14.5, 6; 18.25, 29; 20.5, 6; 21.11, 29; 22.18, 30; 24.21, 23; 25.12; 28.25, 26; 29.16; 30.23; 34.11, 12; 35.12, 13; 36.12, 17; 37.13, 14; 39.23, 24; 43.7, 8; 44.6, 7; 45.8; 46.10, 18 passim.

108. This phrase is similar to the earlier phrase וכל ישראל עוברים in Josh 3.17. See also, 1QM 9.1; 16.7-8.

109. See Kutscher, *Isaiah*, 399; and Qimron, *DSS Hebrew*, 83.

Isa 9.18   ויהי העם
1QIsa^a 9.18   ויהיו העם

Deut 20.11   כל העם הנמצא בה
11QTemple 62.7   כול העם הנמצאים בה

This LBH practice of using the plural verb with the collective noun continued in the MH period. The following examples are illustrative:[110]

m. Ḥor. 1.1   הורו בית דין
m. Šeqal. 4.8[111]   שאר נסים יפלו

By way of summary it should be noted that the tendency to use the plural verb with the collective noun, a characteristic which is prominent in LBH and in post-biblical literature, is a dominant feature of the Book of Ezekiel. Ezekiel thus must be viewed as playing a crucial role in this diachronic shift which finally resulted in understanding the collective as plural.

110. See Segal, *MHG*, 215.
111. It might plausibly be argued that the occurrence of the plural verb in this instance resulted from assimilation to the *nomen rectum*.

ל + *Direct Object*

כפר ל

The tendency for the writers of LBH to employ the preposition ל instead of the particle את to introduce the direct object has been noted by several scholars. Gesenius-Kautzsch for example remarks: 'Another solecism of the later period is finally the introduction of the object by the preposition ל '.[112] This feature is especially prominent in Chronicles as illustrated by the following examples which contrast the Chronicler's practice with the earlier practice in parallel texts:

2 Sam. 8.6	ויושע ה׳ את דוד
1 Chr. 18.6	ויושע ה׳ לדויד
1 Kgs 12.6	להשיב את העם הזה דבר
2 Chr 10.6	להשיב לעם הזה דבר

In the Book of Ezekiel, the use of the preposition ל to introduce the direct object has been observed in the following phrases:

14.7[113]	לדרש לו

---

112. *GKC* § 117 n, 366. See also Smend, *Ezechiel*, 189; Brockelmann, *Hebräische Syntax* § 95, 87; A.B. Davidson, *Introductory Hebrew Grammar. Hebrew Syntax* (Edinburgh, 1894) 107; Hadas-Lebel, *Manuel d'histoire de la langue hébraïque*, 101; and Rendsburg, 'Late Biblical Hebrew and the Date of "P"', 72. It is extant in earlier material as well, as for example the well known phrase ואהבת לרעך(Lev 19.18).

113. Polzin evidently believes the ל preposition introduces the direct object pronominal suffix in this verse. Polzin, *Hebrew*, 65. Two observations about the phrase are noteworthy. First, in the majority of cases in the Bible where the root דרש governs a direct object it is preceded by את. And secondly, the cases where ל does occur with this root are predominantly LBH: Deut 12.5, 30; 2 Sam 11.3; Jer 30.17; Ps 142.5; Job 10.6; Ezra 4.2; 7.21; 1 Chr 22.19; 2 Chr 15.13; 17.3, 4; 20.3; 31.21; 34.3. The preposition could be introducing the indirect object, however. See König, *LHS* III, 273; Smend, *Ezechiel*, 81; Cooke, *Ezekiel*, 155; Keil, *Ezekiel*, 180; Greenberg, *Ezekiel*, 250; and Zimmerli, *Ezekiel* I, 302. If, however, the direct object of לדרוש is בי in Ezek 14.7, then we would observe the same late linguistic feature found only in 1 Chr 10.14 and 2 Chr 34.26. Greenberg, *Ezekiel*, 250.

16.63[114]	בכפרי לך לְכָל אשר עשית
26.3.[115]	כהעלות הים לְגַלָּיו
34.22[116]	והושעתי לְצֹאני
44.8[117]	ותשימון לְשֹׁמרי משמרתי

This tendency for the use of the preposition ל with the direct object is prominent in BA[118] as well as in the Aramaic dialects, including the Babylonian Talmud[119] and Syriac.[120] It is also frequent in MH.[121] Particularly significant is the following illustration from MH which parallels the use of the ל direct object with the root כפר in Ezek 16. 63:

m. Yoma 3.8   כפר נא לעוונות

114. This is the only occurrence in the Bible of the verb כפר in the Piel with the ל preposition preceding the direct object. The significance of the distinctiveness of this usage is reinforced by the frequent occurrence of the phrase אשר ...כל את in the Book of Ezekiel. See Ezek 3.10; 11.25; 16.37; 18.14; 18.31; 20.43; 35.12. 39.26; and especially 16.37b with a perfectly parallel construction to Ezek 16.63 apart from the use of את for ל. The use of את before the direct object of this root is particularly prominent in Lev 16. See for example Lev 16.20, 33.

115. See Selle, *Aramaismis*, 35; Ewald, *Hezeqiel*, 470; Smend, *Ezechiel*, 189; *GKG* § 117 n, 366; and Zimmerli, *Ezekiel* II, 27.

116. This is the only occurrence צאן as the object of the verb ישע in the Bible.

117. Note JPS translation 'but ye have set keepers of my charge'. In addition to these occurrences Selle adds Ezek 34.4, 16; 37.11. See *Aramaismis*, 35.

118. E. Kautzsch, *Grammatik des Biblisch-Aramäischen* (Leipzig, 1884) § 84, 151-52; Selle, *Aramaismis*, 35; and Bauer-Leander, *GBA* § 100, 335. See also, Ewald, *Lehrbuch* § 277 e, 692-93; and § 292 e, 748.

119. See Max L. Margolis, *A Manual of the Aramaic Language of the Babylonian Talmud* (München, 1910) § 61 b, 84.

120. See König, *LHS* III, 275-76; and T. Nöldeke, *Kurzgefasste Syrische Grammatik* (Leipzig, 1898) § 287, 199. The Jerusalem Talmud, however, prefers the direct object marker. See Bendavid, *Leshon* I, 30. Targum Neofiti also prefers the direct object marker, however the preposition ל does occasionally introduce the direct object. See David M. Golomb, *A Grammar of Targum Neofiti* (Chico, California, 1985) 26, 210.

121. Segal, *MHG*, 168. This usage does not occur in the DSS unless ל is used to introduce the direct object in the phrase לכפר לכול המתנדבים in 1QS 5.6. If this is indeed the ל direct object then we have yet another illustration of the pattern כפר ל as in Ezek 16.63.

The widespread nature of the occurrence of the preposition ל preceding the direct object in Aramaic literature should cause us to suspect its occurrence in BH to be due to Aramaic influence.[122] Regardless, its occurrence in Ezekiel, once again suggests a certain association of the language of Ezekiel with the language of LBH.

---

122. Thus Ewald, *Lehrbuch* § 277 e, 692-93; § 292 e, 748; Brockelmann, *Grundriss* II § 211 d, 317-18; *Hebräische Syntax* § 95, 87; and Polzin, *Hebrew*, 65 and n. 100.

והוליד בן

One distinctive feature of LBH is the diminished employment of the
use of the *waw* consecutive tense.[123] This diachronic shift can best be
elucidated by comparing parallel texts from different chronological
periods:[124]

| Gen 25.2 | נַתֵּ֫לֶד לו את זמרן |
| 1 Chr 1.32 | יַלְדָה את זמרן |

| 1 Kgs 8.4 | וַיַּעֲל֫וּ אתם |
| 2 Chr 5.5 | הֶעֱל֫וּ אתם |

| 2 Kgs 8.27 | וַיֵּ֫לֶךְ בדרך בית אחאב |
| 2 Chr 22.3 | הָלַךְ בדרכי בית אחאב |

Accompanying the tendency to avoid the consecutive tense in LBH
is the increase in the use of the simple tense with *waw* conjunction.[125]
Note the following parallel texts where the Chronicler uses the *waw*
conjunction where the parallel text has the *waw* consecutive:

| 2 Sam 24.2 | וְיָדַ֫עְתִּי את מספר העם |
| 1 Chr 21.2 | וְאֵדְעָה את מספרם |

---

123. See Bergsträsser, *Hebräische Grammatik* II § 8 h, 39; § 9 n, 44; Driver,
Tenses § 131, 186; Cooke, *Ezekiel*, 143; and Rabin, 'Hebrew', in *EM* 6, 70. The
reluctance to use the *waw* consecutive tense can be detected as early as the
Lachish letters. See Baumgartner, 'Was wir heute von der hebräischen
Sprache und ihrer Geschichte wissen', 608-609. Huesman's contention that
many of the occurrences of the *waw* conjunction with the perfect tense are no
more than corruptions of actual infinitive absolutes has not gained wide
support. John Huesman, 'The Infinite Absolute and the Waw + Perfect
Problem', *Biblica* 37 (1956) 410-34; cf. 412.
124. See also 2 Sam 24.4 = 1 Chr 21.4; 1 Kgs 15.13 = 2 Chr 15.16; 1 Kgs 15.17 = 2
Chr 16.1; 2 Kgs 15.5 = 2 Chr 26.20; and 2 Kgs 16.7 = 2 Chr 28.16; 2 Kgs 23.16 = 2
Chr 34.5. This trend to avoid the consecutive tense may also be observed in the
Chronicler's substitution of an infinitive or a participle for the consecutive
tense (1 Chr 15.25 = 2 Sam 6.12; 1 Chr 19.6 = 2 Sam 10.6; and 2 Chr 3.13 = 1 Kgs
6.27).
125. See for example, Hadas-Lebel, *Manuel d'histoire de la langue hébraïque*,
98; and Joshua Blau, 'Thoughts on the Tense System in Biblical Literature', in
Festschrift for I.A. Zeligmann. Articles in Bible and Ancient World, eds. Y.
Zakowitz and A. Rofe (Jerusalem, 1982) 20 [In Hebrew].

2 Kgs 12.11[126]	וַיָּעַל ספר המלך
2 Chr 24.11	וַיָּבֹא סופר המלך

2 Kgs 23.6	וַיָּדֶק
2 Chr 34.4	וַהֵדַק

The use of the *waw* conjunction with the simple tense occurs in the Book of Ezekiel in the following examples:

11.6[127]	נמלאתם חוצתיה חלל
18.10[128]	נהוליד בן פריץ שפך דם

The use of *waw* conjunctive with the simple tense occurs at least thirty-two additional times in the Book of Ezekiel.[129]

The preference of the *waw* conjunctive with the simple tense over the employment of the *waw* consecutive increased in post-biblical literature. This phenomenon accounts for the following sequence of verbs in 4QSam[a], which contrasts with the earlier practice in 2 Samuel:

2 Sam 15.2	ועמד ... ויהי ... ויקרא
4QSam[a] 15.2	ועמד ... [והיה] ... וקרא

---

126. The Chronicler's choice of the root בוא to translate the verb וַיָּעַל may suggest that he understood the verb as coming from the Aramaic root עלל, 'enter'. If this is the case, we would have another illustration, on a different level, of the extent of Aramaic influence in LBH. For additional illustrations of the Chronicler using the root בוא where the parallel passage has עלה, see Sara Japhet, 'The Interchange of Verbal Roots in Parallel Texts in the Chronicles', *Leshonenu* 31 (1967) 261 [In Hebrew].

127. See Bergsträsser, *Hebräische Grammatik* II § 9 n, 45.

128. This construction must be viewed as *waw* conjunctive with the simple perfect due to the occurrence of the parallel construction הוליד בן in Ezek 18.14. See Greenberg, *Ezekiel*, 330-31.

129. 9.7, 7, 8; 12.25, 28; 13.6, 8, 11; 14.7; 16.19; 17.18, 24; 18.10, 26; 19.12; 20.22, 37; 23.40, 41; 25.12; 37.2, 7, 8, 10; 40.24, 35; 41.3, 8, 13, 15; 42.15. See Kimchi (on 13.11), Ewald, *Lehrbuch* § 342 b, 841; Cornhill, *Ezechiel*, 246, 348; Ehrlich, *Ezekiel*, 356; Bergsträsser, *Hebräische Grammatik* II § 9 n, 45; Greenberg, *Ezekiel*, 368; Zimmerli *Ezekiel* I, 357-58, 391, 478; *Ezekiel* II, 254; Cooke, *Ezekiel*, 143; and Brownlee, *Ezekiel*, 141.

This tendency to avoid using the consecutive tenses 4QSam[a] should be viewed as the normative practice of DSS Hebrew. It is only in those documents where we observe a calculated imitation of BH that the converted tenses are used as frequently as in EBH.[130] This tendency progressed until in the times of MH the converted tenses were no longer in use.[131]

It is apparent that the proclivity to avoid the consecutive tenses, a feature of LBH and post-biblical Hebrew, was already the practice of the prophet Ezekiel in the exile. The book of Ezekiel should thus be viewed as signaling the beginning of the more frequent use of the simple tenses with the *waw* conjunction. And while Ezekiel's use of the *waw* conjunction with the simple tense has not advanced to the degree of other late biblical books, this feature does occur enough to be considered as a dominant trait of Ezekiel's Hebrew. There is widespread agreement that this avoidance of using the consecutive tenses, with the resultant increase in the use of the *waw* conjunction with the simple tense in BH, is due to Aramaic influence.[132]

---

130. 1QS, for example, completely avoids the use of the *waw* conjunction with the perfect tense. See Leahy, *A Study of the Language of the Manual of Discipline*, 19.
131. See Segal, *MHG*, 151, 154.
132. Thus Driver, *Tenses* § 133, 188; Kropat, *Syntax*, 22; Kutscher, *Isaiah*, 351; Zimmerli, *Ezekiel* I, 478; and Greenberg, *Ezekiel*, 368. By contrast, Rendsburg accounts for the avoidance of the consecutive tenses as merely a reflection of the spoken language. See *Evidence for Spoken Hebrew in Biblical Times*, 103.

Temporal Clause

בצאת

It has long been noted that the employment of the introductory formula ויהי/ה diminished in the biblical period.[133] This diachronic change affected the form of temporal clauses in LBH. This can best be seen from illustrations from parallel texts from Kings and Chronicles:[134]

1 Kgs. 8.54	ויהי ככלות שלמה להתפלל
2 Chr 7.1	וככלות שלמה להתפלל
2 Kgs 12.11	ויהי כראותם כי רב הכסף
2 Chr 24.11	וכראותם כי רב הכסף

Polzin's research has illuminated the clear diachronic demarcation of this phenomenon:

> Confer the concordance where k^e plus *kallôt* occurs twenty-five times. It occurs sixteen times with *hāyāh* and nine times without *hāyāh*; *hāyāh* never occurs in a book later than Jeremiah and the lack of *hāyāh* is found seven times in Chr, Ezr and Dan, and once in Ex and II Sam. Again, the introductory phrase, *wayhî kišmoa'* occurs twice in the Chronicler's language: II Chr 15.8, Ezr 9.3, and not all in Kgs.[135]

The tendency to omit ויהי or והיה before the infinitive construct with ב/כ is particularly evident in the late book of Esther. As Bergey states: 'In Esther, there is a marked preference for the use of the introductory infinitive construct + ב/כ without ויהי or והיה preceding it (1.4, 5: 2.7, 12, 15, 19; 5.9; 9.25) as compared to those with (2.8; 3.4; 5.2)'.[136]

The book of Ezekiel clearly shares this literary feature which was common in the later biblical period as the infinitive construct occurs with ב/כ but without והיה/ויהי forty-eight times as opposed to only

---

133. Driver, *Introduction*, 538; and Kropat, *Syntax,* 23, 74.
134. Kropat, *Syntax,* 23.
135. Polzin, *Hebrew,* 46.
136. *Esther,* 52.

six occurrences of the EBH construction. A few examples of this later
practice are illustrative:[137]

Ezek 1.25	בעמדם תרפינה בנפיהן
Ezek 16.34	ובתחך אתנן ואתנן לא נתן לך
Ezek 39.27	בשובבי אותם מן העמים
Ezek 47.3	בצאת האיש קדים

Particularly noteworthy is the occurrence of the construction ובבוא
in ובבוא הנשיא (Ezek 46.8) and ובבוא עם הארץ (Ezek 46.9).
Every occurrence of כ/ב/בוא with a preceding ויהי or והיה occurs
exclusively in EBH texts—Gen 12.14; Exod 33.9; 1 Sam 4.5; 5.10; 30.1;
2 Sam 17.27; 2 Kgs 10.7.[138] Ezekiel, however, avoids the introductory
והיה/ויהי in typical LBH fashion.

In the DSS this tendency to avoid והיה/ויהי in the temporal clause
is illustrated by the following examples:[139]

1QM 3. 10	ובשובם מן המלחמה
11QTemple 32.12	בבואם לרשת בקודש

The earlier EBH tendency to introduce the temporal clause with
והיה/ויהי does occur in DSS, but only in citations or allusions to
biblical texts.[140]

There can be no doubt that Ezekiel's use of the infinitive construct
with ב or כ in an introductory clause is in harmony with LBH and
DSS, and in contrast to the earlier practice where והיה/ויהי
preceded the infinitive construct. Indeed, Ezekiel prefers this
construction to a greater degree than the late book of Esther as the
ratio of the LBH construction to the EBH construction is 8: 1. This
decided preference certainly indicates that this feature was firmly
established in the exilic period. In post-biblical Hebrew, particularly

---

137. See also Ezek 1.19, 21, 24; 3.18, 20, 27; 5.16; 10.11, 16, 17; 15.5; 16.31; 18.24,
26, 27; 20.31, 34, 39; 26.19; 27.23; 29.7; 32.15; 33.8, 13, 14, 18, 19, 33; 34.12; 35.14;
39.27; 42.14; 43.23; 44.19; 45.1; 46.8, 9, 10; 47.3, 7. The EBH formula with
והיה/ויהי occurs in Ezek 9.8; 10.6; 11.13; 21.8. 37.7; 44.17.
138. The phrase does occur without ויהי/והיה in Exod 34.34; Num 7.89; Deut
31.11; Josh 3.15; 8.29; 1 Kgs 14.12. See Bergey, *Esther*, 53.
139. For additional examples see Bergey, *Esther*, 54-55.
140. Qimron, *DSS Hebrew*, 72-73.

MH, the disuse of ב or כ with the infinitive demonstrates further diachronic change in this construction.[141]

141. Segal, *MHG*, 165; and Kutscher, *EncJud* 16, 'Hebrew Language, Mishnaic Hebrew', 1603.

Infinitive As Indicative

לבוא עתה

Typical of LBH, as well as of the Hebrew of the DSS, is the indicative use of the infinitive construct with *lamed*.[142] Especially noteworthy are the occurrences of this usage of the infinitive construct in Chronicles:[143]

1 Chr 9. 25	ואחיהם בחצריהם <u>לבוא</u>
2 Chr 11.22	ויעמד לראש רחבעם את אביה בן מעכה
	לנגיד באחיו כי <u>להמליכו</u>

The identical practice may be observed in the DSS in the War Scroll:

1QM 6.3	זיקי דם <u>להפיל</u> חללים באף אל
1QM 12.9-10	בעננים וכעבי טל <u>לבסות</u> ארץ וכזרם
	רביבים <u>להשקות</u> משפט לכול צאצאיה

This phenomenon occurs also in the Book of Ezekiel in the following phrase:

| Ezek 22.3[144] | עיר שפכת דם בתוכה <u>לבוא עתה</u> |

The use of the infinitive construct with the preposition ל as an indicative, does not occur very frequently in BH, however the occasions when this phenomenon does occur are apparently restricted to LBH. And, while this trait is by no means common in Ezekiel, Ezekiel does register an early attestation of feature which would later be characteristic of LBH and DSS Hebrew. Thus, once more we see a linguistic feature existing in the Book of Ezekiel that would occur in a

---

142. See Kropat, *Syntax*, 24-25; T. Leahy, 'Studies in the Syntax of 1QS', *Biblica* 41 (1960) 142; and Qimron, *DSS Hebrew*, 70-72.
143. See also 1 Chr 5.1 and 2 Chr 12.12 for similar use of the infinitive preceded by לא.
144. The expression also occurs in Isa 13.22, in the phrase וקרוב לבוא עתה. In the Isaiah passage however, the infinitive has its usual infinitival connotation. Note, for example, how the identical phrases are differently translated in the JPS version.

more widespread fashion later in BH and in post-biblical Hebrew as well.

היה + *Participle*

היה עמד אצלי

The use of the copula היה with the participle, a common feature of
MH,[145] enjoyed an increased frequency in the literature of LBH. As
König remarks: '... so ist es doch zweifellos, dass in den späteren
Schriften des ATs. mehr, als früher, היה mit dem Particip gesetzt
worden ist ...'.[146] Examples of this LBH feature, which connotes the
durative or iterative aspect, include the following:

Neh 2.13	ואהי שבר בחומת ירושלם
2 Chr 24.12	ויהיו שברים חצבים וחרשים

The increased likelihood for the employment of this expression in
LBH may be illustrated by the following parallel passage:

1 Kgs 8.7	כי הכרובים פרשים כנפים
2 Chr 5.8	ויהיו הכרובים פרשים כנפים

This feature is extant in the book of Ezekiel in two places:

Ezek 34.2	הוי רעי ישראל אשר היו רעים אותם
Ezek 43.6[147]	ואיש היה עמד אצלי

This late feature also exists in BA in the phrase עד בטלא עד
שנת תרתין (Ezra 4.24).

In post-biblical literature the היה + participle construction was
used in an even more widespread fashion. This construction, for

145. See Segal, *MHG*, esp. 156-57.
146. König, *LHS* II § 239 c, 132. So also, Bergsträsser, *Hebräische Grammatik*
II § 13 i, 73; Joüon, *Grammaire* § 121 g, 340-41; and most recently Morag,
'Qumran Hebrew: Some Typological Observations', 160. Driver purports to
understand the rationale behind the use of this construction when he suggests
that the more frequent employment of this construction in LBH illustrates the
growing decadence of the language among the later writers who crave for a
greater distinctiveness. See *Tenses* § 135, 198.
147. Bergsträsser, *Hebräische Grammatik* II § 13 i, 73. Perhaps also to be included is the phrase מתבוססת בדמך היית (Ezek 16.22) and the passive
participle סגור with יהיה in Ezek 44.2; 46.1. See, M.H. Segal, 'Mišnaic
Hebrew and its Relation to Biblical Hebrew and to Aramaic', 695, 698.

example, is one of the prominent features of the Temple Scroll.[148] The following is an illustrative list of occurrences in the DSS:[149]

1QM 7.11	הכוהן האחד <u>יהיה מהלך</u>
1QS 1.18-19	<u>והיו הכוהנים</u> והלויים <u>מברכים</u>
11QTemple 34.7	יהיו <u>טובחים</u> אותמה <u>ויהיו בונסים</u> א[ת].7

As noted above, this feature was also part of the language of MH, and could be considered a characteristic feature of the language. The following phrases are some illustrations of the occurrence of this construction in MH:

| *m. Ber.* 1.3 | ואני <u>הייתי בא</u> בדרך |
| *m. Šeb.* 4.1 | <u>היו אומרין</u> |

The following semantically parallel phrase from the BT illustrates both the prevalence of this feature in the Talmud as well as the manner in which the later practice differed from the EBH convention:[150]

| Lev 7.15 | ביום קרבנו <u>יאכל</u> |
| *b. Zebaḥ.* 56b | יכול <u>יהו נאכלין</u> |

By way of summary, we must conclude that Ezekiel sides with LBH and post-biblical Hebrew in the use of the היה + participle construction. The 'intrusion' of this construction into BH was doubtlessly due to Aramaic influence as this feature was widespread in Aramaic, as observed above in the BA illustration, as well as in various Aramaic

148. According to Qimron. See Elisha Qimron, 'The Vocabulary of the Temple Scroll', in *Annual for the Study of the Bible and Ancient East* 4 (1980) 244 [In Hebrew].
149. For other illustrations, see 1QM 9.1; 16.8; 18.15; 11QTemple 34.7.
150. Cited by Bendavid in *Leshon* I, 381. For additional post-biblical examples of this phenomenon see *Leshon* I, 380-81; and *Leshon* II, 540-42.

dialects,[151] including Syriac,[152] Palmyrene,[153] and the Babylonian Talmud.[154]

---

151. For the widespread use of this construction in the Elephantine Papyri see Joseph A. Fitzmyer, *The Syntax of Imperial Aramaic* (Ph.D. dissertation, John Hopkins University, 1956) 221-22.

152. T. Nöldeke, *Kurzgefasste Syrische Grammatik* § 277, 190-92.

153. See J. Cantineau, *Grammaire du Palmyrénien Épigraphique* (Le Caire, 1935) 144.

154. See Michael Schlesinger, *Satzlehre der Aramäischen Sprache des Babylonischen Talmuds* (Leipzig, 1928) § 28, 42; David Marcus, *A Manual of Babylonian Jewish Aramaic* (Washington, DC, 1981) 8; and Margolis, *A Manual of the Aramaic Language of the Babylonian Talmud*, 81. This formation is especially common in Targum Neofiti. See David M. Golomb, *A Grammar of Targum Neofiti*, 188-201.

אֲשֶׁר = 'That'

ידע אשר

The use of the relative pronoun אֲשֶׁר with a subordinate clause increased in frequency in LBH. The particle in these occurrences takes on the meaning 'that' and is used in place of the particle כִּי, common in EBH[155] and in the Lachish letters.[156] A few examples illustrate the growing proclivity toward this trend in LBH:[157]

Est 3.4	כי הגיד להם אֲשֶׁר הוא יהודי
Ezra 2.63	ויאמר התרשתא להם אֲשֶׁר לא יאכלו
Neh 8.14	וימצאו כתוב בתורה אֲשֶׁר צוה ה׳

The following parallel text helps demonstrate this diachronic change:

| 1 Kgs 5.20 | אתה ידעת כִּי אין בנו איש ידע לכרת עצים |
| 2 Chr 2.7 | אני ידעתי אֲשֶׁר עבדיך יודעים לכרות עצי לבנון |

This same diachronic shift may be observed by comparing a text from Ezekiel with an earlier pre-exilic text:

| Ezek 20.26 | למען אשר ידעו אֲשֶׁר אני ה׳ |
| Exod 8.18 | למען תדע כִּי אני ה׳ |

Another example of this use of אֲשֶׁר in the book of Ezekiel might also be evident in the problematic phrase: ועשיתי את אשר בחקי תלכו (Ezek 36.27).[158]

In post-biblical Hebrew, the use of אֲשֶׁר before a subordinate clause discontinued in both DSS Hebrew and in MH. The DSS employed the particle כִּי for this function, while MH used the particle שֶׁ. Note how the use of שֶׁ in MH exactly parallels the use אֲשֶׁר of in LBH:[159]

---

155. See *BDB*, 83; Driver, *Introduction*, 553; and Bergey, *Esther*, 61.
156. See Torczyner, *The Lachish Letters*, 50, 78, and 92.
157. See Bergey, *Esther*, 61.
158. Thus Brockelmann, *Hebräische Syntax* § 161 bβ, 153.
159. See Segal, *MHG*, 205.

m. Ber. 2.5	יודע אני שהוא מקובל
m. 'Abot 4.22	לידע שהוא אל

In conclusion, it is apparent that there was a tendency among the writers of LBH to use אשר for EBH כי in the subordinate clause. This is particularly true of the late books Esther and Nehemiah and is extant as well in the book of Ezekiel.[160] The same trend continued in Tannaitic times although the particle אשר was replaced by ש.

---

160. This feature occurs only once in Chronicles, 2 Chr 2.7. Kropat, *Syntax*, 75.

Dimension Precedes Measure

ורחב חמש אמות

The placement of the measurement dimension before the measurement, is a feature of LBH and differs from the earlier practice of placing the measurement first. A few illustrations will demonstrate the prevailing practice in the the pre-exilic period:[161]

Gen 6.15	שלש מאות אמה אֹרֶךְ
Exod 25.10	אמתים וחצי אֹרְבּוֹ
Deut 3.11	תשע אמות אֹרְבָּה
1 Kgs 6.2	ושלשים אמה קֹומָתוֹ

A measurement attestation from the pre-exilic Siloam Inscription is harmonious with these early biblical sources. In lines five and six of this text we read: ומ[א]ת אמה יהיה גבה.[162] The diachronic shift in BH can be seen by comparing the following parallel texts:

| 1 Kgs 6.2 | ששים אמה ארכו ועשרים רחבו |
| 2 Chr 3.3 | הָאֹרֶךְ ... אמות ששים וְרֹחַב אמות עשרים |

| 1 Kgs 6.20 | עשרים אמה אֹרֶךְ ועשרים אמה רֹחַב |
| 2 Chr 3.8[163] | אֹרְבּוֹ ... אמות עשרים וְרָחְבּוֹ אמות עשרים |

This trend apparently became more intensified late in the pre-exilic period because by the time of the exile the prevalent order appears to be: measurement dimension + measurement. In the book of Ezekiel the measurement dimension is placed before the measurement in fifty-six of seventy-nine possible cases, approximately 71% of the possible chances. A few illustrations of the feature believed to be a characteristic LBH trait are given below:[164]

161. For a comprehensive list of the references see Bergey, *Esther*, 80-81.
162. See Donner-Röllig, *KAI* I, 34.
163. Observe also in this parallel text from Chronicles that the Chronicler, in contrast to the practice in Kings, employs an anticipatory pronominal suffix. This, in conjunction with what we noted above, provides another illustration of a feature characteristic of LBH.
164. The LBH arrangement can also be observed in the following passages: Ezek 40.5, 11, 13, 21, 25, 29, 30, 33, 36, 42, 47, 48, 49; 41.2, 3, 4, 5, 9, 10, 11, 12, 13,

| Ezek 40.5 | וְהָרֹמָה קנה אחד |
| Ezek 40.11 | אֹרֶךְ השער שלוש עשרה אמות |

Particularly illustrative is the following example from Ezekiel, seen
against a parallel, but earlier text:

| Exod 27.1 | וחמש אמות רֹחַב |
| Ezek 40.30 | וְרֹחַב חמש אמות |

This trend continued in the biblical period until by the time of
Esther only the measurement dimension + measurement order was
used.[165] The same order prevailed in BA:

| Dan 3.1 | רוּמֵהּ אמין שתין פְּתָיֵהּ אמין שת |
| Ezra 6.3 | רוּמֵהּ אמין שתין פְּתָיֵהּ אמין שתין |

In the post-biblical period we find that the LBH construction continued in the DSS and MH, as the following examples demonstrate:

1QM 4.15	אוֹרֶךְ ארבע עשרה אמה
11QTemple 30.8-9	רוֹחְבּוֹ ארבע אמות
m. Menaḥ. 11.5	השלחן אָרְכּוֹ עשרה וְרוֹחְבּוֹ חמשה
m. ʿErub. 9.1	גג גְּבֹוּהַ עשרה או נָמוּךְ עשרה

In conclusion, the predominant use of the order, measurement
dimension + measurement in the Book of Ezekiel, in contrast to the
order of EBH, is typical of LBH, DSS Hebrew, and MH. Though the
use of this arrangement in Ezekiel is not exclusive, we can detect a
growing frequency in usage. Moreover, the occurrence of this same
order in BA, as well as in other Aramaic Inscriptions,[166] may suggest
that this shift in Hebrew was due to Aramaic influence.

14, 22; 42.2, 7, 8, 20; 43.14; 45.1, 3, 6; 48.9, 10, 13. In sixteen of the seventy-nine
occurrences alternating LBH/ EBH orders are chiastically arranged.
165. The LBH order occurs in the only two measurements in the book, in Esther 5.14 and 7.9.
166. Cf. A. Cowley, *Aramaic Papyri of the Fifth Century* (Osnabrück, 1967) no.
15, lines 8, 9, and 11, 44-45.

Avoid Repetition

עַל ... וְ

In LBH there was an apparent tendency toward brevity which resulted in the avoidance of repetition. Put differently, there was a tendency among LBH writers to write only once what in EBH would be written twice.[167] This phenomenon was often accompanied by the resultant tendency to form the linkage of two or more linguistic entities simply through the conjunction *waw*. This characteristic trait may best be illustrated in the following parallel passages where the repeated verbs, prepositions, direct object markers, *nomen regens*, and particles of earlier biblical texts are written only once by the Chronicler:[168]

1 Kgs 7.21	וַיָּקֶם אֶת הָעַמֻּדִים לְאֻלָם הַהֵיכָל וַיָּקֶם אֶת
	הָעַמּוּד הַיְמָנִי וַיִּקְרָא אֶת שְׁמוֹ יָכִין וַיָּקֶם אֶת
	הָעַמּוּד הַשְּׂמָאלִי וַיִּקְרָא אֶת שְׁמוֹ בֹּעַז
2 Chr 3.17	וַיָּקֶם אֶת הָעַמּוּדִים עַל פְּנֵי הַהֵיכָל אֶחָד
	מִיָּמִין וְאֶחָד מֵהַשְּׂמָאול וַיִּקְרָא שֵׁם הַיְמָנִי
	יָכִין וְשֵׁם הַשְּׂמָאלִי בֹּעַז
Gen 25.2	וַתֵּלֶד לוֹ אֶת זִמְרָן וְאֶת יָקְשָׁן וְאֶת מְדָן
	וְאֶת מִדְיָן וְאֶת יִשְׁבָּק וְאֶת שׁוּחַ
1 Chr 1.32	יָלְדָה אֶת זִמְרָן וְיָקְשָׁן וּמְדָן וּמִדְיָן
	וְיִשְׁבָּק וְשׁוּחַ
2 Sam 5.19	הַאֶעֱלֶה אֶל פְּלִשְׁתִּים הֲתִתְּנֵם בְּיָדִי
1 Chr 14.10	הַאֶעֱלֶה עַל פְּלִשְׁתִּיִּים וּנְתַתָּם בְּיָדִי

---

167. Extra biblical attestations to the EBH practice may be observed in the Mesha Inscription, lines seven and twelve and Arad 18. 4-5. See Donner-Röllig, *KAI* I, 33; and Y. Aharoni, *Arad Inscriptions* (Jerusalem, 1981) 35. Andersen's statement concerning the occurrence of this feature in the Mesha inscription: 'As in Hebrew, the preposition is repeated before each coordinated noun ...' is accurate for EBH only. Francis I. Andersen, 'Moabite Syntax', *Orientalia* N. S. 35 (1966) 89. This repetition of the preposition is a form of syndeton. Thus Brockelmann, *Grundriss* II § 287 a, 464-65.

168. See also 2 Sam 7.8 = 1 Chr 17.7; 2 Sam 7.10 = 1 Chr 17.9; 2 Sam 7.23 = 1 Chr 17.21; 2 Sam 8.10 = 1 Chr 18.10; 2 Sam 20.23 = 1 Chr 18.17; 1 Kgs 10.29 = 2 Chr 1.17; and 2 Kgs 23.2 = 2 Chr 34.3.

The Chronicler is thus more economic in his use of language, writing only what is necessary and avoiding the repetition of the earlier language.

We find the same tendency to shun repetition prevalent in the book of Ezekiel, as the following examples demonstrate:[169]

Ezek 33.31[170]	ויבואו אליך כמבוא עם וישבו
	לפניך עמי
Ezek 36.3	ותעלו על שפת לשון ודבת עם
Ezek 36.30	והרביתי את פרי העץ ותנובת השדה
Ezek 30.17	בחורי און ופי בסת בחרב יפלו

The same technique can be observed in the DSS, particularly in 1QIsa[a]. Contrast the writer's tendency to abbreviate what might be considered redundant in the MT:

Isa 6.2	שש כנפים שש כנפים לאחד
1QIsa[a] 6.2	שש כנפים לאחד

Isa 6.3	קדוש קדוש קדוש ה׳ צבאות
1QIsa[a] 6.3[171]	קדוש קדוש ה׳ צבאות

In summary, we note again that Ezekiel anticipates another late characteristic prominent in the Chronicles, DSS, and later in the Babylonian Talmud,[172] as his writing is terse when compared with earlier style of EBH. In this we see, once again in the book of Ezekiel, a linguistic phenomenon which was later to become characteristic of the Hebrew of the Chronicler.

---

169. See also Ezek 13.5, 7; 17.9, 15; 22.14; 27.13, 16, 17, 18, 21; 28.2; 32.20; 33.31; 34.14; 35.7, 8; 36.31; 37.19; 38.22; 39.4, 9; 40.5, 42; 43.9; 44.13, 17; and 48.28.
170. See JPS translation.
171. We recognize that this reading could be attributed to haplography.
172. See Margolis, *A Manual of the Aramaic Language of the Babylonian Talmud*, 68.

בין ... ל > בין ... ובין

The diachronic shift illustrated in the above formula was first discovered by G. Haneman in his study of the use of the preposition בין in BH and MH.[173] The formula בין ... ובין is more widespread in BH and occurs with greater frequency in pre-exilic times than the formula בין ... ל. The formula בין ... ובין is used to the exclusion of the formula בין ... ל in Exodus, Joshua, Judges, Jeremiah, and Zechariah; and it is indubitably preferred in Genesis (11: 1), Kings (11: 1), Samuel (7: 1), and Leviticus, Numbers, and Deuteronomy (all 2: 1). The formula בין ... ל first begins to occur on par with the more ancient בין...ובין formula in the book of Ezekiel.[174] This trend toward increased preference for the formula בין ... ל continued as the בין ... ל formula is preferred in Chronicles (2: 1), and is used to the exclusion of the בין ... ובין formula in Jonah, Malachi, Daniel, and Nehemiah.[175] The diachronic shift is beautifully demonstrated in parallel texts from Leviticus and Ezekiel:[176]

Lev 10.10	וּלְהַבְדִּיל בֵּין הַקֹּדֶשׁ וּבֵין הַחֹל
Ezek 22.26	בֵּין קֹדֶשׁ לַחֹל לֹא הִבְדִּילוּ

Lev 10.10	וּבֵין הַטָּמֵא וּבֵין הַטָּהוֹר
Ezek 22.26	וּבֵין הַטָּמֵא לַטָּהוֹר

The late construction favored by the writers of LBH was preferred in post-biblical Hebrew as well. Note the following occurrences in the DSS:

173. On the Preposition בין in the Mishna and in the Bible', *Leshonenu* 40 (1975-76) 33-53. [In Hebrew]. But see also, Bendavid, *Leshon* I, 334.
174. The formula בין ... ובין occurs eight times in Ezek: 4.3; 8.3, 16; 20.12, 20; 34.20; 47.16; 48.22. The formula בין ... ל occurs seven times in Ezek: 18.8; 22.26; 34.17, 22; 41.18; 42.20; 44.23. Doubtlessly, however, the occurrences of the EBH formula in Ezek 20.12, 20 are allusions to an earlier text, Exod 31.13. See Fishbane, 'The "Sign" in the Hebrew Bible', 234. It is also probable that the reference to אות in Ezek 4.3 likewise evokes the more ancient formula בין... ובין from the Exod 31.17 passage. See D.S. Shapira, 'The Literary Sources of the Book of Ezekiel', *Sinai* 66 (1969-70) 7 [In Hebrew].
175. For discussion and chart, see Haneman, 'On the Preposition בין in the Mishna and in the Bible', 43-44.
176. Hurvitz, *Linguistic Study*, 113.

11QTemple 46. 10	מבדיל בֵּין הקודש לָעִיר
4QMMT B.51-52[177]	בֵּין הטמא לַטהור
1QH 14.12	בֵּין טוב לָרשע
1QM 7.6-7	בֵּין כול מחיהמה לַמקום

The inclination for the writers of the DSS to prefer the LBH formula is perhaps best demonstrated by the following phrase from the Manual of Discipline in contrast to a common BH expression:[178]

Exod 18.16; Jer 7.5	בֵּין איש וּבֵין רעהו
1QS 5.20-21	בֵּין איש לָרעהו

In addition, note in the following passage from the Damascus Covenant the similar usage to Ezek 22.26 above in contrast to Lev 10.10:[179]

CD 12.19-20	להבדיל בֵּין הטמא לַטהור
	ולהודיע בֵּין הקדוש לַחול

In MH the formula בֵּין...לְ, which had become the preferred mode of expression in late biblical times, was the dominant formula as it occurs almost one hundred times.[180] The following illustrations constitute a representative list:

m. Nazir 9.3	אם יש בֵּין זה לָזה
m. Ber. 1.2	משיכירו בֵּין תכלת לַלבן
m. Mid. 3.1	בֵּין דמים מעליונים לַדמים התחתונים
	להבדיל

By way of summary, it must be concluded that the book of Ezekiel occupies a critical position in the diachronic history of the use of the formulae בֵּי...וּבֵין and בֵּין...לְ. And while it is precarious to conclude too much from percentages or ratios, we do note that in Ezekiel's more prevalent preference for the LBH formula בֵּין...לְ, he exhibits similar tendencies which we have previously observed—

---

177. Cited by Qimron, *DSS Hebrew*, 83 n. 59.
178. See Haneman, 'On the Preposition בֵּין in the Mishna and in the Bible', 40-41.
179. See Rabin, *Zadokite Documents*, 63.
180. Rabin, *Zadokite Documents*, 37.

Ezekiel often displays linguistic characteristics which approach the linguistic state of the Second Temple period. Ezekiel is the first biblical book to employ the use of the formula בֿין ... לֿ equally as much as the more ancient בֿין ... וּבֿין. This shift represents an apparent inner-Hebrew development with the book of Ezekiel nicely illustrating the transitionary stage.

Asyndetic Imperfect Apodosis

כי...ימות

The apodosis of the conditional sentence in LBH differs from the apodosis in EBH in two ways. First of all, the apodosis in LBH tends to be asyndetic in contrast with the syndetic apodosis in EBH: 'There is a steady advance in the use of the asyndetic apodosis as the sources become later in date ...'.[181] Secondly, the *waw* consecutive perfect, commonly employed in the apodosis in EBH, is replaced by the imperfect.[182] The following is a list of passages which reflect the common EBH pattern:[183]

Deut 21.14	והיה אם לא חפצת בה <u>ושלחתה</u>
2 Sam 15.33	אם עברת אתי <u>והית</u> עלי למשא
2 Kgs 7.4	ואם ישבנו פה <u>ומתנו</u>

The emerging pattern of the imperfect apodosis and the resultant avoidance of the *waw* consecutive apodosis, is best illustrated in the book of Esther. In each of the nine conditional sentences in Esther the apodosis is syndetic and in each apodosis the main verb of the clause is in the imperfect tense. A few examples will illustrate not only the pattern which occurs in Esther but the distinctive nature of the apodosis of the conditional clause in LBH:[184]

Est 1.19	אם על המלך טוב <u>יצא</u> דבר מלכות מלפניו
Est 6.13	אם מזרע היהודים מרדכי אשר החלות
	לנפל לפניו <u>לא תוכל</u> לו

In Ezekiel the apodosis of the conditional sentence unequivocally resembles the LBH composition. The apodosis occurs with the initial *waw* in twelve out of the thirteen conditional sentences. In addition, the imperfect tense is utilized instead of the perfect in nine out of the

---

181. Rebecca Corwin, *The Verb and the Sentence in Chronicles, Ezra, and Nehemiah* (Ph.D. dissertation, University of Chicago, 1909) 14.
182. Guenther, *Diachronic Study*, 218.
183. For additional examples and discussion, see Brockelmann, *Grundriss* II § 432, 646; § 465, 673; and Driver, *Tenses* § 136, 203.
184. The other conditional sentences occur in Est 3.9; 4.14; 5.4, 8; 7.3; 8.5; and 9.13.

possible ten situations.[185] Note the following illustrations of the use of
the conditional sentence in Ezekiel:[186]

3.6	אם לא אליהם שלחתיך <u>המה ישמעו</u> אליך
3.19	כי הזהרת רשע ולא שב מרשעו ומדרכו
	הרשעה <u>הוא</u> בעונו <u>ימות</u>
33.2-4[187]	כי... <u>דמו</u> בראשו <u>יהיה</u>

In BA the imperfect tense is used exclusively in the apodosis, to the
exclusion of the *waw* consecutive construction with the perfect tense.
The following examples are representative:[188]

Dan 2.5	הן לא תהודעונני חלמא ופשרה הדמין
	<u>תתעבדון</u>
Ezra 5.17	הן על מלכא טב <u>יתבקר</u> בבית גנזיא

This pattern in BA is consistent with what we find in other Aramaic
Inscriptions from about the fifth century BC.

Cowley # 5.7, 13[189]	הן בליתך <u>אנתן</u>
Cowley # 8.20-21[190]	הן מחר או יום אחרן ארשנכי דין...
	<u>אנה אנתן</u>
Kraeling # 3.14-15[191]	הן גרינך דין... <u>אנחן ננתן</u>

185. The apparent discrepancy in the number of conditional sentences results
from the fact that in three of the apodoses, neither the *waw* consecutive perfect
nor the imperfect occurs but rather the participle (14.15), perfect tense (33.6),
and imperative (43.11). For the apodosis of 14.15 beginning with the term
חבלי, see the JPS translation and *BDB*, 115.
186. The other verses which have both the asyndetic apodosis and the verb in
the imperfect include 3.21; 18.5-9, 21; 21.18; 33.9; 46.16. Ezek 46.17 is in fact the
only pure occurrence of the EBH conditional construction in Ezekiel.
187. The translations of both Cooke and Zimmerli disclose their acknowledgement of the long protasis. Cooke, *Ezekiel*, 364; and Zimmerli, *Ezekiel* II, 179.
188. See also Dan 2.6; 3.15; 5.16; Ezra 4.13, 16.
189. See A. Cowley, *Aramaic Papyri of the Fifth Century B.C.*, 11.
190. Cowley, *Aramaic Papyri of the Fifth Century B.C.*, 22.
191. See Emil G. Kraeling, *The Brooklyn Museum Aramaic Papyri*, 154. In the
recently published Aramaic papyri from Wadi ed-Daliyeh, it is clear that the
apodosis of the conditional clause in line six is asyndetic, though it is impossible to determine the tense of the verb due to the damaged text. See Cross,
'Samaria Papyrus 1: An Aramaic Slave Conveyance of 335 B.C.E. Found in the
Wadi Ed-Daliyeh', 8. The Ammonite Inscription from Deir 'Alla, on the other

The construction of the apodosis in the conditional sentence in the DSS does not present the consistent trend which we see emerging in LBH. Often, in fact, the earlier pattern of EBH is employed. Concerning the construction of the apodosis in 1QS, Leahy observes: 'Waw consecutive perfect frequently constitutes "waw-apodosis" for complex sentences beginning with a conditional, relative, or temporal expression'.[192] The Temple Scroll seems to slightly favor the earlier practice as well, although the later pattern of LBH is not infrequent. Note the alternating LBH/EBH pattern in the following contiguous conditional clauses from 11QTemple 47.15-17:

אם במקדשי תזבחוהו יטהר למקדשה ואם
בעריכמה תזבחוהו וטהר לעריכמה

Later in post-biblical Hebrew, in MH, the avoidance of the *waw* consecutive pattern which began in LBH is exclusively adopted while the main verb of the apodosis may take various forms. Note the following the examples:

m. Ber. 1.1	אם לא עלה עמוד השחר מותרין אתם
m. Ber. 2.1	אם ביוון את לבו יצא
m. Yoma 8.7	ואם מת יניחוהו

In conclusion, it should be noted that the shift from the *waw* consecutive perfect of EBH to the use of the simple imperfect in the apodosis in LBH and Aramaic texts in the apodosis, is certainly the prevailing pattern in the book of Ezekiel. And while post-biblical Hebrew did not completely adopt the LBH pattern, the avoidance of the *waw* consecutive in the apodosis is clearly evident, especially in MH and in the Babylonian Talmud.[193] The cause for this diachronic change should be sought from Aramaic influence as BA and Aramaic inscriptions consistently reflect this pattern which was to characterize LBH.

---

hand, has an asyndetic apodosis with an imperfect verb in each of the two conditional clauses of the inscription. See Jo Ann Hackett, *The Balaam Text From Deir 'Alla* (Chico, California, 1980) 26.

192. *A Study of the Language of the Essene Manual of Discipline*, 19 (italics his).

193. See Michel Schlesinger, *Satzlehre der Aramäische Sprache des Babylonischen Talmuds*, 269-91.

Conclusion

In the discussion of the orthographical, morphological, and syntactical qualities of the book of Ezekiel we observed twenty features which differ from the practice of EBH and are in harmony with LBH conventions. Of these twenty traits, nineteen continued to be employed in post-biblical Hebrew (אשר = 'that', being the lone exception). Furthermore, we noted that six of the twenty features may be attributed to Aramaic influence.[194]

Having thus a picture of the diachronic status of the grammar of Ezekiel, we now turn to the lexical features of the book to determine the extent to which late post-classical terms of BH are prevalent.

---

194. The six features include the shift to the Piel (הקים > קים), ל before the direct object (כפר ל), *waw* conjunction before finite verb (והוליד בן), היה + Participle (היה צמד אצלי), Dimension Precedes Measurement (ורחב חמש אמות), and Asyndetic Imperfect Apodosis (כי ... ימות).

Chapter 6

LATE LEXICAL FEATURES IN THE BOOK OF EZEKIEL

As indicated above, in our discussion concerning the methodology of diachronic study, lexical analysis is a viable method for measuring language change. Indeed, it is true of all languages that terms which are in vogue in one period subsequently die out or come to be used less frequently as a competing term replaces the earlier term and becomes the convention. Almost all categories of vocabulary in a given language's lexical stock may be candidates for extinction, apart from core words which refer to kin relations or body parts. Lexical change in the latter categories is quite rare.

Given the Hebrew Bible's rich lexical stock,[1] the chances that language change can be detected are considerable. As noted above, Hurvitz anticipated our analysis in his *Linguistic Study* where he contrasted the later lexical terms in Ezekiel with the earlier correspondents in the material attributed to the P source.[2] In this chapter we will seek to find additional support for his findings as well as discuss lexemes he did not consider, given the restricted aim of his inquiry.

The two columns below represent the lexical developments of the book of Ezekiel treated in this chapter. The left column represents EBH lexemes, while the right column lists the LBH counterparts which are extant in the book of Ezekiel. The columns are arranged according to the order of the appearance of the LBH term in the book of Ezekiel. As in the previous chapter our operating controls in detecting linguistic change are the principles of contrast and distribution.

1. Kutscher, *History* §§ 77-82, 54-56.
2. See also a related work by Hurvitz, 'The Evidence of Language in Dating the Priestly Code', *RB* 81 (1974) 24-56.

EBH lexeme	LBH lexeme
אל	על
מחתה	מקטרת
צעק	זעק
ספר, מכתב	כְּתָב
נתץ, הרס	נָתַ֫ץ
עדה	קָהָל
קצף,	כעס
חרה אף	
קום	עמד
הלך	הָלַ֫ךְ
אסף, קבץ	כנס
שש	בוץ
קרקע, מרצפת	רצפה
רחץ	הדיח
דרך	מהלך
חצר	עֲזָרָה

Expressions

אשר לא, לבלתי	למען לא
כסף וזהב	זהב וכסף

אל/על

It has been widely known that the preposition עַל became more prominent in LBH at the expense of the preposition אֶל.[3] The shift becomes readily apparent when one compares texts from Samuel/Kings with later, parallel texts from Chronicles:[4]

1 Sam 31.3	ותכבד המלחמה אֶל שאול
1 Chr 10.3	ותכבד המלחמה עַל שאול
2 Kgs 22.16	הנני מביא רעה אֶל המקום הזה
2 Chr 34.24	הנני מביא רעה עַל המקום הזה

This same diachronic contrast may also be observed in the following alternative ways of expressing a priestly formula:[5]

---

3. Ewald, *Lehrbuch* § 217 i, 566-67; Bendavid, *Leshon* II, 453, n.; Hurvitz, *Lashon*, 22 and n. 25; and Qimron, 'The Vocabulary of the Temple Scroll', 252. The issue is thus apparently lexical in nature and not phonological. It is true that later Aramaic had the tendency to confuse the phonemes א and ע, but this occurred at a substantially later time and thus this exchange of phonemes should not be construed as the cause for the confused state in the book of Ezekiel. For the phonetic interchange in later Aramaic, see Edwin M. Yamauchi, *Mandaean Incantation Texts* (Ph.D. dissertation, Brandeis University, 1964) 109; and David Marcus, *A Manual of Babylonian Jewish Aramaic,* 3. Cohen and Brownlee, on the other hand, insist that the change is phonological in nature. See A. Cohen, 'עַל instead of אַל', *BM* 15, 2 (1969-70) 206 [In Hebrew]; and Brownlee, *Ezekiel*, 189.

4. Other examples of this shift include the following parallel texts: 2 Sam 5.19 = 1 Chr 14.10; 2 Sam 23.23 = 1 Chr 11.25; 2 Sam 6.3 = 1 Chr 13.7; 2 Sam 6.10 = 1 Chr 13.13; 2 Sam 7.19 = 1 Chr 17.17; 2 Sam 7.28 = 1 Chr 17.26; 2 Sam 8.7 = 1 Chr 18.7; 2 Sam 10.2 = 1 Chr 19.2; 2 Sam 20.23 = 1 Chr 18.15; 2 Sam 23.13 = 1 Chr 11.15; 2 Sam 23.23 = 1 Chr 11.25; 2 Sam 24.3 = 1 Chr 21.3; 2 Sam 24.4 = 1 Chr 21.4; 2 Sam 24.16 = 1 Chr 21.15; 1 Kgs 10.7 = 2 Chr 9.18; 1 Kgs 10.19 = 2 Chr 9.18; 1 Kgs 22.17 = 2 Chr 18.16; 2 Kgs 11.14 = 2 Chr 23.13; and 2 Kgs 16.7 = 2 Chr 28.16. In three texts Chronicles has אֶל for עַל of Kings! These texts are 1 Kgs 15.20 = 2 Chr 16.4; 2 Kgs 22.16 = 2 Chr 34.15; and 2 Kgs 22.20 = 2 Chr 34.28. These exceptions, however, in no way diminish the strength of the thesis that there is a clear אֶל > עַל in shift in LBH.

5. Cited by Ewald, *Lehrbuch* § 217 i, 566. This diachronic contrast which establishes the chronological priority of the Priestly Blessing of Num 6 also supports Fishbane's thesis that the Priestly Blessing of Num 6.24-26 influenced Ps 4. See Michael Fishbane, 'Form and Reformulation of the Biblical Priestly Blessing', *JAOS* 103 (1983) 116.

| Num 6.25 | יאר ה׳ פניו אֵלֶיךָ |
| Ps 4.7 | נסה עָלֵינוּ אור פניך ה׳ |

It has long been observed that there is great confusion in the use of the prepositions עַל/אֶל in the book of Ezekiel. For example, Zimmerli states: 'However, the book of Ezekiel shows throughout a quite surprising blurring of the distinction between עַל and אֶל, which can be interchanged without fixed rules'.[6] The following parallel examples illustrate the confusion in the use of these prepositions.

Ezek 1.12	אֶל אשר יהיה שמה
Ezek 1.20	עַל אשר יהיה שם
Ezek 11.10	עַל גבול ישראל
Ezek 11.11	אֶל גבול ישראל
Ezek 12.7	בעלטה הוצאתי עַל כתף נשאתי
Ezek 12.12	אֶל כתף ישא בעלטה ויצא
Ezek 14.3	העלו גלוליהם עַל לבם
Ezek 14.4	יעלה את גלוליו אֶל לבו

The following examples provide additional support to the claim that the prepositions עַל/אֶל are used disconcertingly in the book of Ezekiel. In each instance of the occurrence of אֶל or עַל the other preposition is what would be expected according to general BH usage:[7]

---

6. Zimmerli, *Ezekiel* I, 86. See also Cooke, *Ezekiel*, 26; and Keil, *Ezekiel*, 202.
7. See also 29.18; 30.22; 31.13; 34.13, 14; 35.3; 38.3, 7; 39.1; 41.12, 19, 25; 42.7, 10, 13; 43.3; 44.4; 48.21, 32. Sperber, largely because of the 'inconsistent' usage of these prepositions in Ezekiel, maintains that in fact אֶל and עַל are used indiscriminately in the Bible. Alexander Sperber, *A Historical Grammar of Biblical Hebrew* (Leiden, 1966) 59-63, esp. 59. Similarly, Cohen, 'עַל instead of אֶל', 207; and George M. Landes, 'Linguistic Criteria and the Date of the Book of Jonah', *Eretz Israel* 16 (1982) 158. While this assertion is certainly not without basis, it does fail to recognize the clear diachronic distinction in the employment of these two prepositions. Thus it fails to account for a possible cause behind the confusion.

Ezek 2.10[8]	וכתוב אליה
Ezek 13.8[9]	הנני אליכם
Ezek 27.29	אל הארץ יעמדו
Ezek 40.2	ויניחני אל הר גבה

The confusion in the employment of these two terms may be the source behind the unusual occurrence of the phrase על תחס עיניכם in Ezek 9.5. Here we see the preposition על being substituted for the precative אל.[10] The most likely explanation for this occurrence is that, due to the state of confusion in the employment of the prepositions אל and על in the book of Ezekiel, על has even mistakenly replaced the precative אל, the homomorph of the אל preposition![11]

It has been suggested that the impetus for the preference for על in BH is the result of Aramaic influence. In BA, we find the preposition על used in lieu of EBH אל as the following examples illustrate:

Dan 2.24	כל קבל דנה דניאל על עַל אריוך
Ezra 4.11	דנה פרשגן אגרתא די שלחו
	עלוהי עַל ארתחששתא מלכא

Perhaps this tendency in Aramaic is best demonstrated, however, by examining illustrations from the Targum where the Aramaic version substitutes על for BH אל:

Gen 20.2	ויאמר אברהם אֶל שרה אשתו
Tg. Onq.	ואמר אברהם עַל שרה איתתיה

Gen 43.30	רחמיו אֶל אחיו
Tg. Onq.	רחמרהי עַל אחוהי

---

8. The only other illustrations of this pattern occur in Jer 36.2 and 51.60. See, *BDB*, 507.

9. In this formulaic expression ('the challenge formula'), the preposition אל is in fact favored over the expected על in the book of Ezekiel by a ratio of 10: 4. Zimmerli, *Ezekiel* I, 286.

10. Thus Cooke, *Ezekiel*, 109. Most commentators, however, opt for reading the Q אל for this difficult reading. See Kraetzschmar, *Ezechiel*, 101; Smend, *Ezechiel*, 56; and Fohrer-Galling, *Ezechiel*, 53.

11. Selle cites this reference as an example of Aramaic influence in Ezekiel. *Aramaismis*, 14-15.

In the Hebrew of the DSS as well as in Ben Sira, the preference of
the preposition עַל for אֶל is even more prominent than in LBH. This
fact can be observed by merely comparing the sharp contrast of the
quantity of entries of the two terms in these two works.[12] The following examples may help to illustrate the increasing tendency for the
preposition עַל to be used at the expense of BH אֶל at Qumran:

Ps 129.8	ברכת ה׳ <u>אֲלֵיכֶם</u> ברכנו אתכם
4QpPs[b] 4.2	[ברכת] ה׳ <u>עֲלֵיכֶם</u> בר[כנו אתכם
Hab 1.2	אזעק <u>אֵלֶיךָ</u>
1QpHab 1.4	[ז]עקו <u>עַל</u>
2 Sam 20.10	<u>אֶל</u> החמש
4QSam[a] 20.10[13]	<u>עַל</u> החמש
2 Sam 14.30[14]	<u>אֶל</u>
4QSam[c] 14.30	<u>עַל</u>
2 Sam 15.3	<u>אֵלָיו</u>
4QSam[c] 15.3[15]	<u>עֲלָיו</u>

The notion that the preposition אֶל occurred only infrequently in the
Hebrew of the DSS is also supported by the the use of the formula
שלח עַל in the Temple Scroll instead of the formula שלח אֶל of
EBH:[16]

---

12. See Kuhn, *Konkordanz,* 14-15, 163-64; and *Ben Sira, Concordance,* 85-86,
238-42. It should also be noted that in the 'Songs of the Sabbath Sacrifice' from
Qumran Cave 4, the preposition עַל occurs on approximately ten occasions
while the preposition אֶל does not occur. See Carol Newsom, *Songs of the
Sabbath Sacrifice: A Critical Edition* (Atlanta, 1985) 436.
13. For these readings from 4QSam[a], see Ulrich, *The Qumran Text of Samuel
and Josephus,* 79, 89, 126. For five additional illustrations of עַל read in place
of אֶל, see *ibid.,* 78, 82, 83, 96. The opposite substitution, אֶל for עַל, in 4QSam[a]
occurs only on two occasions. *Ibid.,* 105, 126.
14. See Emmanuel Tov, 'Determining the Relationship between the Qumran
Scrolls and the LXX: Some Methodological Issues', 59.
15. For this reading see, Kenneth Alan Mathews, *The Paléo-Hebrew Leviticus
Scroll From Qumran* (Ph.D. dissertation, University of Michigan, 1980) 110.
16. The late formula also occurs in three LBH texts, Ezra 5.6, 7; 1 Chr 13.2. See
Qimron, 'The Vocabulary of the Temple Scroll', 252.

11QTemple 58. 4   וישלח עַל שרי האלפים
                            ועַל שרי המאות

In conclusion, it is readily apparent that the inconsistent usage of the prepositions אֶל and עַל in the book of Ezekiel reflects a period of transition.[17] This state has certainly arisen due to Aramaic influence which predominantly uses the preposition עַל at the expense of אֶל.[18] The אֶל preposition does occur in Aramaic texts but only those which are of an early provenance.[19] Later texts from BA, as noted above, clearly illustrate the shift to the preposition עַל. In light of these facts some believe that the confusion that exists in the book of Ezekiel over the employment of these two prepositions is due to the influence of Aramaic.[20] This trend continued into Tannaitic times where the preposition עַל was used to the virtual exclusion of אֶל.[21]

---

17. The confusion in the use of the prepositions עַל/אֶל is evident in Jeremiah, but to a lesser degree. See Jer 11.22; 23.35; 33.14; 35.11; 36.31; 50.35; 51.1.
18. Bendavid, *Leshon* II, 453, n.; *KB*, 1107; and Hadas-Lebel, *Manuel d'Histoire de la Langue Hébraïque*, 100-101.
19. See Stanislav Segert, *Altaramäische Grammatik* (Leipzig, 1975) 526.
20. See Zimmerli, *Ezekiel* I, 86; and Greenberg, *Ezekiel*, 234.
21. אֶל occurs only on rare occasions in both the Mishnah and Tosefta. עַל, on the other hand, occurs thousands of times in these works. Contrast this state of affairs with the earlier Lachish letters where the preposition אֶל is used profusely while עַל occurs only two times. See Torczyner, *Lachish Letters*, 199, 202. A similar shift may be observed in the preference for the phrase שלום עַל in LBH and post-biblical literature for the earlier שלום ל. For complete discussion see, Avi Hurvitz, 'When Was The Expression שלום עַל ישראל Coined'? *Leshonenu* 27-28 (1964) 297-302 [In Hebrew].

מקטרת

The terms מחתה and מקטרת are apparent BH synonyms referring to vessels of the tabernacle/temple involved in the cult.[22] The terms are usually rendered in English as 'censer' or 'fire-pan'.[23] An examination of the lexical distribution of these synonyms in BH reveals a distinct apportionment. The earlier term מחתה occurs twenty-two times in BH and is used exclusively in EBH. Nineteen occurrences of this technical cultic term are from the Pentateuch with two more coming from 1 Kings and 2 Kings respectively.[24] מקטרת, on the other hand, occurs only two times in BH, in the following later texts:

Ezek 8.11	ואיש <u>מקטרתו</u> בידו
2 Chr 26.19	ויזעף עזיהו ובידו <u>מקטרת</u> להקטיר

Perhaps the diachronic contrast can best be observed by distinguishing different modes of expressing the following parallel phrases:

<u>ואיש מקטרתו</u>	<u>איש מחתתו</u>
Ezek 8.11	Lev 10.1
	Num 16.17 (2x)
	Num 16.18

Note also the following contrastive ways of expressing a similar expression:

Num 16.17	וקחו איש <u>מחתתו</u> ונתתם עליהם <u>קטרת</u>
2 Chr 26.19	ויזעף עזיהו ובידו <u>מקטרת להקטיר</u>

In early post-biblical Hebrew מקטרת is restricted to the following texts:[25]

---

22. Cooke, *Ezekiel*, 102.
23. See *BDB*, 367, 883; *KB*, 515, 560; and translations in JPS.
24. The occurrence of the term in 2 Chr 4.22 is ruled out as this verse is clearly borrowed from 2 Kgs 22.15.
25. The form מחתה occurs but once in the DSS in 4QTestim 24. This nominal form however is from the root חתה and has the meaning 'destruction, ruin'. See J.M. Allegro, 'Further Messianic References In Qumran Literature', *JBL* 75 (1956) 185. The EBH term מחתה returned to popular usage in later post-biblical Hebrew, however, as the term occurs on numerous occasions in MH as

1QM 2.5   אלה יתיצבו ... לעדוך <u>מהטרת</u>
4Q512, vii.11[26]   <u>מהטרת</u> קודשב]ה

In the use of the term מקטרת we find the unique situation of a
term gaining lexical dominance in the LBH period only to later fall
out of use. The term clearly occurs in situations where in the earlier
period we would expect מחתה but this substitution apparently was
only short-lived. מחתה again gained dominance in the Mishnaic and
Talmudic periods. We suspect that the rare occasion that would elicit
this type of term in the post-biblical period, coupled with the exclusive
occurrence of מחתה in the Pentateuch, contributed to the re-
emergence of the earlier term. However brief was the period of the
employment of the lexeme מקטרת in the history of the Hebrew language, it should be emphasized that it can not be doubted that the
term is LBH and that its first recorded occurrence is in Ezek 8.11.

well as in BT. See for example *m. Yoma* 5.1; *m. Tamid* 1.4; 6.2; *m. Kelim* 2.3-7;
and *b. Yoma* 47a.
26. For transcription, see *DJD* VII, 265.

זעק

The verbs זעק/צעק function as true synonyms in BH. Both terms connote the meaning 'cry, cry out, call'.[27] What is of interest in the occurrence of these terms in BH is the dissemination of the two terms in EBH and LBH literature. As Kutscher states concerning the distribution of these two verbs:

> In the Bible as a whole they are both used approximately the same number of times (צעק is slightly more common). However, upon closer scrutiny one discovers that the two words are very unequally distributed between the early and late parts of the Bible. Whereas in the Pentateuch צעק is used almost exclusively, (the ratio there of זעק :צעק = 26:2), in Chron., Neh. and Esther for example the picture is very very different. In these books the ratio of צעק :זעק = 3:11! We thus see that זעק (apparently thanks to Aramaic influence) was commoner by far during the Second Temple Period.[28]

As Kutscher states in EBH the two verbs occur with about the same frequency, with צעק being slightly favored by a ratio of 37: 33. In LBH, however, a sharply different picture arises. In these texts the use of the verb זעק clearly predominates. The verb צעק occurs only in two indisputably late texts, Neh 9.27 and 2 Chr 13.14.[29] זעק on the other hand occurs twelve times in later texts, in the following texts: Jer 11.11, 12; Ezek 9.8; 11.13; 21.17; Est 4.1; Neh 9.4, 28; 1 Chr 5.20; 2 Chr 18.31; 20.9; and 32.20.[30] The following parallel usages of זעק/צעק demonstrate not only the semantic equivalency of these

---

27. Not only are the identical definitions given for the meaning of each verb in *BDB*, but in each entry the lexicon notes that the verbs are parallel. See pp. 277, 858.

28. Kutscher, *Isaiah*, 34. Due to the similarity of these two roots the nature of the diachronic shift might be viewed as phonemic rather than lexical. The shift would then merely involve a change from an emphatic sibilant צ to a voiced sibilant ז. Yet, for this to be the reason for our diachronic shift in this instance it must be demonstrated that this shift was common in the post-exilic period. Other examples, apart from Syriac זדיק for צדיק, must be produced to show that this is the reason for the change. Since other examples are not forthcoming it is preferable to maintain that the reason for the change is merely lexical preference.

29. The verb also occurs three times in poetic texts which might be considered as early: Jer 22.20; 49.3; and Lam 2.18.

30. See Bergey, *Esther*, 119.

two verbs but also the LBH tendency to prefer זעק over the earlier צעק:[31]

Exod 5.8	עַל כֵּן הֵם צֹעֲקִים לֵאמֹר
Ezek 11.13	וָאֶזְעַק קוֹל גָדוֹל וָאֹמַר
Exod 14.15	מַה תִּצְעַק אֵלָי
Jer 11.12	וְזָעֲקוּ אֶל הָאֱלֹהִים
1 Chr 5.20	כִּי לֵאלֹהִים זָעָקוּ
Gen 27.34	וַיִּצְעַק צְעָקָה גְדֹלָה וּמָרָה
Est 4.1	וַיִּזְעַק זְעָקָה גְדֹלָה וּמָרָה

For our interests it is important to point out that only the term זעק, which is more prevalent in LBH texts, occurs in Ezekiel (9.8; 11.13; 21.17); צעק, on the other hand, the lexeme which is virtually restricted to EBH texts, is not attested in Ezekiel.

Similarly, in BA, only זעק is attested:[32]

Dan 6.21	לְדָנִיֵּאל בְּקָל עֲצִיב זְעִק

This example suggests that the increase in frequency of זעק may be due to Aramaic influence. This hypothesis is strengthened by the following illustration of the use of זעק in the Aramaic Targum:

Exod 14.10	וַיִּצְעֲקוּ בְּנֵי יִשְׂרָאֵל
Tg. Onq.	וְזָעִיקוּ בְּנֵי יִשְׂרָאֵל

In the post-biblical period, the tendency for writers of Hebrew to prefer זעק over צעק apparently continued. The use of זעק clearly dominates in frequency in the DSS. This tendency can be best illustrated by noting that the writer of 1QIsa[a] frequently substituted זעק for צעק of the MT. The following parallel texts graphically demonstrate this phenomenon:[33]

Isa 42.2	לֹא יִזְעַק וְלֹא יִשָּׂא

---

31. For other examples, see Exod 22.22 = Jer 11.11; Num 20.16 = Neh 9.4.
32. The same can be said for the Samaritan Pentateuch. See Kutscher, *Isaiah*, 233.
33. See Kutscher, *Isaiah*, 233; and Bergey, *Esther*, 120.

1QIsaᵃ 42.2	לוא <u>יזעק</u> ולוא ישא
Isa 46.7	אף <u>יצעק</u> אליו ולא יענה
1QIsaᵃ 46.7	אף <u>יזעק</u> עליו ולוא יענה
Isa 65.14	ואתם <u>תצעקו</u> מכאב לב
1QIsaᵃ 65.14	ואתם <u>תזעקו</u> מכאיב לב

Kutscher sums the significance of this interchange between צעק and זעק in MT Isa and 1QIsaᵃ:

> This being one of the few instances where we find the same substitution in the Scr. more than once, it is particularly significant for the understanding of the Scr.'s system, since they cannot then be ascribed to chance. This is further attested by the fact that זעק (9 times!) was not changed to צעק.[34]

The preference of זעק over the earlier צעק was not due to the stylistic tendencies of the writer of 1QIsaᵃ. This is conclusively demonstrated by what we observe in the Temple Scroll, which has no attestations of the earlier צעק but employs the later זעק quite frequently. Particularly significant are the following parallel passages which differ from EBH usage:[35]

Deut 22.24	לא <u>צעקה</u> בעיר
11QTemple 66.2-3	לוא <u>זעקה</u> בעיר
Deut 22.27	כי בשדה מצאה <u>צעקה</u> הנער המארשה
11QTemple 66.7-8	כי בשדה מצאה <u>זעקה</u> הנצרה המאורשה

זעק also occurs in the DSS in the following texts: 11QTemple 59.6, 6; 1QpHab 9.15; 4QIsaᶜ 23, 2.16; 4Q511, 31.2; 11QPsᵃ 24.14, 11QPsᵃ 155, 24.14.[36] The verb צעק, rare in LBH, occurs only one time in the DSS (1QIsaᵃ 5.7); but here the use of this verb in this context is probably due to the author's intention to maintain a play on words.[37]

---

34. Kutscher, *Isaiah*, 233.
35. See Yadin, *Temple Scroll* II, 296.
36. All but 4Q511, 31.2 and 11 QPsa 155, 24.14 are cited by Bergey, *Esther*, 120-21.
37. The phrase in question is ויקו למשפט והנה משפח לצדקה והנה צעקה. The use of the verb צעק may have been influenced by the occurrence of

זעק is curiously absent from MH[38] but occurs in the Tosefta. Note the use of the verb in the following passages:

זוֹעֵק לשמים

t. Ma'as´ S. 3.9 = *t. Ma'as´ S.* 3.10

Similar to the diachronic contrast observed in the occurrence of צעק and זעק in the MT and 1QIsa^a cited above is the following midrash[39] on the phrase ויצעק צעקה גדלה ומרה of Gen 27.34:

זעקה אחת הזעיק יעקב לעשו

This confirms the contention that in the post-biblical period, the verb זעק was more commonly used in the spoken language than the earlier צעק.

In conclusion, it is readily apparent that beginning in LBH there was a tendency to prefer the use of the term זעק in lieu of its synonym צעק. This statement is reinforced by the distribution of the nominal forms, זעקה and צעקה:

> Here also LBH prose shows a higher incidence of the form having the voiced sibilant (five times) as compared to the use of the emphatic (two times). EBH prose again shows a preference for the form having the emphatic (ten times) rather than the voiced (once).[40]

The following parallel texts illustrate the preference of זעקה over צעקה in LBH:

Gen 27.34	ויצעק <u>צעקה</u> גדלה ומרה
Est 4.1	ויזעק <u>זעקה</u> גדלה ומרה
Exod 3.7	ואת <u>צעקתם</u> שמעתי מפני נגשיו
Neh 9.9	ואת <u>זעקתם</u> שמעת על ים סוף
1 Sam 4.14	וישמע עלי את <u>קול הצעקה</u>
Jer 51.54	<u>קול זעקה</u> מבבל

the emphatic sibilant צ in the previous noun צדקה. Bergey, *Esther*, 121 and n. 1.

38. צעק occurs quite frequently in the Mishnah, however. See *m. Ber.* 9.3, 3; *m. Sanh.* 4.5, 11(3); *m. Ta'an.* 2.4, 5(4), 6(4), 7(4), 8(4), 9(4), 10(4), 11(5); 3.7. Most of these citations are noted by Bergey, *Esther*, 122 n. 1.

39. *Gen. Rab.* II, 757-58.

40. Bergey, *Esther*, 121.

Ezek 27.28   לְקוֹל זַעֲקַת חֹבְלַיִךְ יִרְעֲשׁוּ מִגְרֹשׁוֹת

It is striking that Ezekiel makes use of neither the verb צָעַק nor the
noun צְעָקָה but prefers זָעַק as noted in the above discussion and
זְעָקָה in the poetic text 27.28! In this usage Ezekiel again resembles
LBH, as well as the Hebrew of the DSS and the Tosefta. The shift from
צָעַק with the emphatic sibilant צ to זָעַק with the voiced sibilant is
thought by some to have resulted from Aramaic influence,[41] or
perhaps reflects a dialectal variant which enjoyed a greater
frequency after the exile to Babylon.[42] The possibility of Aramaic
influence is perhaps strengthened by the fact that only the equivalent
of the later זָעַק occurs in Syriac. Particularly noteworthy is the fact
that in the Peshitta the latter term is employed to translate BH
צָעַק.[43]

41. Thus Kutscher, *Isaiah*, 34, 233; and Qimron, 'The Vocabulary of the Temple Scroll', 244. This possibility is also hinted at by Bendavid. See *Leshon* I, 33.
For the occurrence of the verb in an Aramaic inscription, see Cowley,
Aramaic Papyri, 180, # 71, line 17. For the frequent occurrence of the nominal
and verbal form in Palestinian Aramaic, see Joseph A. Fitzmyer, *A Manual of
Palestinian Aramaic Texts* (Rome, 1978) 24, 32, 36, 40, 76.
42. This hypothesis has never been substantiated, however. See G. Hasel,
TDOT IV, 114.
43. See Payne-Smith, *Thesaurus Syriacus* I, 1143.

כְּתָב

The noun כתב occurs seventeen times in BH. The term is restricted to Ezekiel, Esther, Daniel, Ezra, Nehemiah, and Chronicles. The following are a representative list of the occurrences of this word in BH:[44]

Ezek 13.9	בסוד עמי לא יהיו <u>ובכתב</u> בית ישראל לא יכתבו
Est 8.8	כי <u>בכתב</u> אשר נכתב בשם המלך
1 Chr 28.19	הכל <u>בכתב</u> מיד ה׳ עלי השכיל

The lexeme should thus be considered as late and as the equivalent of EBH terms ספר and מכתב.[45] Note some examples of the latter terms, semantically parallel to LBH כתב in the following EBH texts:[46]

Exod 32.33[47]	מי אשר חטא לי אמחנו <u>מספרי</u>
2 Sam 11.14	ויהי בבקר ויכתב דוד <u>ספר</u> אל יואב
2 Kgs 10.1	ויכתב יהוא <u>ספרים</u>

Exod 32.16	<u>והמכתב מכתב</u> אלהים הוא חרות על הלחת
Exod 39.30	ויכתבו עליו <u>מכתב</u> פתוחי חותם
Deut 10.4	ויכתב על הלחת <u>במכתב</u> הראשון
Isa 38.9	<u>מכתב</u> לחזקיהו מלך יהודה

Though כתב is the preferred lexeme in LBH, it occurs unequivocally only one time in the Dead Sea Scrolls:[48]

44. The term also occurs in Est 1.22; 3.12, 14; 4.8; 8.9, 13; 9.27; Dan 10.21; Ezra 2.62; 4.4; Neh 7.64; 2 Chr 2.10; 35.4.
45. Kautzsch, *Aramaismen*, 44; Hurvitz, *Lashon*, 58-59; and Polzin, *Hebrew*, 139.
46. While ספר occurs frequently in the Bible, c. 185 times, מכתב occurs only nine times. Hence, a limited number of illustrations are given for ספר while all EBH occurrences of מכתב are listed. Consistent with this diachronic distinction is the lexical preference of the Lachish letters of the early sixth century. In these letters the early term ספר occurs repeatedly, while the late term כתב is not attested. See Torczyner, *Lachish Letters*, 202.
47. The sentiment expressed in this verse appears to be conceptually parallel to Ezek 13.9 with the EBH term ספר for LBH כתב.
48. For a photograph of this text, see J.C. Trever, 'Completion of the Publication of Some Fragments From Qumran Cave I', *RQ* 5 (1965) 340. For a

1Q34 3b.7	ונכתב ימינך להודיעם יסורי כבוד
	ומעלי עולם

The term is used quite frequently in Ben Sira, however. Note the following examples of the occurrences of this term in Ben Sira:[49]

(ב) 39.32	והתבונני ובכתב הנחתי
(ב) 44.5	נושאי משל בכתב

The term is even more prevalent in MH. The following examples are representative of the widespread usage of this lexeme in MH:[50]

m. Šabb. 12.5	כתב אות אחת סמוך לכתוב כתב
	על גבי כתב
m. Yebam. 15.14	שהכתב מוכיח
m. Yad. 4.5	וכתב עברי אינו מטמא את הידים

Especially noteworthy, are those instances where the translators of Targum Onqelos translate Hebrew מכתב with the word כתב.

Exod 32.16	והמכתב מכתב
Tg. Onq.	וכתבא כתבא

Exod 39.30	ויכתבו עליו מכתב
Tg. Onq.	וכתבו עלוהי כתב

Deut 10.4	ויכתב על הלחת כמכתב הראשון
Tg. Onq.	וכתב על לוחיא כבתבא קדמאה

In conclusion, the use of the term כתב in the Book of Ezekiel, represents the first written attestation of this lexeme in Hebrew literature. The term continued to be used in later texts of LBH and became even more widespread in post-biblical Hebrew, particularly

---

transcription, see *DJD* I, 154. There is another possible occurrence of this term from the caves of Murabba'at. See *DJD* II, 142 for a reconstruction.

49. Additional examples may be found in 42.7 (ב); 45.11 (ב).

50. The term also occurs about fourteen times in the Tosefta apart from the widespread occurrence of the idiom כתב יד. See Kasovsky, *Tosephta Concordance* IV, 187.

MH.[51] It is relatively certain that this term is an Aramaic loanword as the word is attested in various dialects, including Nabatean and Palmyrene, as well as in the Aramaic Targum as observed above.[52] Moreover, the noun has the *q^etal* pattern which is a morphological pattern of Aramaic nouns.[53] Most lexemes with this morphological pattern in BH are late.[54] The term thus represents another possible example of Aramaic influence in the book of Ezekiel, an influence which especially affected the writers of LBH. Ezekiel, is thus similar to LBH in the employment of this term and in fact signals a biblical innovation in the usage of this term in BH.

51. In its relation to the earlier מכתבה, the preference for the כתבה in the Mishnah may be viewed as an illustration of the tendency in MH to omit the ת prefix of earlier BH nouns. See Bendavid, *Leshon* II, 444. This may be analogous to the occasional omission of the participial preformative ת in MH. See Segal, *MHG*, 63. For the numerous occurrences of כתבה in the Midrashim and Talmudic literature, see Jastrow, *Dictionary* I, 679.
52. See Ryssel, *De Elohistae Pentateuchici Sermone*, 39-40; Selle, *Aramaismis*, 31; Kautzsch, *Aramaismen*, 44; Jean-Hoftijzer, *Dictionnaire*, 129; Bendavid, *Leshon* I, 62; Wagner, *Aramaismen*, 69; Cooke, *Ezekiel,* 143; and Zimmerli, *Ezekiel* I, 294. For attestations of the term in late Nabataean, see Cooke, *NSI*, 217, 220.
53. This nominal morphology is thus believed to have entered Hebrew as the result of Aramaic influence. See *GKC* § 93 ww, 274; and Kraetzschmar, *Ezechiel*, 133.
54. Kutscher, *History* § 103, 75; Hurvitz, *Lashon*, 59 n. 158; and Hadas-Lebel, *Manuel d'Histoire de la Langue Hébraïque*, 102.

נָתַץ

The Piel of the root נ ת ץ occurs only seven times in BH, almost exclusively in LBH texts.[55] The later term is used instead of the Qal stem of נ ת ץ and of הרס in EBH literature. The diachronic shift can easily be demonstrated by comparing the use of the Piel נ ת ץ in later texts of the Chronicler with the practice of earlier texts:[56]

| 2 Kgs 23.15 | ואת הבמה נתץ |
| 2 Chr 33.3 | את הבמות אשר נתץ יחזקיהו |

Deut 7.5[57]	מזבחתיהם תתצו
1 Kgs 19.10	את מזבחתיך הרסו
2 Chr 34.7	וינתץ את המזבחות

| Jer 39.8 | ואת חמות ירושלם נתצו |
| 2 Chr 36.19 | וינתצו את חומת ירושלם |

Similarly, in Ezek 16.39, we find the Piel of נ ת ץ in the phrase:

והרסו גבך ונתצו רמתיך

In post-biblical literature the use of both the EBH נ ת ץ and LBH נ תֵ ץ are rather restricted. There is slight evidence for the use of the Qal of נ ת ץ[58] and הרס while the Piel of נ ת ץ fell out of use.[59] Thus we have the unique situation where a term gained dominance in LBH only to later give way to the earlier EBH practice. At any rate, the Book of Ezekiel elicits evidence of this use of the Piel of נ ת ץ as do other LBH texts, and in so doing demonstrates its affinity once again with LBH literature.

55. Deut 12.3 being the lone EBH text.
56. The Piel of נ ת ץ also is substituted for הסיר in 2 Kgs 18.4 = 2 Chr 31.1 and אבד in 2 Kgs 21.3 = 2 Chr 33.1. See Sara Japhet, 'The Interchange of Verbal Roots in Parallel Texts in Chronicles', 265. Japhet erroneously asserts that only the Chronicler employs the Piel stem of נ ת ץ. *Ibid.*, n. 75.
57. For other EBH uses with מזבח as the object, see Exod 34.13; Judg 6.25, 30.
58. See, e.g., Jastrow, *Dictionary* II, 945.
59. None of the terms occurs in Ben Sira and only הרס occurs one time in the DSS, in 1QpHab 4.8. For the few occurrences of the Qal of נ ת ץ in post-biblical literature, see Ben-Yehuda, *Thesaurus* V, 3884.

קָהָל

The biblical term קָהָל, though not absent from EBH, became more widespread in the literature of LBH and post-biblical period than its earlier counterpart עֵדָה. The term עֵדָה, on the other hand, occurs profusely in the EBH, particularly in the Pentateuch and Early Prophets.[60] But what is particularly significant about the occurrence of the term עֵדָה in BH is its lack of attestation in LBH. Hurvitz explains the significance of this phenomena as follows: 'The total absence of *ʿēdāh* in the distinctively late biblical works—Ezra, Nehemiah and Chronicles—is, therefore, a clear indication of the term's gradual falling into disuse'.[61] Significantly, for our purposes, is the fact that the early term is also absent from Ezekiel. This avoidance of using the early term on the part of Ezekiel is graphically illustrated by observing the following early, analogous texts, which employ the term:[62]

Exod 16.2	וילינו <u>כל עדת</u> בני ישראל ... במדבר
Ezek 20.13	וימרו בי <u>בית ישראל</u> במדבר
Num 16.9	ולעמד <u>לפני העדה</u> לשרתם
Ezek 44.11	והמה יעמדו <u>לפניהם</u> לשרתם

The latter illustration is particularly significant. As we noted above in our discussion of Ezekiel's use of sources, Ezekiel 44, as the Korahite incident in Numbers 16-18, is concerned with the establishment of the priestly and levitical hierarchy. Thus Ezekiel used this text to legislate proper priestly relations in response to an apparent crisis, in the same manner that the content of the Korahite rebellion was intended to convey the proper role of the respective priestly groups. And yet, when Ezekiel borrows the phrase which describes the function of the levitical priests as serving the people (לשרתם Num

---

60. It is a characteristic term of the material attributed to the P source. Thus Driver, *Introduction*, 133. For full discussion, see Jacob Milgrom, 'Priestly Terminology and the Political and Social Structure of Pre-Monarchic Israel', *JQR* 69 (1978) 66-76.
61. *Linguistic Study*, 66. Actually, עֵדָה does occur one time in Chronicles, in 2 Chr 5.6. This text however is parallel to 1 Kgs 8.5 and hence we should assume that the reference to עֵדָה in 2 Chr 5.6 is the result of Chronicler's borrowing of the language of his *Vorlage*.
62. See Hurvitz, *Linguistic Study*, 65-66.

16.9 = Ezek 44.11), he omits the EBH noun צדה. This probably
suggests that the the conventional status of EBH noun was losing
ground at the time of the writing of Ezekiel 44.

The use of קהל, as noted above, on the other hand, is very
widespread in LBH. Particularly significant are the numerous occasions where the Chronicler uses this lexeme in passages which have
no parallel in Samuel/Kings.[63] This might reinforce the contention
that the term was part of the language of the post-exilic community,
as the Chronicler substituted his own language in places where he
was not following an earlier source. The prevalence of the term קהל
by the Chronicler might also be illustrated by observing the preference for קהל in the following passage, which is very similar to the
parallel passages in 2 Kings apart from the addition of the term קהל:

2 Kgs 11.4   ויבא אתם אליו בית ה׳ ויברת להם ברית
2 Chr 23.2-3   ויבאו אל ירושלם ויברת _בל הקהל_ ברית
בבית האלהים

We see the same substitution in the book of Ezekiel. Notice how the
judicial punishment is carried out by צדה in EBH, while Ezekiel
employs the later synonym קהל:

Lev 24.16   _רגום ירגמו_ בו כל _העדה_
Num 15.35   _רגום אתו באבנים כל העדה_
Ezek 23.47   _ורגמו_ עליהן אבן _קהל_

קהל continued to be employed in post-biblical sources. Here are
some examples from the numerous occurrences of this term in the
DSS and Ben Sira:[64]

---

63. The term קהל occurs in the additional material of the Chronicler on
twenty-seven occasions. See 1 Chr 13.2, 4; 28.8; 29.1, 10; 2 Chr 1.3, 5; 6.13; 20.5,
14; 24.6, 6; 28.14, 28; 29.23, 31, 32; 30.2, 4, 13, 17, 23, 24, 25; 31.18. This situation
should be contrasted with the only six occurrences of קהל in Samuel/Kings.
64. See also, 1QM 4.10; 11.16; 14.5; 15.10; 18.1; 1QH 2.30; Sa 1.25; 29; 4QMa 3;
CD 7.17; 11.22-33; 12.5-6; 14.18; 11QTemple 16.15, 16, 18; 18.7; 20.4; 26.7, 9; Ben
Sira 11.6 (ב); 30.27 (ה); 34.11 (ב); 44.15 (ב); 44.15 (מ); 46.7 (ב); 50.13, 20 (ב).
Although there is abundant evidence for the use of קהל in the DSS and Ben
Sira, the earlier equivalent צדה is actually more abundant in this literature.
Hurvitz attributes this reality to be due to the tendency which exists in both Ben
Sira and the DSS to adopt antiquarian biblical expressions. See *Linguistic
Study*, 66 n. 33.

1QSa 2.4   אל יבוא בקהל
4Q403 1, ii.24[65]   רוש מכוהן קורת וראשי עדת
                         המלך בקהל
Ben Sira 15.5 (א)   ובתוך קהל תפתח פיו

It is, however, in the Aramaic Targum that we sense the clearest example of the ascendency of קהל over עדה. In the Aramaic translations of the Hebrew text the noun קהל is consistently translated by the Aramaic cognate קהלא. The form כנשתא, on the other hand, is the term that is consistently used to translate the earlier term עדה. This suggests that עדה was no longer part of the linguistic milieu.[66]

עדה vied with קהל as alternative, synonymous terms in Tannaitic literature in the same way that the terms were alternatively used in the DSS and Ben Sira,[67] although the evidence suggests that עדה was falling into disuse.[68] The following examples provide further illustrations of the use of קהל from post-biblical literature:[69]

m. Sanh. 4.10(4)   עוד אחד מן הקהל
t. Yad. 2.18   מותר לבוא בקהל
Sipre Deut. 160   ביום הקהל

The lexeme קהל, which became prominent in LBH texts, continued to be used in the post-biblical period although it did not by any means completely replace its earlier synonym עדה. The latter may have continued to enjoy frequent use in post-biblical literature because of its prominence in the Pentateuch. Special mention should perhaps be made of the phrase עדת קרח (cf. Num 17.5; 26.9). This phrase, which is particularly conspicuous in Rabbinic literature, is

---

65. For reading see Newsom, *Songs of the Sabbath Sacrifice: A Critical Edition*, 226. The reference in the citation to וראשי עדת in the citation is probably an allusion to Num 31.26. *Ibid.*, 241.
66. Avi Hurvitz, 'The Use of the Priestly Term *ʿēdāh* in Biblical Literature', *Tarbiz* 40 (1971) 263 [In Hebrew].
67. That is, in the written records. See Hurvitz's remark above. עדה occurs eighty-two times in the DSS and fourteen times in Ben Sira. See Kuhn, *Konkordanz*, 156-57; and *Ben-Sira, Concordance*, 233.
68. Hurvitz, 'The Use of the Priestly Term *ʿēdāh* in Biblical Literature', 263.
69. Other illustrations include *m. Ber.* 7.5(3); *m. Pesaḥ.* 7.6; *m. Qidd.* 4.3; *t. Hor.* 1.1.

frequently recited to refer to those who will have no portion in the world to come.[70] Nevertheless, it is clear that קָהֵל was the more prominent term in LBH, and the fifteen occurrences of this term in the book of Ezekiel, with the same technical meaning as the earlier עֵדָה[71] decisively associate this book with other works of LBH. The prominence of קָהֵל in the time of Ezekiel, may indicate that עֵדָה was beginning to ebb from the contemporary linguistic currency.[72]

---

70. See *m. Sanh.* 10.5(3); *t. B.Bat.* 7.9, 10; *t. Sanh.* 13.9; and *b. Sanh.* 109b. This repeated allusion to the Korahite incident with the retention of the early Hebrew noun עֵדָה has a biblical precedent. Psalm 106, in reference to the Korahite incident also employs the use of the EBH noun עֵדָה (Ps 106.17).
71. Thus Milgrom, 'Priestly Terminology and the Political and Social Structure of Pre-Monarchic Israel', 73.
72. Milgrom's contention that the lack of evidence for עֵדָה in Ezekiel meant that the lexeme had disappeared seems to overstate the case. Milgrom believes it was the establishment of the monarchy that signalled the beginning of the diminished use of עֵדָה. 'Priestly Terminology and the Political and Social Structure of Pre-Monarchic Israel', 73, 75.

כעס

The verb כ ע ס which has the connotation of 'expressing anger', occurs in the Qal almost exclusively in LBH.[73] The verb is thus used in post-exilic Hebrew in place of קצף and the expression חרה אף of earlier texts.[74] Observe the following usages of the Qal in BH:[75]

Ezek 16.42	ושקטתי ולא אכעס עוד
Neh 3.33	ויחר לו ויכעס הרבה
2 Chr 16.10	ויכעס אסא אל הראה

As noted above the the Qal of כעס does not occur in a text which is unequivocally EBH. Notice how the semantic parallel was expressed in earlier Hebrew:[76]

Gen 30.2	ויחר אף יעקב ברחל
Hos 8.5	זנח עגלך שמרון חרה אפי בם
Deut 9.19	קצף ה' עליכם להשמיד אתכם

The tendency to use כעס for 'expressing anger' continued in post-biblical literature, particularly in Rabbinic literature.[77] Note the following illustrations:[78]

m. 'Abot 2.10	ואל תהי נוח לכעוס
t. Sukk. 2.6	כעס עליהם
Pesiq. R. 11.1 (p. 94)	והקב״ה כועס עליהם

73. The verb occurs in the Qal in Ps 112.10. The date of this Psalm is open to question. This one possible exception, however, does not lessen the force of the basic premise that כעס in the Qal is a feature of LBH. See Hurvitz, *Lashon*, 174 n. 303; and *Linguistic Study*, 115.
74. Bendavid, *Leshon* I, 361; and Hurvitz, *Lashon*, 174 n. 303; *Linguistic Study*, 115.
75. See also, Eccl 5.16; 7.9.
76. Other examples of the EBH usage include Gen 41.10; Lev 10.16; Num 11.33; 16.22; Deut 6.15.
77. For example, see Jastrow, *Dictionary* I, 656. The verb in the Qal is absent from the DSS and Ben Sira. These documents, however, do attest the occurrence of the common EBH idiom חרה אף. כעס does occur in the story of Ahikar, line 189. See Cowley, *Aramaic Papyri*, 218. Furthermore, the Hiphil stem is extant at Qumran in 4Q504, 26.7. For transcription, see *DJD* VII, 166.
78. Among the numerous other examples from Rabbinic literature include *m. 'Abot* 5.11; *Deut. Rab.* 97b; *b. Ber.* 7a; and *b. Sanh.* 103a.

Observe how the same concept expressed in classical Hebrew occurs in later Hebrew with the verb כעס:

1 Sam 20.30	וַיִּחַר אַף שָׁאוּל בִּיהוֹנָתָן
Sipre Num. 86,15 (p. 85)	למלך בשר ודם שֶׁבָּעַס עַל בנו
b. Ber. 32a	משל למלך שֶׁבָּעַס עַל בנו

Particularly significant is the the following diachronic contrast:[79]

Exod 16.20	וַיִּקְצֹף עֲלֵהֶם מֹשֶׁה
Mek. Besh. IV (p. 167)	ויקצוף עליהם משה,
	כָּעַס עליהם ואמר להם

In conjunction with the prevailing tendency of post-classical writers to use the Qal of כעס for expressing anger, we find evidence from the exilic period in the book of Ezekiel. This verb increased in frequency at the expense of the earlier expressions with קצף and חרה אף. As Hurvitz states:[80]

> Clearly, the actual living verb used in post-classical Hebrew to denote the meaning 'be vexed, wroth, angry' was *kāʿas*. *Qāṣaph* and *ḥārah*, to be sure, had not altogether vanished, for they appear in some late sources. However, they are nothing more than ancient survivals or archaizing devices, inherited from a previous phase of the language. The late distribution of *kāʿas* within the Bible faithfully reflects an actual linguistic situation.

The book of Ezekiel represents the earliest attestation of the replacement of the earlier semantic parallels with the Qal of כעס.

79. Bendavid, *Leshon* I, 332. Cited by Hurvitz, *Linguistic Study*, 116.
80. *Linguistic Study*, 116.

עמד

In the later history of BH the term עמד was employed more and
more in contexts where EBH used the approximate synonym קום.
This can even be observed already in BH where it is possible to recognize the 'intrusion' of עמד into the semantic domain of the earlier
lexeme קום.[81] The semantic similarity, as well as the diachronic shift,
can be viewed in BH by noting the following parallel usages of the two
terms:[82]

Lachish Letter 13.1[83]	קם לעשת מלאבה
1 Sam 3.6	ויהם שמואל וילך אל עלי
Ezra 2.63 = Neh 7.65	לא יאבלו ... עד עמד (ה)כהן
Exod 1.8	ויהם מלך חדש על מצרים
Dan 8.23	יעמד מלך עז פנים
Judg 9.18	ואתם הקמתם על בית אבי היום
Dan 11.14	רבים יעמדו על מלך הנגב
Deut 19.15	על פי שלשה עדים יקום דבר
Est 3.4	לראות היעמדו דברי מרדכי

Thus we are able to see that the connotations 'rise up, appear, rise up
against, and establish', expressed in EBH by the verb קום were indicated in LBH by עמד. In the book of Ezekiel, this semantic shift has
not taken place to the degree that it occurs in other books of LBH.
There are some indications, however, that the LBH lexeme was
beginning to be used in lieu of the earlier קום. Note the following
example which is parallel to Ezra 2.63 = Neh 7.65 and thus differs
from the earlier usage in 1 Sam 3.6 as seen above:

Ezek 37.10	ותבוא בהם הרוח ויחיו ויעמדו
	על רגליהם

81. E.Y. Kutscher, 'Aramaic Calque in Hebrew', *Tarbiz* 33 (1964) 124 [In He-
brew].
82. See Hurvitz, *Linguistic Study*, 95; and Bergey, *Esther*, 126-27.
83. Torczyner, *Lachish Letters*, 159. This is the only occurrence of the root in
the Lachish letters. The later parallel עמד however, does *not* occur in these
letters from the early sixth century.

In addition, the following citation from the book of Ezekiel apparently
is used analogously to the LBH passage from Dan 11 cited above:

Ezek 44.24[84]	ועל ריב המה <u>יעמדו</u> לשפט

Perhaps, the best illustration of Ezekiel's affinity with LBH in the use
of this term occurs in Ezek 17.14. There Ezekiel uses the later עמד in
contrast to the earlier technical language which was used in reference to establishing a covenant.[85] Note how the language of Ezekiel
differs from that which was commonly used in pre-exilic Hebrew:[86]

Gen 26.3	<u>והקמתי</u> את השבעה אשר נשבעתי
	לאברהם אביך
Lev 26.9	<u>והקימתי</u> את בריתי אתכם
Num 30.14	כל נדר וכל שבעת אסר לענת נפש
	אישה <u>יקימנו</u>
Ezek 17.14	לשמר את בריתו <u>לעמדה</u>

The trend for to use עמד in contexts where EBH employed the
term קום continued in post-biblical Hebrew as well. The following are
but a few of the examples from the DSS and Ben Sira which illustrate
this proclivity:[87]

1QS 10.2	<u>נעמד</u> הכוהן ודבר אל העם
CD 1.14[88]	כן סרר ישראל <u>בעמוד</u> איש הלצון
11QTemple 56.9	שמוע אל הכוהן <u>העומד</u> שמה לשרת
Ben Sira 47.1	וגם אחריו <u>עמד</u> נתן

---

84. It might be maintained that this phrase illustrates a diachronic contrast
with the phrase על כן לא יקמו רשעים במשפט of Ps 1.5.
85. Both Cooke and Zimmerli understand the syntax of Ezek 17.14 in this way.
Cooke, *Ezekiel*, 193; and Zimmerli, *Ezekiel* I, 357.
86. Hurvitz, *Linguistic Study*, 94.
87. The verb also occurs in the Proverbs of Ahikar, line 160. See Cowley, *Aramaic Papyri*, 218.
88. Rabin observes that this usage of עמד is harmonious with LBH. *Zadokite
Documents*, 4 n. 14,2.

The shift from קום > צמד in post-biblical Hebrew is best illustrated, however, by contrasting the following post-biblical passages with EBH:[89]

Judg 10.1	ויקם אחרי אבימלך להושיע את ישראל
4QFlor 1.13	דויד יעמוד להושיע את ישראל
2 Kgs 13.21	ויקם על רגליו
b. Sanh. 47a	על רגליו עמד ולביתו לא הלך
Num 24.17	וקם שבט מישראל
CD 7.19-20	וקם שבט מישראל
	השבט הוא נשיא כל העדה ובעמדו
Deut 6.7	ובקומך
Sipre Deut. 34 (p. 62)	ובקומך, יכול אפילו עמד
	בחצי הלילה
Ps 1.5	לא יקמו רשעים במשפט
m. Sanh. 10.3	ואין עומדין בדין ... שנאמר על כן
	לא יקומו רשעים במשפט

The latter illustration is particularly illuminating. The biblical citation from Ps 1 is cited as a proof text to the dictum stated in *m. Sanh.* 10.3. The expression in the Mishnah, reflecting contemporary speech, used the verb צמד, for the BH term קום. This vividly illustrates not only the קום > צמד shift, but that צמד was considered synonymous with the earlier קום.

In conclusion, it should be noted that although Ezekiel does not demonstrate the קום > צמד shift to the same degree as other post-exilic books or post-biblical Hebrew in general, the employment of צמד in Ezek 17.14; 37.10; and 44.24 indicate that the shift was underway in the exilic period. Thus, Ezekiel shares a lexical affinity with LBH and post-biblical Hebrew in contrast to the practice of the earlier, classical period. This preference for צמד over קום continued

---

89. Cf. Bendavid, *Leshon* I, 332, 360; Hurvitz, *Linguistic Study*, 95-96; and Bergey, *Esther*, 127. The last four citations are particularly significant as the post-biblical texts are explicit commentaries on the parallel EBH passages. In all four instances the earlier EBH verb קום is replaced by the verb צמד, which had obviously replaced the earlier EBH synonym.

as shown above until Tannaitic times when virtually only צָמַד is used.[90]

90. Kutscher, *History* § 123, 84; and Bendavid *Leshon* I, 2, 62, 65, 66, 84, 114, 132, 327. The root קוּם occurs in the Mishnah only about five times in all stems. The root עָמַד on the other hand occurs over 200 times. The same state of affairs is also reflected in the Tosefta. See Kasovsky, *Mishnah Concordance* III, 1380-83; IV, 1566. In addition, in the Mishnah, עָמַד is the verb that is used to explain BH נצב. Because of the prominent occurrence of עָמַד in MH, Greenfield believes the lexeme should be considered a MH verb. *The Lexical Status of Mishnaic Hebrew*, xxi.

הָלַךְ

The Qal of the root הלך occurs over a thousand times in the Hebrew Bible in virtually every conceivable genre and context. The use of the Piel, on the other hand, occurs only twenty-five times and is virtually restricted to late and poetic texts.[91] The Piel should be considered a late linguistic development,[92] analogous to the preference for the Piel in the קיים > הקים shift discussed in Chapter 4. The following parallel passages between early biblical and extra-biblical Hebrew texts on the one hand, and later biblical and post-biblical Hebrew on the other, may illuminate the הָלַךְ > הלך diachronic shift:[93]

Isa 8.6	מי השלח ההלכים לאט
Siloam 4-5[94]	וילבו המים מן המוצא
m. Kelim 22.9[95]	אלא שיהוא המים מהלבין תחתיהן
2 Sam 11.2	ויהי לעת הערב ויקם דוד מעל משכבו
	ויתהלך על גג
Dan 4.26[96]	לקצת ירחין תרי עשר
	על היכל מלכותא די בבל מהלך הוה
Lev 11.27	וכל הולך על כפיו בכל החיה
b. Ḥul. 70b	כל מהלבי כפיים בחיה

The last parallel is especially significant as the Talmudic text is an explicit commentary of Lev 11.27.[97]

The occurrence of the Piel in Ezek 18.9 similarly appears to be an allusion to an earlier expression, yet the normative Qal has been

---

91. The Piel occurs in Isa 59.9; Ezek 18.9; Hab 3.11; Ps 38.7; 55.15; 81.14; 85.14; 86.11; 89.16; 104.3, 10, 26; 115.7; 131.1; 142.4; Job 24.10; 30.28; Prov 6.11, 28; 8.20; Eccl 4.15; 8.10; 11.9; Lam 5.18. The term occurs in only one non-poetic text that is clearly considered pre-exilic, 1 Kgs 21.27. See Smend, *Ezechiel*, 118.
92. *BDB*, 235.
93. See Bendavid, *Leshon* I, 376; and Hurvitz, *Linguistic Study*, 50.
94. See *KAI* I, # 189, 34.
95. This reading is from the Lowe edition. See W.H. Lowe, *The Mishnah On Which The Palestinian Talmud Rests* (Cambridge, 1883).
96. An analogous expression is found in the phrase ואנה מהלך בין ברמיא of Ahiqar, line 40. See Cowley, *Aramaic Papyri*, 213.
97. The term מהלבי occurs twelve additional times in *b. Ḥul.* 70b.

changed to the Piel. Note the following illustrations of the earlier expression, which differ from the later use in Ezek 18.9:[98]

Lev 18.3	וּבְחֻקֹּתֵיהֶם לֹא תֵלֵכוּ
Lev 20.23	וְלֹא תֵלְכוּ בְּחֻקֹּת הַגּוֹי
Lev 26.3	אִם בְּחֻקֹּתַי תֵּלֵכוּ
Ezek 18.9	בְּחֻקּוֹתַי יְהַלֵּךְ

In post-biblical Hebrew the Piel of הלך is quiet frequent. This formation occurs in the DSS and in Ben Sira in the following passages:[99]

| 1QS 8.18 | לְהַלֵּךְ בְּתָמִים דרך |
| Ben Sira 10.6(א) | וְאַל תְּהַלֵּךְ בדרך גאוה |

The preference for the Piel stem of הלך is also prevalent in the Aramaic Targum. Note the following instances where the MT used the Qal, and the Aramaic translation preferred to substitute the Piel stem:

Gen 7.18	וַתֵּלֶךְ התבה על פני המים
Tg. Onq.	וּמְהַלְּבָא תיבותא על אפי מיא
Exod 2.5	וְנַעֲרֹתֶיהָ הֹלְכֹת על יד היאר
Tg. Onq.	וְעוּלֵימָתְהָא מְהַלְּכָן על כיף נהרא

The occurrence of the Piel of הלך is especially prevalent in MH. The following examples are but a few of the numerous occurrences of the Piel stem in Rabbinic literature:[100]

| *m. Roš Haš*. 1.11(9) | וְאֵינוּ יכול לְהַלֵּךְ |
| *m. 'Abot* 3.9(7) | הַמְהַלֵּךְ בדרך |

98. The expression with the Qal does occur in Ezek in 11.12; 20.18; 36.27.
99. See also 1QS 8.18; Ben Sira 12.11(א); Ben Sira 13.13(א). Ben Sira 42.5 (מ) may qualify as another occurrence, although the text is damaged at the place where the the lexeme in question occurs. Some would argue that the above forms are indeed Qal. The Piel stem, however, appears to be more likely. E.g., see Hurvitz, *Linguistic Study*, 50 n. 76.
100. For further examples from MH, Tosefta, and Midrashim, see Ben-Yehuda, *Thesaurus* II, 1097-98.

t. B. Bat. 2.11   הִילֵּךְ בה בין לאוּרכה
Gen. Rab. (II, p. 632)   ומהלֵּךְ קודם כליא

It can easily be demonstrated that the Piel stem of הלך continued to enjoy widespread usage in the post-exilic period and continued in MH and later in both the Jerusalem and Babylonian Talmuds.[101] The occurrence of this form in Ezek 18.9 demonstrates not only Ezekiel's association with LBH and post-biblical Hebrew, but also registers one of the earliest occurrences of the root הלך in the Piel stem. Consequently, we have another example of a lexeme that became widespread in the post-biblical period which is attested in the exilic period, in the book of Ezekiel. The extensive usage of הלך in the Piel in Aramaic texts might indicate that the term's occurrence in BH is due to Aramaic influence.

---

101. The occurrences of the Piel of הלך in the Talmud are considerable. Ben-Yehuda, *Thesaurus* II, 1097-98; and Jastrow, *Dictionary* I, 352-53.

כנס

The verb כנס, in the Qal and Piel stems, is restricted to LBH passages with the connotation 'gather, collect'.[102] The verb is thus the later equivalent of the EBH verbs אסף/קבץ.[103] Note some illustrations of the later usage in some LBH texts:[104]

Neh 12.44	ויפקדו ... <u>לכנוס</u> בהם
1 Chr 22.2	ואמר דויד <u>לכנוס</u> את הגרים

This later practice of using כנס can be contrasted to the situation which existed in EBH where the verb כנס does not occur:[105]

Gen 29.22	<u>ויאסף</u> לבן את כל אנשי המקום
Gen 41.35	<u>ויקבצו</u> את כל אכל
Deut 30.4	משם <u>יקבצך</u>
Mic 2.12	<u>אסף אאסף</u> יעקב כלך <u>קבץ אקבץ</u>
Hos 8.10	עתה <u>אקבצם</u>

Note particularly how these EBH verbs are replaced by כנס in parallel expressions in later texts:[106]

Isa 11.12	ו<u>אסף</u> נדחי ישראל
Isa 56.8	<u>מקבץ</u> נדחי ישראל
Ps 147.2	נדחי ישראל <u>יכנס</u>
2 Sam 12.29	<u>ויאסף</u> דוד את כל העם
2 Sam 2.30	<u>ויקבץ</u> את כל העם
Est 4.16	<u>כנוס</u> את כל היהודים

---

102. *BDB*, 488; and *KB*, 444. The verb occurs one time in the Hithpael conjugation, in Isa 28.20. This reference is, however, not relevant to this discussion as the verb not only differs morphologically, belonging to a different stem, but is semantically obscure as well. See Hurvitz, *Linguistic Study*, 124 n. 201.
103. Bendavid, *Leshon* I, 338.
104. See also, Ezek 22.21; 39.28; Ps. 33.7; 147.2; Est 4.16.
105. The occurrence of the term אסף in the phrase ירחו אסף in the pre-exilic Gezar Inscription is apparently harmonious with what occurred in EBH. See *KAI* I, 182.1, 34.
106. See Hurvitz, *Lashon*, 175 n. 308; 'Linguistic Criteria For Dating Problematic Biblical Texts', *Hebrew Abstracts* 14 (1973) 77; and Bergey, *Esther*, 130.

Isa 13.14	וּכְצֹאן וְאֵין <u>מְקַבֵּץ</u>
Jer 23.3	וַאֲנִי <u>אֲקַבֵּץ</u> אֶת שְׁאֵרִית צֹאנִי
m. B. Qam. 6.1	<u>הַכּוֹנֵס</u> צֹאן לְדִיר

Exod 3.16[107]	לֵךְ וְ<u>אָסַפְתָּ</u> אֶת זִקְנֵי יִשְׂרָאֵל
Tg. Onq.	אִיזֵיל וְ<u>תִכְנוֹשׁ</u> יָת סָבֵי יִשְׂרָאֵל

1 Kgs 18.19[108]	<u>קְבֹץ</u> אֵלַי אֶת כָּל יִשְׂרָאֵל
Tg. Neb.	<u>כְּנוֹשׁ</u> לְוָתִי יָת כָּל יִשְׂרָאֵל

It can be easily observed from the illustrations cited above, that EBH
אסף/קבץ and LBH and post-biblical כנס are parallel semantically.
These verbs may refer in a general sense to gathering or collecting
something materially, such as food or tithes; they refer specifically to
collecting or gathering a people for a specific purpose. The latter
usage, as in Ps 147.2 and Est 4.16, cited above, is what we find in
Ezekiel:[109]

22.21	וְ<u>כִנַּסְתִּי</u> אֶתְכֶם
39.28	וְ<u>כִנַּסְתִּים</u> עַל אַדְמָתָם

The cognate כנש is also the preferred term in BA. Note the following illustrations from the Book of Daniel:[110]

3.2	וּנְבוּכַדְנֶצַּר מַלְכָּא שְׁלַח לְ<u>מִכְנַשׁ</u>
3.27	וּמִתְ<u>כַּנְּשִׁין</u> אֲחַשְׁדַּרְפְּנַיָּא סִגְנַיָּא

In post-biblical Hebrew, the verb כנס continued to be used. The
term occurs three times in the DSS:[111]

---

107. The Aramaic Targum also translates אסף with כנש in Gen 29.22; 30.23;
42.17; 49.33; Exod 4.29; Num 11.16, 24, 32; 21.16, 23; Deut 28.38; and passim.
108. The Aramaic Targum also translates קבץ with כנש in Gen 41.35, 48;
Deut 13.17; 30.3, 4, etc.
109. The earlier terms אסף and קבץ occur often in Ezekiel as well. See Ezek
11.17; 16.37; 20.34, 41; 22.19, 20; 24.4; 28.25; 29.5; 34.13; 36.24; 27.21; 39.17, 27.
110. See also Dan 3.3.
111. Only two occurrences are cited since כנס is the only word that has surviv-
ed in 4QpIsa[c] 163, 55.1. For transcription, see *DJD* V, 27. The first attested
Hebrew reading of the nominal form כנסת occurs in the Temple Scroll. See
Qimron, 'The Vocabulary of the Temple Scroll', 245.

4Q159 1,2.4[112]   אין לו יאוכלנה וְכנס לו
11QTemple 34.7   ויהיו כונסים [א]ת במזרקות

The verb increased in usage in MH as the term occurs quite
frequently, in place of אסף/קבץ.[113] The following examples are
illustrative:

m. Šeb. 4.8   הבאיש כונס לתוך ביתו
m. B. Bat. 3.1   כנס את תבואתו
m. Mid. 3.1   עלה אמה וכנס אמה

In conclusion, we see that Ezekiel again displays lexicographical
affinities with LBH by the use of the later Hebrew lexeme כנס. This
verb, used in place of the earlier, corresponding verbs in LBH, continued to be preferred by the writers of post-biblical Hebrew. The
occurrence of the verb in Ezekiel, not only illustrates the attestation of
a late term in the book of Ezekiel,[114] but also points out the book's
transitionary status, in that the verb כנס occurs first in written
Hebrew documents in the book of Ezekiel. It is probable that the verb
owes its existence in Hebrew vocabulary, as well as in Akkadian
vocabulary, to the influence of Aramaic.[115] כנש (BH כנס) was
widespread in Imperial Aramaic, Aramaic Targums,[116] Palmyrene,
and BA.[117]

---

112. For a photograph, see J.M. Allegro, 'An Unpublished Fragment of Essene Halakhah (4 Q Ordinances)', *JSS* 6 (1961) 72. For a transcription, see *DJD*
V, 6.
113. Thus Bendavid, *Lashon* I, 46, 109. For the scores of occurrences of this
root in MH, see especially Kasovsky, *Mishnah Concordance* III, 974. אסף, on
the other hand, occurs only rarely in MH, about eleven times for all stems. The
root קבץ does not occur in MH and only one time in the Tosefta, *t. Sanh.* 14.5.
Greenfield has called the substitution of כנס for earlier קבץ/אסף a
'mishnaism'. See *The Lexical Status of Mishnaic Hebrew*, xvii.
114. Acknowledged to be late by *BDB*, 488; *KB*, 443; and Driver, *Introduction*,
475.
115. Kautzsch, *Aramaismen*, 107; Driver, *Introduction*, 475; and von Soden,
Aramäische Wörter, 12-13. The latter reference was cited by Hurvitz, *Lashon*,
175 n. 308. See also, Cooke, *Ezekiel*, 247.
116. The Targum used the root to translate the EBH terms, אסף and קבץ,
and many other Hebrew roots as well. Cf., Kasovsky, *Targum Concordance* I,
245-46.
117. See Jean-Hoftijzer, *Dictionnaire*, 123; and *BDB*, 1027.

בוץ

The term בוץ , a 'fine white linen',[118] common in both Akkadian and Aramaic,[119] is restricted to late biblical texts in BH.[120] The lexeme occurs only eight times in BH in the following texts: Ezek 27.16; Est 1.6; 8.15; 1Chr 4.21; 15.27; 2 Chr 2.13; 3.14; 5.12.

The earlier correspondent for בוץ, in EBH, was the Egyptian loanword שש.[121] As בוץ is restricted to LBH, שש is virtually restricted to EBH texts. The latter term occurs in Gen 41.42; Ezek 16.10, 13; 27.7; Prov 31.32; and thirty-three times in the book of Exodus with reference to temple paraphernalia. The diachronic shift in the occurrence of these two synonyms is best illustrated by noting the occurrence of the two terms in the following parallel passages:[122]

Exod 36.35	ויעש את הפרכת תכלת וארגמן ותולעת
	שני ו<u>שש</u> משזר מעשה חשב עשה אתה כרבים
2 Chr 3.14	ויעש את הפרכת תכלת וארגמן וכרמיל
	ו<u>בוץ</u> ויעל עליו כרובים

Similarly, note the absence of בוץ in the earlier, but parallel passage below:

2 Sam 6.14	ודוד מכרכר בכל עז לפני ה'
	ודוד חגור אפוד בד
1 Chr 15.27	ודויד מכרבל במעיל <u>בוץ</u> ...
	ועל דויד אפוד בד

The conclusion one should draw from the latter illustration, with the addition of the term בוץ in Chronicles, is that the lexeme was the term of choice by the Chronicler. Put differently, when the Chronicler would add material which was absent from his *Vorlage*

---

118. Jean-Hoftijzer, *Dictionnaire*, 41.
119. See Selle, *Aramaismis*, 40-41; von Soden, *AHW* I, 143; and Brockelmann, *Lexicon*, 63. In Akkadian literature, the term is primarily restricted to Neo-Assyrian and Neo-Babylonian texts. See *CAD* II, 350.
120. *BDB* observes that this term is late. See p. 101.
121. See Thomas O. Lambdin, 'Egyptian Loan Words in the Old Testament', *JAOS* 73 (1953) 155.
122. See Smend, *Ezechiel*, 204; Kraetzschmar, *Ezechiel,* 211; Avi Hurvitz, 'The Usage of שש and בוץ in the Bible and its Implication for the Date of P', *HTR* 60 (1967) 117-18. See also, Bergey, *Esther*, 94.

he would be prone to use the living language of his contemporaries. The addition of בוץ by the Chronicler in this type of situation thus reinforces the idea that the lexeme is from the language of the Second Temple period rather than the pre-exilic period.

The synonyms בוץ/שש are rather scarce in the post-biblical period, probably as a result of the limited contexts which would call for either of these two terms in the post-biblical literature.[123] Yet, it is not without significance, that only בוץ occurs in MH and the Aramaic Targums. The following passages record all of the occurrences of בוץ in MH:[124]

m. Yoma 3.4	פרסו סדין של<u>בוץ</u> בינו לבין העם
m. Yoma 3.7(6)	פרסו לו סדין של<u>בוץ</u> בינו לבין העם
m. Yoma 7.1[125]	אם רוצה בבגדי <u>בוץ</u> קורא
m. Yoma 7.2(3)	ואם בבגדי <u>בוץ</u> קרא קידש

Note below how the Aramaic Targum often translates BH שש with בוץ:[126]

Gen 41.42	וילבש אתו בגדי <u>שש</u>
Tg. Onq.	ואלביש יתיה לבושין <u>דבוץ</u>
Exod 27.9	לחצר <u>שש</u> משזר
Tg. Onq.	לדרתא <u>דבוץ</u> שזיר
Exod 39.27	ויעשו את הכתנת <u>שש</u>
Tg. Onq.	ועבדו ית כיתונין <u>דבוץ</u>

The distribution of the synonyms בוץ/שש in BH clearly indicates that these terms were prevalent at different chronological stages in

123. Only שש occurs in the DSS in the passage 1QM 7.10. This attestation is of limited significance, however, as the citation is an obvious allusion to Exod 39.27-29. Thus Hurvitz, 'The Evidence of Language in Dating the Priestly Code', *RB* 81 (1974) 34 n. 21.
124. שש does occur in *t. Menaḥ.* 9.17. On the preference for בוץ in the post-biblical period, see Bendavid, *Leshon* I, 338.
125. This example is especially significant as the phrase refers to the holy garments of the priesthood which in the Pentateuch are always referred to by the lexeme שש.
126. This same phenomenon can be observed in the Targum to Exod 26.1; 27.18; 36.8; 38.9, 16; 39.28, 29.

the Hebrew Bible. The Egyptian loanword שׁשׁ being the term employed in the pre-exilic period was later replaced by בוץ, a term more at home to the north and east of Israel. It is especially significant that the book of Ezekiel, not only is the only book of the Hebrew Bible which employs both of these terms, but apparently records the earliest attestation of the term בוץ in written sources. As Bergey states: 'The lexical variation in Ezekiel suggests that בוץ penetrated the Hebrew vocabulary early in the LBH period, at which time it began to displace the use of שׁשׁ'.[127] The supposition that the term entered the Hebrew vocabulary subsequent to the exile is reinforced by the fact that the provenance of the term was from the Northeast (i.e. Akkadian, Aramaic).[128] Thus it is reasonable to suppose that the term first came to be used by speakers of Hebrew during the period of the nation's greatest exposure to this foreign influence from the Northeast—the time of the exile and deportation to Babylon! As the book of Ezekiel reflects a Babylonian setting,[129] we should perhaps not be surprised that the first occurrence of בוץ in BH is in this book. It is thus clear then that in the use of the term בוץ, Ezekiel is the forerunner to what would become the common lexical practice in both the post-exilic period and later.

127. *Esther*, 95.
128. For an illustration of this term in Phoenician, see Mark Lidzbarski, *Ephemeris für Semitische Epigraphik* (Giessen, 1909-15) 223, lines 12-13. The term is attested also in a late Punic text, c. the fourth century BC. See Cooke, *NSI*, 125; and *KAI* I, #76.6, 17.
129. E.g. Greenberg, *Ezekiel*, 106.

רצפה

The term רצפה[130] occurs only seven times in the Bible. Each occurrence is in a LBH text and refers to the floor or 'pavement'[131] of a building structure. The term occurs once in Esther, once in Chronicles, and five times in Ezekiel. Observe the usages of this lexeme in the following late texts:[132]

Est 1.6	מטות זהב וכסף על רצפת
2 Chr 7.3	ויכרעו אפים ארצה על הרצפה
Ezek 40.17	והנה לשכות ורצפה
Ezek 40.18	והרצפה אל כתף השערים

The term is apparently a later equivalent for the EBH Hebrew words קרקע or מרצפת.[133] Note the following illustrations of EBH texts which call for the use of the lexeme רצפה had the term existed in the early writer's lexical stock:[134]

1 Kgs 6.15	מהרקע הבית עד קירות הספן
1 Kgs 6.30	ואת קרקע הבית
1 Kgs 7.7	וספון בארז מהקרקע עד הקרקע
2 Kgs 16.17[135]	ויתן אתו על מרצפת אבנים

The diachronic contrast can be prominently noted by observing the contrastive method of employing the common BH idiom, 'bowing to the ground'. What is of particular significance is that the following

130. The פ is a spirant. Hence, the term is not to be confused with the term רצפה, 'glowing stone (or coal)', which has the פ labial stop. See Cooke, *Ezekiel*, 443. Analogous constructions with spirants include ירכתו in Gen 49.13, פטדה in Exod 28.17, and שפכה in Deut 23.2. See Bauer-Leander, *HG* § 75 f., 603; and Bergey, *Esther*, 96 n. 1.
131. Thus *BDB*, 954 and consistently by JPS translators.
132. The word occurs again in Ezek 40.17; 40.18; and 42.3.
133. Polzin acknowledges רצפה as the later equivalent of מרצפת. *Hebrew*, 150. With reference to the diachronic contrast with מרצפת, it is possible to see a morphological change, in that post-biblical Hebrew, particularly MH, tended to avoid the nominal pattern with the מ prefix. See Bendavid, *Leshon* II, 444 and the discussion of בתב above.
134. Hurvitz, *Linguistic Study*, 135-36; and Bergey, *Esther*, 96.
135. The Aramaic Targum translates this phrase ויהב יתיה על רצפת אבניא. The choice of the word רצפה to translate מרצפת indicates both the lateness of the former and possibly its Aramaic provenance.

earlier texts do not use the LBH term רצפה in the idiom—whereas the term does occur in the LBH text:[136]

Gen 42.6	ויבאו אחי יוסף וישתחוו לו אפים ארצה
2 Sam 14.22	ויפל יואב אל פניו ארצה וישתחו
1 Kgs 1.31	ותקד בת שבע אפים ארץ ותשתחו למלך
2 Chr 7.3	ויכרעו אפים ארצה על הרצפה וישתחוו

The term continued to be used in post-biblical Hebrew. Note the following occurrences from MH:[137]

m. Zebaḥ. 2.1 = *Zebaḥ.* 11.3	נשפך על הריצפה
m. Mid. 3.3	למטה בריצפה באתה הקרן
m. Tamid 1.5(4)	הגיע לריצפה

By way of summary, it must be concluded that רצפה, a technical term of the temple court, is characteristic of LBH and post-biblical Hebrew, replacing the earlier, equivalent terms קרקע and מרצפת.[138] The latter two terms do not occur in fact after the First Temple period in BH. The Aramaic tendency to avoid the מ prefix in the nominal pattern may not only suggest that רצפה was derived from מרצפת but that the former term's existence in Hebrew is ultimately the result of Aramaic influence. At any rate, Ezekiel records the first attestation of this term in Hebrew sources which suggests that it was not until the exilic period that the term first penetrated BH.[139]

---

136. The context supports the contention that each event occurs in a building complex. Other EBH examples of the idiomatic expression could be cited which do not occur within a building edifice and likewise avoid the use of the term רצפה. See Gen 19.1; 1 Sam 24.9; 25.41; 28.14.

137. See Ben-Yehuda, *Thesaurus* VII, 6720; Hurvitz, *Linguistic Study*, 136-37; and Bergey, *Esther*, 96-97. The term also occurs in *m. Šeqal.* 6.2; *m. Yoma* 1.7; and *m. Zebaḥ.* 3.2. For the numerous occurrences of this term in the Tosefta, see Kasovsky, *Tosephta Concordance* VI, 289. רצפה is absent from DSS. The term קרקע, however, does occur in 11QTemple 49.12.

138. It is perhaps also significant that the word רצפה was used to translate the difficult term משכית of Lev 26.1 in *b. Meg.* 22b. See Jastrow, *Dictionary* II, 1495. This possibly illustrates the continued use of this term in the common speech in contrast to the earlier EBH terms.

139. Bergey, *Esther*, 97.

הדיח

The root דוח, in its cultic-technical meaning, 'cleaning the sacri-
fices', occurs only four times, but always in the Hiphil stem in BH.
The following is a comprehensive list of all attestations of this root in
BH:

Isa 4.4	אם רחץ אדני את צאת בנות ציון
	ואת דמי ירושלם <u>ידיח</u> מקרבה
Jer 51.34[140]	מלא כרשו מעדני <u>הדיחנו</u>
Ezek 40.38	ולשכה ופתחה באילים השערים
	שם <u>ידיחו</u> את העלה
2 Chr 4.6	את מעשה העולה <u>ידיחו</u> בם

What is first of all worthy of mention about the above citations is that
the occurrence of this root is primarily restricted to LBH. Another
noteworthy factor concerning the use of דוח is observed from the last
two quoted examples. We see in the Ezekiel passage, and in the passage from 2 Chronicles, the use of the root דוח to refer specifically to
the 'cleansing of the sacrifice'. In the Hebrew of the classical period
this concept was expressed by use of the verb רחץ, shown to be parallel to דוח in the citation from Isa 4.4 above. Contrast the following
citations from EBH which employ the verb רחץ rather than דוח in
reference to 'cleansing of the sacrifice':[141]

Exod 29.17	<u>ורחצת</u> קרבו וכרעיו ...
Lev 1.9	וקרבו וכרעיו <u>ירחץ</u> במים
Lev 8.21	ואת הקרב ואת הכרעים <u>רחץ</u> במים
Lev 9.14	<u>וירחץ</u> את הקרב ואת הכרעים

There is an additional line of evidence which may be brought forth to
support the contention that דוח replaces the earlier רחץ in referring
to the 'cleaning the sacrifice'; or at least that the Hiphil of דוח was
the term employed in the Second Temple period to refer to the prepa-
ration of sacrifices. This corroboration is derived from the addition of
the root דוח in 2 Chr 4.6, in contrast to the earlier, parallel passage of
1 Kgs 7.38-39. Observe the diachronic contrast:

140. The meaning of the term in this passage is obscure. See Hurvitz, 'The
Evidence of Language in Dating the Priestly Code', 35 n. 24.
141. See Hurvitz, *Linguistic Study*, 63; and Zimmerli *Ezekiel* II, 367.

1 Kgs 7.38-39

ויעש עשרה בירות ...
חמש על כתף הבית מימין וחמש
על כתף הבית משמאלו ואת הים נתן

2 Chr 4.6

ויעש כיורים עשרה
ויתן חמשה מימין וחמשה משמאול לרחצה בהם
את מעשה העולה <u>ידיחו</u> בם והים לרחצה לכהנים בו

Two salient observations concerning the 'added' material in the above parallel texts are worthy of comment. First of all, it is to be noted, that the Chronicler has additional material concerning cleansing practices which does not occur in the earlier text from Kings. In describing the cleansing of the offering he uses the root דוח. The addition of this term supports the argument that this was the common term used to refer to the cleansing of the sacrifice in his day, in the Second Temple period. It is also striking that in the additional material in the Chronicler's account, the earlier term for cleansing the sacrifice, רחץ, occurs two times. However, the Chronicler employs רחץ to refer to the cleaning of non-sacrificial material, i.e. the laver and the priests. This suggests that the use of רחץ in referring to 'cleansing of sacrifices' was no longer part of the living language at the time of the Chronicler's writing and had been in fact replaced by the later Hiphil דוח.

In post-biblical Hebrew the practice which began in LBH of using the Hiphil of דוח to refer to 'cleaning the sacrifice' was continued. The employment of the Hiphil to refer to the 'cleaning of the cultic sacrifice', is the exclusive practice in MH. Hurvitz points out the diachronic distinction concerning the employment of the roots דוח/רחץ with regard to the cleaning of sacrifices in post-biblical Hebrew:[142]

> This picture changes completely in Rabbinic literature. Here one may note that both *rāḥaṣ* and *hēdhîₐḥ* enjoy a wide distribution; but, nevertheless, a clear semantic differentiation has developed between the two roots: whereas *rāḥaṣ* continues to serve as the regular term for 'washing' in general, *hēdhîₐḥ* is found specifically in the cultic context of 'cleansing the sacrifices'. This process of differentiation is already an accomplished fact in the Mishnah, where (in connection with sacrifices) numerous occurrences of *hēdhîₐḥ* are found—to the total exclusion of *rāḥaṣ*.

142. *Linguistic Study*, 64.

Note the following illustrations of the use of דוח in reference to 'cleaning the sacrifices' in the Mishnah and Tosefta:[143]

m. Ṭamid 4.2	הקרביים מְדִיחִין אותן
m. Seqal. 6.(4)5[144]	שעליהן מְדִיחִין את הקרבים
t. Zebaḥ. 9.9-10	מוריד את הקרבים וּמְדִיחָן במים
t. Ḥul. 8.7	אסור חם לתוך צונן מְדִיחָן ואוכלו

From the above discussion, it is clear that the root דוח is a late term in BH and that it took on the connotation 'cleansing the sacrifice', in the Hiphil stem. In adapting this particular semantic nuance, LBH דוח replaced the earlier רחץ. In post-biblical Hebrew the replacement was complete. The book of Ezekiel records the first attested usage of the Hiphil of דוח with this connotation which was an innovation in the history of the Hebrew language.

---

143. An example of the more general connotation may be found in *m. Miqw.* 7.3. The root דוח does not occur in the DSS. רחץ does occur at Qumran but only in the Piel and once in the nominal form. See Kuhn, *Konkordanz*, 204. It is important to note that though the root רחץ does occur in the DSS, it no longer has the specific connotation it had in EBH. The term is used exclusively for cleaning the body; it does not occur in the classical sense of 'cleaning the sacrifice'. For the first Mishnaic citation, see Hurvitz, *Linguistic Study*, 64.

144. For this reading see, Lowe, *The Mishnah On Which The Palestinian Talmud Rests*.

מהלך

Although the verbal root הלך is one of the most frequently occurring verbs in BH, the nominal form occurs only five times. The term מהלך is restricted to the following passages: Ezek 42.4; Jonah 3.3, 4; Zech 3.7; and Neh 2.6. The substantive has several semantic nuances, such as 'walk, journey, going, distance',[145] similar to the more common biblical term דרך. The following passages illuminate different modes of expression, comparing early texts with later biblical writings:

Num 9.10	בדרך רחקה
Exod 3.18	דרך שלשת ימים
Jonah 3.3	מהלך שלשת ימים
Deut 14.24	וכי ירבה ממך הדרך כי לא תוכל שאתו כי ירחק ממך המקום
Ezek 42.4	ולפני הלשכות מהלך עשר אמות רחב

The lexeme מהלך continued to be used in post-biblical Hebrew. The following passages are illustrative:

Ben Sira 11.12 (א)	אש רשש ואבד מהלך
m. Ma'as.' Š 5.2	מהלך יום אחד לכל צד
t. Soṭa 8.7	מהלך ששים מיל

Particularly significant are the following explanations of the phrase דרך רחוקה cited above from Num 9.10 in the Mishnah and Tosefta respectively. In both texts the interpretation uses the term מלהך to interpret דרך:[146]

m. Roš Haš. 1.11(9) ואם היתה דרך רחונה לוקחין בידן מזוזות שעל מהלך לילה ויום מחללים את השבת

t. Pesaḥ. 8.3 ר יוסה הגליל או דרך רחונה, שומע אני מהלך יום אחד

---

145. See *BDB*, 237; and *KB*, 499. *BDB* says the term is 'late'. *Ibid*.
146. The term also occurs in this literature in the following texts: *m. Ma'as.' Š* 5.2; *t. Ma'as. Š.* 5.14; *t. Soṭa* 8.7.

The same practice can be observed in Sipre Deuteronomy. In the discussion of Deut 1.2, Num 10.33 is brought into the discussion. In both instances the term דרך of the Hebrew text is reiterated as מהלך in the language of the Rabbis:[147]

Sipre Deut. 2 (p. 8)   אחד עשר יום מחרוב דרך
הר שעיר עד קדש ברנע ... והלא אינו אלא
מהלך שלשה ימים ... דרך שלשת ימים
... והלא אינו אלא מהלך ארבעים יום

Analogous to the above phenomenon is the use of מהלך by the translators of the Aramaic Targum to translate דרך of the Hebrew text.[148] The following is a selection of the examples of the the rendering of דרך as מהלך in the Aramaic Targum:[149]

Gen 30.36	וישם דרך שלשת ימים
Tg. Onq.	ושוי מהלך תלתה יומין
Exod 5.3	נלכה נא דרך שלשת ימים במדבר
Tg. Onq.	ניזיל כען מהלך תלתה יומין במדברא
2 Kgs 3.9	ויסבו דרך שבעת ימים
Tg. Neb.	ואסתחרו מהלך שבעא יומין

The use of the lexeme מהלך is restricted to only a select number of passages in BH and we should suspect that it was not part of the vocabulary of the earlier standard Hebrew. The frequent occurrence of the term in the Aramaic Targum might cause us to suspect its existence in BH to be due to Aramaic influence.[150] Landes, on the other hand does not believe there is enough data available to be able to come to such a conclusion: 'Our present meagre evidence certainly does not preclude the possibility that it came into Aramaic from Hebrew, and does not lend convincing support to the reverse'.[151] The

147. Observed by Hurvitz, *Linguistic Study*, 93.
148. See Hurvitz, *Linguistic Study*, 93; and Athalya Brenner, 'The Language of the Book of Jonah as a Measurement for the Time of its Composition', *BM* 24 (1979) 400 [In Hebrew].
149. See also, Exod 3.18; 8.23; Num 10.33, 33; 11.31; 33.8; Deut 1.2.
150. Thus Brenner, 'The Language of the Book of Jonah as a Measurement for the Time of its Composition', p 400.
151. 'Linguistic Criteria and the Date of the Book of Jonah', 159.

frequent occurrence of מהלך in the Aramaic Targum in translating דרך does seem, however, to give greater support to the suggestion that the direction of influence is from Aramaic. Regardless, the existence of the term in the book of Ezekiel illustrates again that this book has a tendency to employ terms which are considered to be 'late'. Also, the occurrence of מהלך in Ezek 42.4 may be the first attestation of this late term in our available Hebrew sources.

עֲזָרָה

The term עזרה, usually translated 'temple court', occurs only nine
times in BH (Ezek 43.14, 14, 14, 17, 20; 45.14; 2 Chr 4.9, 9; 6.13),[152] and
is considered to be the later equivalent for the more frequent חצר.[153]
   This LBH term occurs but once in both the DSS and in Ben Sira.
Observe the restricted use of this lexeme in the following passages:

| 11QTemple 23.13[154] | ועל ארבע פנות <u>עזרת</u> המזבח |
| Ben Sira 50.11 (ב)[155] | ויהדר <u>עזרת</u> מקדש |

Whereas this LBH term occurs only rarely in the DSS and in Ben
Sira, it is more widespread in later Hebrew, notably in the Mishnah
and Tosefta. The term may be found, for example, in *m. Sanh.* 1.5; *m.
Mid.* 2.6 (6X); *t. Pesah.* 4(3).12; *t. Zebah.* 7.1; *t. Kip.* 1.3.[156]
   עזרה is also attested in the Aramaic Targum. Notice how the
widespread occurrence of this lexeme is illustrated by its use in
translating the nouns היכל and גבעה in the following passages:

1 Sam 3.3	ושמואל שכב <u>בהיכל</u> ה'
Tg. Neb.	ושמואל שכיב <u>בעזרת</u> ליואי
Isa 10.32	הר בית ציון <u>גבעת</u> ירושלם
Tg. Neb.	דבציון ועל <u>עזרתא</u> דבירושלם

More significant for our purposes, however, is the use of the later
עזרה to translate MT חצר:[157]

---

152. Each the three occurrences of the term in Chronicles has no parallel in
Samuel/Kings. It is probable, therefore, that the term was part of the *living*
language of the Chronicler.
153. First observed by Hurvitz, in 'The Evidence of Language in Dating the
Priestly Code. A Linguistic Study in Technical Idioms and Terminology', 41-
43. See also Polzin, *Hebrew*, 147. Levy also states that the Hebrew term עזרה is
late Hebrew. See *Wörterbuch* III, 633. For a possible distinctive semantic value
of the term in Ezekiel, see Hurvitz, *Linguistic Study*, 81, 162.
154. Yadin acknowledges that the term is late. *Temple Scroll* I, 185.
155. See Ben-Yehuda, *Thesaurus* V, 4416.
156. There are at least sixty occurrences of this lexeme in the Tosefta. Mention
should also be made of the famous expression ספר העזרה as for example in
m. Kelim 15.6 and *m. Mo'ed Qat.* 3.4.
157. Also noted by Hurvitz. See *Linguistic Study*, 80.

Isa 1.12   מי בקש זאת מידכם רמס חצרי

Tg. Neb.   מן תבע דא מידבון למיתי לא תדושון עזרתי

It is clear that the term עזרה should be considered a late lexeme in BH which became preferred over חצר[158] in the post-biblical period. In the Bible the term is restricted to LBH with its first recorded usage occurring in the book of Ezekiel. The term probably entered the Hebrew lexical stock from the influence of Aramaic. Howie comments on the significance of the occurrence of this lexeme in Aramaic and Syriac: 'Late and scant usage in the Bible plus a later development in Aramaic and Syriac indicate a probable Aramaic origin'.[159] The term continued to be used and enjoyed widespread usage in the Tannaitic period.

158. It should be observed that this term, which was prevalent in EBH, does not occur in the DSS or Ben Sira.
159. Carl Gordon Howie, *The Date and Composition of Ezekiel* (Philadelphia, 1950) 57.

Expressions

למען לא

The first line of evidence for the proposition that the phrase למען לא is late is the complete absence of this phrase in the writings from the First Temple period. The phrase occurs only in Psalms, Ezekiel, and Zechariah among the biblical books.[160] In the Hebrew of EBH a number of expressions were used to express the same semantic range as the later למען לא. These include the expressions: לבלתי, פן, אשר לא, למען לא, or למען אשר לא.[161] The following passages demonstrate the different modes of expression by pre-exilic and post-exilic writers:

Exod 23.33	לא ישבו בארצך פן יחטיאו אתך לי
Ps 119.11	בלבי צפנתי אמרתך למען לא אחטא לך

Judg 7.2	פן יתפאר עלי ישראל לאמר ידי הושיעה לי
Zech 12.7	והושיע ה' את אהלי יהודה בראשנה
	למען לא תגדל תפארת בית דויד

Josh 23.6	וחזקתם מאד לשמר ולעשות את כל הכתוב
	בספר תורת משה לבלתי סור ממנו ימין ושמאול
Ezek 14.10-11	ונשאו עונם כעון הדרש כעון הנביא
	יהיה למען לא יתעו עוד בית ישראל מאחרי

Deut 17.12	והאיש אשר יעשה בזדון לבלתי שמע
	אל הכהן
Ezek 19.9	יבאהו למען לא ישמע קולו עוד

Gen 11.7	ונבלה שם שפתם אשר לא ישמעו
	איש שפת רעהו
Deut 20.17-18	כאשר צוך ה' אלהיך
	למען אשר לא ילמדו
	אתכם לעשות ככל תועבתם
Ezek 25.10	ונתתיה למורשה למען לא תזכר
	בני עמון בגוים

160. Ezek 14.10; 19.9; 25.10; 26.10; Zech 12.7; Ps 119.11, 80; 125.3.
161. See Hurvitz, *Lashon*, 147-48 for this discussion. See also, Cooke, *Ezekiel*, 156.

The evidence for the continuation of the use of the phrase in non-biblical sources is scanty. Thus far, only three examples have been discovered. The phrase occurs once in the Temple Scroll (11QTemple 35.13), and twice in Ben Sira (Ben Sira 38.8 (ב); Ben Sira 45.26 (ב).[162]

The phrase לׄמעֵן לׄא was used only rarely in BH and is restricted to texts which were not written in the classical period. The phrase continued to be used only sparingly, yet there is some evidence of its occurrence in post-biblical Hebrew texts. The fact that the phrase occurs four times in Ezekiel suggests that the phrase was in wide use in the exilic period.

---

162. Hurvitz suggests that a seventh-century BC Aramaic inscription provides a fourth example. The text in question is Nerab 2.7-8: עם לבשי שמוני לׄמעֵן לׄאֵחרה לתהנם ארצתי. For text, see Cooke, *NSI*, 190. Cited by Hurvitz, *Lashon*, 148 n. *213. This interpretation is, however, open to question.

זהב וכסף > כסף וזהב

A casual survey of the occurrences of the above phrases in BH will
demonstrate, that while both phrases occur in both pre-exilic and
post-exilic BH, the first phrase occurs primarily in EBH texts, while
75% of the occurrences of the latter phrase are in LBH.[163] The
diachronic shift can be detected by observing the following parallel
passage:

2 Sam 8.10	כלי כסף וכלי זהב
1 Chr 18.10	וכל כלי זהב וכסף

Nonbiblical sources support the proposition that the phrase כסף
וזהב, common in pre-exilic biblical Hebrew, was more prevalent
before the Persian period than after. Early Ugaritic, Phoenician, and
Aramaic inscriptions exhibit the כסף וזהב order.[164] By contrast,
later Egyptian, Akkadian, and BA sources well attest the arrangement זהב וכסף which is more common in LBH.[165] The LBH order
is attested both in the DSS as well as in Rabbinic literature in such
texts as 1QM 5.5; 1QM 5.7-8; Ben Sira 40.25 (ב); *t. Sukk.* 4.6; *Lev.
Rab.* 1.6(3a).[166] The following are a few of the examples of the LBH
formula in late non-Hebrew sources:

Dan 5.2	להיתיה למאני דהבא וכספא

163. See Avi Hurvitz, 'Diachronic Chiasm in Biblical Hebrew', in *The Bible
and the History of Israel. Studies in Honor of Jacob Levor,* ed. Benjamin
Uffenheimer (Tel Aviv, 1969) 248-51 [In Hebrew]; and *Lashon*, 146. The order
כסף וזהב occurs in: Gen 13.2; 24.35, 53; 44.8; Exod 3.22; 11.2; 12.35; Num
22.18; 24.13; Deut 7.25; 8.13; 17.17; 29.16; Josh 6.19, 24; 22.8; 2 Sam 8.10, 11; 21.4;
1 Kgs 7.51; 10.25; 15.15, 18, 19; 20.3, 7; 2 Kgs 7.8; 16.8; 20.13; 23.35; Isa 2.7; 39.2;
Jer 10.4; Ezek 7.19; 38.13; Hos 8.4; Joel 4.5; Nah 2.10; Hag 2.8; Zech 6.11; Ps
105.37; 115.4; 135.15; Prov 17.3; 22.1; 27.21; Eccl 2.8; Dan 11.8; Ezra 1.4; 8.25, 28,
30, 33; 1 Chr 18.11; 2 Chr 1.15; 5.1; 15.18; 16.2, 3; 2 Chr 21.3; 32.27. The order
זהב וכסף occurs in Exod 23.3; 31.4; 35.5, 22; Num 31.22; 2 Kgs 12.14; 14.14;
25.15; Jer 52.19; Ezek 16.17; 17.13; 28.4; Nah 2.10; Hab 2.19; Zech 14.14; Mal 3.3;
Ps 119.72; Prov 25.11; Est 1.6; Dan 11.38, 43; Ezra 1.1; 1 Chr 19.10; 22.16(15);
29.2, 3, 5; 2 Chr 2.6, 13; 9.4, 21; 24.14.
164. See Hurvitz, 'Diachronic Chiasm in Biblical Hebrew', 249.
165. Hurvitz, 'Diachronic Chiasm in Biblical Hebrew', 250-51.
166. The Temple Scroll consistently follows the EBH pattern. This practice by
the writer(s) of the Temple Scroll may be another example of conscious imitation of EBH style, a custom of DSS writers observed in the previous chapter.

Ezra 5.14   בית אלהא די דהבה וכספא
Eleph Pap 30.12[167]   שרפו ומזרקיא זי זהבא וכסף
Eleph Pap 31.11   שרפו ומזרקיא זי זהבא ווי בספא
Matt 10.9   Μὴ κτήσησθε χρυσὸν μηδὲ ἄργυρον

Furthermore, the LBH order is also attested in the third century AD in a Palmyrene inscription:[168]

קיניא עבדא דהבא וכספא ליקרה

The source of this change in word order may have resulted from the change of the respective worth of these metals. Silver was rare in earlier times, and hence it occurs first in the early formulae. Gold, subsequently increased in value and this may explain why this metal occupied the first position more often in the post-exilic period and beyond.[169] Regardless, we observe that the occurrence of the phrase זהב וכסף in Ezek 16.17; 17.13; and 28.4 again illustrates another manner in which the book of Ezekiel resembles LBH and post-biblical Hebrew.[170]

---

167. Both this text and the following text are numbered after Cowley's method. See, Cowley, *Aramaic Papyri*, 112, 120.

168. See Cooke, *NSI*, 286.

169. See Hurvitz, 'Diachronic Chiasm in Biblical Hebrew', 250 n. 14 for discussion and references.

170. It should also be noted that the occurrence of the earlier phrase in Ezek 7.19 was probably borrowed from Zeph 1.18. For substantiating evidence that Ezekiel was familiar with this work, see above, p. 63.

Conclusion

In this chapter we have observed seventeen lexemes and expressions in the book of Ezekiel which are characteristic of LBH. Of these seventeen terms and expressions, fifteen continued to have widespread usage in post-biblical literature.[171] In addition, six of the LBH terms found in Ezekiel could be attributed to Aramaic influence.[172]

Particularly noteworthy, were the two occasions in Ezekiel where an allusion or reference to an earlier text was apparent. First, we saw that the Piel stem, in harmony with later Hebrew practice, was employed rather than the Qal in the phrase בחזקתי יהלך (28.9), in contrast to the earlier בחזקתי תלבו (Lev 26.3). In a similar fashion, we noted that Ezekiel used the LBH term קהל (23.47) to designate the agents of capital punishment in contrast to the earlier frozen expression ירגמו... כל העדה (Lev 24.16; Num 15.35). Also, in reference to our discussion of EBH עדה versus LBH קהל, we observed how Ezekiel, in reinterpreting the earlier account of the Korahite affair, avoided using עדה in Ezek 44.11. This omission clearly demonstrated that the use of עדה had begun to wane at the time of the writing of Ezekiel 44. This example of Ezekiel's reinterpretation of the Korahite incident illustrates, in particular, the manner in which inner-biblical exegesis assists the diachronic analysis of BH.

---

171. The exceptions being the terms מקטרת and נתץ (Piel).
172. These include צל, זעק, כתב, הלך (Piel), בנס, בוץ.

Chapter 7

CONCLUSION

In our analysis of the language of the book of Ezekiel we have set out to measure linguistic developments in the book based on the linguistic principles of contrast and distribution. Our ability to isolate late language features was augmented by the recognition that Ezekiel, as an heir to a rich literary tradition, made use of earlier sources and frozen forms. In our study of the language of Ezekiel we were able to identify thirty-seven grammatical and lexical features which are characteristic of LBH. Of these thirty-seven characteristics, fifteen were attributed to Aramaic influence. Thus through the external factor of language contact we can account for many LBH features in the book of Ezekiel. The influence of Aramaic upon Hebrew actually began late in the eighth century as Rabin has stated:[1]

> In 721 the Assyrians had introduced into the former kingdom of Israel exiles from southern Mesopotamia (Kutha, Avva, Sepharvaim = Sippar, 2 Kings 17:24) and northern Syria (Hamath), and these, if they did not already speak Aramaic at home, certainly spoke this lingua franca in their new seats in Palestine, thus aiding its spread to that country.

The most intense period of Aramaic influence, however, did not occur until the Persian period. Chomsky, commenting on the impact of Aramaic at this crucial period of the history of the Hebrew language, noted:[2]

> ... Later, the prophet Jeremiah, in addressing himself to the Jews living in Babylonia, employed a whole Aramaic verse (Jeremiah 10.11), in which he bade them tell the idol worshippers in Babylonia that the idols were helpless, futile and doomed to perdition. The reason for rendering this verse in Aramaic is that this language was then popular in the Near East, and it must have gained wide currency among the Hebrews, especially those residing in the Babylonian exile.

1. Chaim Rabin, 'Hebrew and Aramaic in the First Century', 1013.
2. William Chomsky, *Hebrew: The Eternal Language* (Philadelphia, 1957) 157-58.

Chomsky's suggestion that Aramaic influence would be particularly significant for the Jews living in the Babylonian exile, has special relevance for Ezekiel. Rabin comments on how this crucial period in the history of the people of Israel, affected the Israelites speaking habits, particularly as reflected in the book of Ezekiel:[3]

> During the exile, no doubt, the popular language changed more rapidly (as language often does in times of social upheaval), and the educated classes in Babylonia learnt to speak Aramaic, which by then had replaced Babylonian (Akkadian) as the spoken language of Mesopotamia. This, and the disturbance of life and education, impaired the stability of the written language, as we can observe in the peculiarities of the book of Ezekiel.

It is possible that the prestige factor played a role in the Israelites' adopting the Aramaic language given the impact this language had upon the educated classes as noted above. Regardless, at the beginning of the exile the prominence of EBH began to wane, largely as a result of the influence of Aramaic.[4] The following charts illustrate the late linguistic features in the book of Ezekiel which may be attributable to Aramaic influence and provide the pages where the features are discussed in this work.

---

3. Rabin, 'Hebrew and Aramaic in the First Century', 1013.
4. See Bendavid, *Leshon* I, 60. Hence, we take exception to Driver's contention that Aramaic influence is prevalent in the Bible only in the books of Ecclesiastes, Esther, and Chronicles. *Introduction*, 156.

Aramaic Influence on the Grammar of Ezekiel

קים > הקים	83-85
(בבאו האיש) > בבא משה	91-93
כפר ל > כפר את	97-99
והוליד בן > ויולד בן	100-102
היה עמד אצלי > עמדים אצל	108-110
ורחב חמש אמות > וחמש אמות רחב	113-114
כי...ימות > ואם...והמתני	120-122

Aramaic Influence on the Vocabulary of Ezekiel

על/אל	127-131
זעק > צעק	134-138
כתב > ספר, מכתב	139-141
והלּךֶo > הלך	153-155
כנס > קבץ, אסף	156-158
בוץ > שש	159-161
רצפה > מרצפת, קרקע	162-163
מהלך > דרך	167-169
{עֲזָ;רָה > חצר	170-171

While this external factor of language contact is rather easy to detect, other linguistic changes, notably from internal factors, are more difficult to recognize. We propose, however, following our discussion of language change in the opening chapter (pp. 1-21 above), that the following change which we discovered in the book of Ezekiel may be attributable to the analogic mechanism.

a	:á
b	: X= b´
יהי	: יחי
היה	: X=חיה[5]

In this example, we see the utilization of the analogical mechanism to effect language change. The analogic mechanism explains how the EBH יח began to be replaced by היה in LBH. Given the similar pro-nunciation and graphemic form of יח(ה) to the ubiquitous היה (ו]היי]) it is not unreasonable to assume that the יח > חיה shift resulted from an underlying attempt to represent a more uniform morphological pattern.

Furthermore, in our discussion of linguistic change we stressed the importance of the concept of variation in language change. Thus we have reason to assume that all the LBH shifts from the earlier, classi-cal language initially occurred as dialectical differences or variations which may have penetrated the linguistic currency from outside influence, particularly Aramaic and certainly other dialectical pockets which must have existed in Israel. Some of these variations may have already existed in the EBH period functioning as a synonym to a feature which would later become extinct or occur in an increasingly diminished capacity. Most of the LBH changes which existed initially as variant forms continued in the DSS and the rest of post-biblical literature. This fact, as was discussed above, was substantiating evidence that the features we designated as LBH were in fact late. Of the thirty-seven LBH features we examined in the book of Ezekiel, only three did not survive in post-biblical literature. In

---

5. It is possible that the חום > חומה shift observed in Ezek 30.18; 34.27 and the שבע > שבעה shift (Ezek 16.28, 49; 39.19) can also be explained by the shift observed in the בז > בזה analogy. With regard to the latter Ezekielian shift it is worth noting that שבעה has one attestation in the DSS (1QpHab 3.12) while שבע does not occur.

each of these three cases either the earlier EBH feature re-emerged, or continued adaptation occurred to the point that the LBH characteristic was replaced by a post-biblical innovation.[6] We must assume that these features did not attain wide acceptance and that their challenge to the earlier EBH forms was short-lived. The variant form was used for only a short period in the life of the Hebrew language. Nevertheless, these variations which effectuated a flucuation in the frequency of both the variant forms and their EBH counterparts, constitute the essence of linguistic change.[7]

The late grammatical and lexical features we observed in the book of Ezekiel were considerable. To gain a better perspective of Ezekiel's place in the history of a Biblical Hebrew continuum, however, examine the following charts which record the distribution of the LBH features of the book of Ezekiel in other biblical works, deemed to be late.

---

6. Two of the three LBH features which did not continue in post-biblical literature are lexical: מקטרת, נתץ (Piel). The only grammatical feature which did not continue in the post-biblical literature is the ידי אשר construction.
7. Thus Bloomfield, *Language*, 409, 435.

Distribution of Ezekiel's Late Grammatical Features[8]

LBH Feature of Ezekiel	Jer	Est	Dan	Ezra	Neh	Ch	DSS	MH
דויד		ø	ø	X	X	X	X	X
אני	X	X	X	X	X	X	X	X
ארצות	X	X	X	X	X	X	X	X
הם			X	X	X	X	X	X
חיה		X			X		X	
קים		ø		ø			CD	X
חללוהו		X	X	X	X	X	X	X
את הנשיא	X		X		X	X	X	X
בבאו...	X		X	X	X	X	X	X
וראו...		X				X	X	X
כפר לֹ	X		X	X	X	X		X
והוליד	X	X	X	X	X	X	X	X
בצאת		X	X	X	X	X	X	
לבוא עתה	X	X	X	X	X	X	X	
היה עמד			X	X	X	X	X	X
ידע אשר		X	X	X	X	X		ø
ורחב חמש אמות	X	X	ø	ø	ø	X	X	X
על ... וֹ						X	X	
בין לֹ		ø	X	ø	X	X·	X	X
בי ... ימות	X	X	X	X	X	X		X

8. The symbol 'X' designates the existence of the late feature, a blank space signifies that only the earlier corresponding feature occurs, while the symbol 'ø' designates that neither the early or late trait is extant.

Distribution of Ezekiel's Late Lexical Features

LBH Lexeme	Jer	Est	Dan	Ezra	Neh	Ch	DSS	MH
עַל	X		X	X		X	X	X
מקטרת		ø	ø	ø	ø	X	X	
זעק	X	X	ø	ø	X	X	X	
כתב		X	X	X	X	X	X	X
ניתץ		ø	ø	ø	ø	X		
קהל	X	ø	ø	X	X	X	X	X
כעס			ø	ø	X	X		X
עמד		X	X	X	X	X	X	X
הילך			X				X	X
כנס	X	X			X	X	X	X
בוץ	ø	X	ø	ø	ø	X		X
רצפה	ø	X	ø	ø	ø	X		X
הדיח	X	ø	ø	ø	ø	X	ø	X
מהלך		ø	ø		X		BS	X
עזרה			ø	ø		X	X	X
למען לא		ø		ø	ø		X	
זהב וכסף	X	X	X	X	ø	X	X	

Based upon our analysis of the late features of the book of Ezekiel, specifically as illustrated in the above charts, it might be argued that Ezekiel be considered as a component of LBH. It is understandable that this might be the perception as it has been our purpose to demonstrate the linguistic shifts in the book of Ezekiel which are harmonious with LBH. Consequently, the isolation of other factors which would demonstrate Ezekiel's affinity with EBH have been omitted. It could be pointed out, on the other hand, that all of the EBH grammatical qualities which we contrasted with later developments in Ezekiel are also extant in the book of Ezekiel. In addition, of the seventeen lexical developments in the book, only six occur to the exclusion of their earlier EBH counterpart.[9] This, as we noted above, is to be expected given both the short diachronic time span we are analyzing as well as the transitional status of the book of Ezekiel. To add a more balanced perspective to our study, the following chart will provide a more complete picture of the language of Ezekiel, as we point out the features of the book which are harmonious with EBH style in contrast to later developments in other LBH books. It should be noted in the chart below that Ezekiel employs the EBH feature to the exclusion of the LBH counterpart. We have listed the grammatical features first which are followed by the the lexemes.[10]

---

9. These are the lexemes הדיח, רצפה, בעט, קהל, זעק, מקטרת.
10. Much of this information is found in Bergey's *Esther*, 178-80.

EBH in the Book of Ezekiel

EBH FEATURE	LBH FEATURE
שבט	שרביט
ירושלם	ירושלים
עשו יעשה	יעשה
לבלתי הוציא	אין לבוא
מ	יותר מ
o	יום ויום
בז	בזה
חג , מועד	יום טוב
חזקה	תקף
חק	דת
חרד	זוע
יתר	שאר
כבוד	יקר
משל	שלט
לקח	קבל
עטרה	כתר
ממלכה	מלכות

The late features in the charts on pp. 182-83 are thus selective, representing only the late features found in Ezekiel. For a more balanced perspective of Ezekiel's place in the history of BH we should remember that while the forty-eight chapters of Ezekiel contain thirty-seven illustrations of LBH, the book of Esther with only ten chapters contains fifty-eight grammatical and lexical LBH characteristics.[11] Similarly, there are far fewer late features in Ezekiel than in other LBH works such as Ezra, Nehemiah and Chronicles.[12] Thus we should be hesitant to classify the book of Ezekiel as LBH. Given the fact that Ezekiel contains many late biblical features, though not to the extent of other LBH books, it is better to understood the book as a

11. Bergey, *Esther*.
12. Thus Hurvitz, *Linguistic Study*, 161-62.

transitional work. In fact, this book appears to be the best candidate in the biblical corpus to typify the transitional link between pre-exilic and post-exilic BH—a view consistent with the exilic setting reflected in the book. As we noted in Chapter 3, Ezekiel demonstrated more affinity to LBH than the alleged P source, Polzin's choice as the mediating representative between EBH and LBH literature. And as we may note above in the charts of Ezekiel's grammatical and lexical developments, Jeremiah, which appears to share a greater linguistic affinity to EBH,[13] contained only fifteen of Ezekiel's thirty-seven late features.[14] Thus Ezekiel appears to be the best representative of the mediating link between pre-exilic and post-exilic Hebrew and hence the exemplar of Biblical Hebrew in Transition.

13. This is the conclusion of Guenther's study. See Guenther, *Diahcronic Study*, esp. 225.
14. This observation substantiates Rabin's comment above concerning the effect of social upheaval (i.e. exile) upon language. Landes in 'Linguistic Criteria and the Date of the Book of Jonah', suggests that the book of Jonah represents a transitional work. We believe this premise is difficult to prove given the restricted size of the document. Nida comments on the necessity of a sizable corpus as a safeguard against statistical distortion : 'One must have a far larger corpus to be certain of statistical analyses of isolated features'. Eugene A. Nida, 'Implications of Contemporary Linguistics for Biblical Scholarship', *JBL* 91 (1972) 79. See also, Garr, *Dialect Geography of Syria-Palestine, 1000-586 B.C.E.*, 1-2. Furthermore, Qimron argues that it is impossible to precisely pinpoint the date of the writing of the book of Jonah. Elisha Qimron, 'The Dating of the Book of Jonah', *BM* 81 (1980) 182 [In Hebrew].

BIBLIOGRAPHY

PRIMARY SOURCES

Bible
Biblia Hebraica Stuttgartensia, Stuttgart, 1966.
Aramaic Targum. A. Sperber, *The Bible in Aramaic*, Leiden, 1959-73.

Rabbinic Literature
Mishnah. G. Beer, *Faksimile-Ausgabe des Mischna-Codex Kaufmann A50*, The Hague, 1929.
Tosefta. S. Lieberman, *The Tosefta According to Codex Vienna*, New York, 1955 [Zera'im, Mo'ed, Nashim].
—M.S. Zuckermandel, *Tosephta Based on the Erfurt and Vienna Codices*, Jerusalem, 1970 [Neziqim, Qodashim, Tohorot].
Mechilta. *Mechilta d'Rabbi Ismael*. Vienna edition, 1968.
Pesikta Rabbati. Warsaw edition, 1912-13.
Sipre Numbers. H.S. Horovitz, *Sipre d'Be Rab*, Leipzig, 1917.
Sipre Deuteronomy. H.S. Horovitz and L. Finkelstein, *Sipre ad Deuteronomium*, Berlin, 1939.
Midrash Rabbah. J. Theodor and Ch. Albeck, *Midrash Bereshit Rabba*, 3 vols., Jerusalem, 1965.
—Grossman's *Midrash Rabbah*, 2 vols., New York, 1952.
Babylonian Talmud. Gur-Ary, *Vilna Edition*, New York, 1972.

Dead Sea Scrolls
Cave 1. *Qumrân Cave I*, ed. D. Barthélemy and J.T. Milik; Discoveries in the Judean Desert, 1; Oxford, 1955.
Cave 4. *Qumrân Cave 4*, ed. J.M. Allegro; Discoveries in the Judean Desert, 5; Oxford, 1968.
—*Qumrân Cave 4*, ed. J.T. Milik and R. de Vaux; Discoveries in the Judean Desert, 6; Oxford, 1977.
—*Qumrân Cave 4*, ed. M. Baillet; Discoveries in the Judean Desert, 7; Oxford, 1982.
Damascus Covenant. S. Zeitlin, *The Zadokite Fragments*, Philadelphia, 1952.
Genesis Apocryphon. J.A. Fitzmyer, *The Genesis Apocryphon of Qumran Cave I*, Rome, 1966.
Hodayot. E.L. Sukenik, *Treasury of the Hidden Scrolls*, Jerusalem, 1954.
Isaiah Scroll. John C. Trever, *Scrolls from Qumran Cave I*, Jerusalem, 1974.
Psalms Scroll. *The Scriolls of Qumrân Cave 11*, ed. J.A. Sanders; Discoveries in the Judean Desert, 4; Oxford, 1965.
Manual of Discipline. John C. Trever, *Scrolls from Qumran Cave I*, Jerusalem, 1974.
Murabba'at. *Les Grottes de Murabba'at*, ed. P. Benoit, J.T. Milik and R. de Vaux, Discoveries in the Judean Desert, 2; Oxford, 1961.

Ben-Sira. The Historical Dictionary of the Hebrew Language, *The Book of Ben Sira. Text, Concordance and Analysis of the Vocabulary.* Jerusalem, 1973.

Inscriptions
Donner, H., and W. Röllig, *Kanaanäische und Aramäische Inschriften,* 3 vols., Wiesbaden, 1973-79.
Gibson, J.C.L. *Textbook of Syrian Semitic Inscriptions, I. Hebrew and Moabite Inscriptions,* Oxford, 1973.
—*Textbook of Syrian Semitic Inscriptions, II. Aramaic Inscriptions,* Oxford, 1975.
—*Textbook of Syrian Semitic Inscriptions, III. Phoenician Inscriptions, including Inscriptions in the Mixed Dialect of Arslan Tash,* Oxford, 1982.

SECONDARY SOURCES

Adams, William James and L. La Mar Adams, 'Language Drift and the Dating of Biblical Passages', *Hebrew Studies* 18 (1977), pp. 160-64.
Aharoni, Y., *Arad Inscriptions,* Jerusalem, 1981.
Albrecht, K., *Neuhebräische Grammatik auf Grund der Mishna,* München, 1913.
Albright, W.F., 'The Old Testament and the Canaanite Language and Literature', *CBQ* 7 (1945), pp. 5-31.
—*Yahweh and the Gods of Canaan,* London, 1968.
Allegro, J.M., 'Further Messianic References in Qumran Literature', *JBL* 75 (1956), pp. 174-87.
—'An Unpublished Fragment of Essene Halakhah (4Q Ordinances)', *JSS* 6 (1961), pp. 71-73.
Andersen, F.I., 'Moabite Syntax', *Orientalia* 35 (1966), pp. 81-119.
—and David Noel Freedman, *Hosea,* Anchor Bible, New York, 1980.
—and A. Dean Forbes, ' "Prose Particle" Counts in the Hebrew Bible', in *The Word of the Lord Shall Go Forth. Essays in Honor of David Noel Freedman,* pp. 165-83; ed. Carol L. Meyers and M. O'Conner, Winona Lake, 1983.
Anttila, Raimo, *An Introduction to Historical and Comparative Linguistics,* New York, 1972.
Arlotto, Anthony, *Introduction to Historical Linguistics,* Lanham, 1972.
The Assyrian Dictionary of the University of Chicago, Chicago, 1956–
Avinery, I. 'The Aramaic Influence on Hebrew', *Leshonenu* 3 (1930-31), pp. 273-9Q [in Hebrew].
Barr, James, 'Linguistic Liteature, Hebrew', *EncJud* 16, Jerusalem, 1972.
—'The Ancient Semitic Languages—The Conflict between Philology and Linguistics', *Transactions of the Philological Society* (1983), pp. 37-66.
—*Comparative Philology and the Text of the Old Testament,* 2nd edn, Winona Lake, 1987.
Bauer, H. and P. Leander, *Grammatik des Biblisch-Aramäischen,* Halle, 1927.
—*Historische Grammatik der hebräischen Sprache des Alten Testaments,* Halle, 1922.
Baumgartner, Walter, 'Was wir heute von der hebräischen Sprache und ihrer Geschichte wissen', *Anthropos* 35-36 (1940-41), pp. 593-616.

—ed. *Hebräisches und Aramäisches Lexikon zum Alten Testament*, Leiden, 1967.

Bendavid, A., *Biblical Hebrew and Mishnaic Hebrew*, 2 vols., Tel Aviv, 1967 [in Hebrew].

—*Parallels in the Bible*, Jerusalem, 1972.

Ben Hayyim, A., 'The Samaritan Tradition and its Relation to the Tradition of the Language of the Dead Sea Scrolls and Rabbinic Literature', *Leshonenu* 22 (1958), pp. 233-45 [in Hebrew].

—*The Contribution of the Samaritan Heritage to the Investigation of the History of Hebrew*, Jerusalem, 1968 [in Hebrew].

Ben Yehuda, E., *Thesaurus Totius Hebraitatis*, 8 vols., Jerusalem and Tel Aviv, 1947-59 [in Hebrew].

Bergey, Ronald L., *The Book of Esther—Its Place in the Linguistic Milieu of Post-Exilic Biblical Hebrew Prose. A Study in Late Biblical Hebrew*, Ph.D. dissertation, Dropsie College for Hebrew and Cognate Learning, 1983.

Bergstrasser, G., *Hebräische Grammatik*, Leipzig, 1918-29.

—*Einführung in die semitischen Sprachen*, Munich, 1963.

Bierwisch, Manfred, 'Poetics and Linguistics', in *Linguistics and Literary Style*, trans. Peter H. Salus; ed. Donald C. Freeman; New York, 1970.

Birnbaum, Henrik, 'Notes on Syntactic Change Cooccurrence vs. Substitution. Stability vs. Permeability', in *Historical Syntax*, pp. 25-46; ed. Jacek Fisiak; Berlin, 1984.

Blau, J. 'Zum angeblichen Gebrauch von '*t* vor dem Nominativ', *VT* 4 (1954), pp. 7-19.

—'Some Difficulties in the Reconstruction of "Proto-Hebrew" and "Proto-Canaanite"', in *In Memoriam Paul Kahle*, BZAW 103, pp. 23-43; ed. Matthew Black and Georg Fohrer; Berlin, 1968.

—'Hebrew Language, Biblical Hebrew', *EncJud* 16, Jerusalem, 1972.

—'The Historical Periods of the Hebrew Language', in *Jewish Languages Theme and Variations*, pp. 1-13; ed. Herbert H. Paper; Cambridge, Mass.: Association for Jewish Studies, 1978.

—'Thoughts on the Tense System in Biblical Literature', in *Festschrift for I.A. Seeligmann. Studies in Bible and the Ancient World*, pp. 19-23; ed. I. Zakovich and A. Rofe; Jerusalem, 1982 [in Hebrew].

Bloomfield, Leonard, *Language*, Chicago, 1983.

Blount, Ben G. and Mary Sanches, *Sociocultural Dimensions of Language Change*, New York, 1977.

The Book of Ben Sira—Text, Concordance and an Analysis of the Vocabulary, Jerusalem, 1973.

Brenner, Athalyah, 'The Language of the Book of Jonah as a Measurement for the Time of its Composition', *BM* 24 (1979), pp. 396-405 [in Hebrew].

Brettler, Marc, 'Ideology, History and Theology in 2 Kings XVII 7-23', *VT* (forthcoming).

Bright, William and A.K. Ramanujan, 'Sociolinguistic Variation and Language Change', in *Proceedings of the Ninth International Congress of Linguistics*, pp. 1107-13; ed. Horace G. Lunt; Cambridge, Mass., 1964.

Brin, Gershon, 'The Bible as Reflected in the Temple Scroll', *Annual for the Study of the Bible and the Ancient Near East* 4 (1980), pp. 182-225 [in Hebrew].

Brockelmann, C., *Lexikon Syriacum*, Berlin, 1895.

—*Grundriss der vergleichenden Grammatik der semitischen Sprachen*, 2 vols., Berlin, 1913.

—'Stand und Aufgaben der Semitistik', in *Beiträge zur Arabistik, Semitistik und Islamwissenschaft*, pp. 3-41; ed. Richard Hartman; Leipzig, 1944.
—*Hebräische Suntax*, Neukirchen, 1956.
—*Syrische Grammatik*, Leipzig, 1960.
Brown, F., S.R. Driver, and C. Briggs, eds., *A Hebrew and English Lexicon of the Old Testament*, Oxford, 1907, reprint edn, 1974.
Brownlee, W.H., *Ezekiel 1–19*, Word Biblical Commentary, Waco, 1986.
Burrows, Millar, *The Literary Relations of Ezekiel*, Philadelphia, 1925.
—'Orthography, Morphology, and Syntax of the St. Mark's Isaiah Manuscript', *JBL* 68 (1949), pp. 195-211.
Bynon, Theodora, *Historical Linguistics*, Cambridge, 1977.
Cantineau, J., *Grammaire du Palmyrénien Épigraphique*, Cairo, 1935.
Carpenter, J. Estlin and George Harford, *The Composition of the Hexateuch*, London, 1902.
Carroll, John B., 'Vectors of Prose Style', in *Style in Language*, pp. 283-92; ed. Thomas Sebeok; New York, 1960.
Chase, Mary Ellen, *Life and Language in the Old Testament*, New York, 1955.
Chomsky, W., 'How the Study of Hebrew Grammar Began and Developed', *JQR* 35 (1944-45), pp. 281-301.
—*Hebrew. The Eternal Language*, Philadelphia, 1957.
—*David Kimchi's Grammar*, New York, 1952.
Cohen, A., *'kg* instead of *kt'*, *BM* 15,2 (1969-70), pp. 206-207 [in Hebrew].
Cooke, G.A., *A Text-Book of North-Semitic Inscriptions*, Oxford, 1903.
—*The Book of Ezekiel*, International Critical Commentary, Edinburgh, 1936.
Cornhill, C.H., *Das Buch des Propheten Ezechiel*, Leipzig, 1886.
Corwin, R., *The Verb and the Sentence in Chronicles, Ezra and Nehemiah*, Ph.D. dissertation, University of Chicago, 1909.
Costello, John R., *Syntactic Change and Syntactic Reconstruction, A Tagmemic Approach*, Dallas, 1983.
Cowley, A., *Aramaic Papyri of the Fifth Century BC*, Oxford, 1913.
Cross, F.M. and D.N. Freedman, *Early Hebrew Orthography*, New Haven, 1952.
—*Studies in Ancient Yahwistic Poetry*, Missoula, 1975.
—'Samaria Papyrus . An Aramaic Slave Conveyance of 335 BCE. Found in the Wadi Ed-Daliyeh', *Eretz-Israel* 18 (1985), pp. 7-17.
Dahood, M., 'Canaanite-Phoenician Influence in Qoheleth', *Biblica* 33 (1952), pp. 30-52.
—'Ugaritic-Hebrew Syntax and Style', *UF* 1 (1969), pp. 15-36.
Dalman, Gustaf, *Grammatik des Jüdisch-Palästinischen Aramäisch*, Leipzig, 1905.
Davidson, A.B., *Hebrew Syntax*, 3rd edn, Edinburgh, 1901.
Dietrich, F.E.C., *Abhandlungen zur hebräischen Grammatik*, Leipzig, 1846.
Driver, G.R. 'Ezekiel Linguistic and Textual Problems', *Biblica* 35 (1954), pp. 145-59, 299-312.
Driver, S.R., 'On Some Alleged Linguistic Affinities of the Eliohist', *Journal of Philology* 2 (1882), pp. 201-36.
—*A Treatise on the Use of the Tenses in Hebrew*, 3rd edn, Oxford, 1892.
—*An Introduction to the Literature of the Old Testament*, Cleveland and New York, 1956.
Ehrlich, A.B., *Ezekiel. Mikrâ ki-Pheschutô*, New York, 1968 [in Hebrew].

Epstein, J.N., *A Grammar of Babylonian Aramaic*, Jerusalem and Tel Aviv, 1960 [in Hebrew].

Ewald, H., *Die Propheten des Alten Bundes. Jeremja und Hezeqiel mit ihren Zeitgenossen*, Göttingen, 1868.

—*Ausführliches Lehrbuch der hebräischen Sprache des Alten Bundes*, 8th edn, Göttingen, 1870.

Fishbane, Michael, 'The "Sign" in the Hebrew Bible', *Annual for the Study of the Bible and the Ancient Near East* 1 (1975), pp. 213-34 [in Hebrew].

—'Torah and Tradition', in *Tradition and Theology in the Old Testament*, 275-300; ed. Douglas Knight; Philadelphia, 1976.

—'The Qumran Pesher and Traits of Ancient Hermeneutics', in *Proceedings of the Sixth World Congress of Jewish Studies* I, pp. 97-114; Jerusalem, 1977.

—'Revelation and Traditon. Aspects of Inner-Biblical Exegesis', *JBL* 99 (1980), pp. 343-61.

—'Famine', *EM* 7, Jerusalem, 1981 [in Hebrew].

—'Form and Reformulation of the Biblical Priestly Blessing', *JAOS* 103 (1983), pp. 115-21.

—'Sin and Judgment in the Prophecies of Ezekiel', *Interpretation* 38 (1984), pp. 131-50

—*Biblical Interpretation in Ancient Israel*, Oxford, 1985.

Fitzmyer, J.A., *The Syntax of Imperial Aramaic*, Ph.D. dissertation, Johns Hopkins University, 1956.

Fohrer, G. and K. Galling, *Ezekiel*. Handbuch zum Alten Testament, Tübingen, 1955.

Fredericks, Daniel C., *Qoheleth's Language: Re-evaluating its Nature and Date*, Lewiston, 1988.

Freedman, David Noel, 'Pottery, Poetry, and Prophecy. An Essay on Biblical Poetry', *JBL* 96 (1977), pp. 5-26.

—'The Spelling of the Name "David" in the Hebrew Bible', *HAR* 7 (1983), pp. 89-102.

—'Another Look at Biblical Hebrew Poetry', in *Directions in Biblical Poetry*, 11-28; ed. Elaine R. Follis; Sheffield, 1987.

Freedy, K.S., *The Literary Relations of Ezekiel. A Historical Study of Chapters 1-24*, Ph.D. dissertation, University of Toronto, 1969.

Friedman, Jerome, *The Most Ancient Testimony*, Athens, Ohio, 1983.

Friedrich, J. and W. Röllig, *Phönizisch-Punische Grammatik*, Rome, 1970.

Gardiner, Sir Alan, *Egyptian Grammar*, Oxford, 1927.

Garr, Randall, *Dialect Geography of Syria-Palestine, 1000–586*, Philadelphia, 1985.

Gesenius, Wilhelm, *Geschichte der hebräischen Sprache und Schrift*, Leipzig, 1815.

Gevirtz, Stanley, *Patterns in the Early History Poetry of Israel*, 2nd edn, Chicago, 1973.

Giesebrecht, F., 'Zur Hexateuchkritik. Der Sprachgegrauch des Hexateuchischen Elohisten', *ZAW* 1 (1881), pp. 177-276.

Goetze, Albrecht, 'Is Ugaritic a Canaanite Dialect?', *Language* 17 (1941), pp. 127-38.

Goldberg, Ariella, *Northern-Type-Names in the Post-Exilic Jewish Onomasticon*, Ph.D. dissertation, Brandeis University, 1972.

Golomb, David M., *A Grammar of Targum Neofiti*, Chico, California, 1985.

Gordis, Robert, 'Studies in the Relationship of Biblical and Rabbinic Hebrew', in *Louis Ginzberg Jubilee Volume*, pp. 173-99; New York: American Academy for Jewish Research, 1945.

Gordon, Cyrus, 'Azitwadd's Phoenician Inscription', *JNES* 8 (1949), pp. 108-15.

—'Northern Israelite Influence on Post-Exilic Hebrew', *Eretz-Israel* 3 (1954), pp. 104-105 [in Hebrew].

—'North Israelite Influence on Postexilic Hebrew', *EncJud* (1955), pp. 85-88.

—*Ugaritic Textbook*, Rome, 1967.

Goshen-Gottstein, M.H., 'The History of the Bible-Text and Comparative Semitics—A Methodological Problem', *VT* 7 (1957), pp. 195-201.

—'Linguistic Structure and Tradition in the Qumran Documents', in *Scripta Hierosolymitana* 4, pp. 101-37; Jerusalem, 1958.

—*Text and Language in Bible and Qumran*, Jerusalem and Tel-Aviv, 1960.

—*Hebrew and Semitic Languages*, Tel-Aviv, 1964 [in Hebrew].

—'Comparative Semitics—A Premature Obituary', in *Essays on the Occasion of the Seventieth Anniversary of Dropsie University*, pp. 141-50; ed. Abraham Isaac Katsh, Philadelphia, 1979.

—'The Textual Criticism of the Old Testament—Rise, Decline, Rebirth', *JBL* 102 (1983), pp. 365-99.

Greenberg, Moshe, *Ezekiel 1–20*, Anchor Bible, New York, 1983.

—'The Design and Themes of Ezekiel's Program of Restoration', *Interpretation* 38 (1984), pp. 181-208.

Greenfield, Jonas, *The Lexical Status of Mishnaic Hebrew*, Ph.D. dissertation, Yale University, 1956.

Guenther, A.R., *A Diachronic Study of Biblical Hebrew Prose Syntax. An Analysis of the Verbal Clause in Jeremiah 37–45 and Esther 1–10*, Ph.D. dissertation, University of Toronto, 1977.

Habberman, A.M., *Scrolls of the Judean Desert*, Israel, 1959 [in Hebrew].

Habel, N., 'The Form and Significance of the Call Narratives', *ZAW* 77 (1965), pp. 297-323.

Hackett, Jo Ann, *The Balaam Text from Deir 'Alla*, Chico, California, 1980.

Hadas-Lebel, Mireille, *Manuel d'histoire de la langue hébraïque*, Paris, 1976.

Haneman, G., 'On the Preposition בין in the Mishna and in the Bible', *Leshonenu* 40 (1975-76), pp. 33-53 [in Hebrew].

Harris, Z.S., *Development of the Canaanite Dialects*, New Haven, 1978.

—'The Linguistic Structure of Hebrew', *JAOS* 61 (1941), pp. 143-67.

Hill, Andrew E., *The Book of Malachi. Its Place in Post-Exilic Chronology Linguistically reconsidered*, Ph.D. dissertation, University of Michigan, 1981.

—'Dating Second Zechariah. A Linguistic Reexamination', *HAR* 6 (1982), pp. 105-34.

Hock, Hans Heinrich, *Principles of Historical Linguistics*, Berlin, 1986.

Höhne, Ernst, *Die Thronwagenvision Hesekiels. Echtheit und Herkunft der Vision Hes. 1,4-28 und ihrer einzelnen Züge*, Ph.D. dissertation, Friedrich-Alexander Universität, 1953.

Hoftijzer, J., 'Remarks Concerning the Use of the Particle *'t* in Classical Hebrew', *Oudtestamentische Studiën* 14 (1965), pp. 1-99.

Holzinger, Heinrich, *Einleitung in den Hexateuch*, Leipzig, 1893.

Hospers, J.H., 'A Hundred Years of Semitic Comparative Semitics', in *Studia Biblica et Semitica* (Festschrift T.C. Vriezen) , Wageningen, 1966.

Howie, Carl Gordon, *The Date and Composition of Ezekiel*, Philadelphia, 1950.

Hurvitz, A., 'When Was the Expression שלום על ישראל' Coined?', *Leshonenu* 27-28 (1964), pp. 297-302 [in Hebrew].

—The Usage of שש and בוץ in the Bible and its Implication for the Date of P', *HTR* 60 (1967), pp. 117-21.

—'The Chronological Significance of 'Aramaisms' in Biblical Hebrew', *IEJ* 18 (1968), pp. 234-40.

—'The Use of the Priestly Term 'ēdāh in Biblical Literature', *Tarbiz* 40 (1970-71), pp. 261-67 [in Hebrew].

—*Biblical Hebrew in Transition—A Study in Post-Exilic Hebrew and its Implications for the Dating of Psalms*, Jerusalem, 1972 [in Hebrew].

—' "Diachronic Chiasm" in Biblical Hebrew', in *The Bible and the History of Israel. Studies in Honor of Jacob Levor*, pp. 248-55; Tel-Aviv, 1972 [in Hebrew].

—'Linguistic Criteria for Dating Problematic Biblical Texts', *Hebrew Abstracts* 14 (1973), pp. 74-79.

—'The Date of the Prose-Tale of Job Linguistically Reconsidered', *HTR* 67 (1974), pp. 17-34.

—'The Evidence of Language in Dating the Priestly Code. A Linguistic Study in Technical Idioms and Terminology', *RB* 81 (1974), pp. 24-56.

—'The Language and Date of Psalm 151 from Qumran', *Eretz Israel* 8 (1967), pp. 82-87 [in Hebrew].

—*A Linguistic Study of the Relationship between the Priestly Source and the Book of Ezekiel*, Cahiers de la Revue Biblique 20, Paris, 1982.

Jakobson, Roman, 'Linguistics and Poetics', in *Style in Language*, pp. 350-77; ed. Thomas A. Sebeok; New York, 1960.

Japhet, S., 'The Interchange of Verbal Roots in Parallel Texts in the Chronicles', *Leshonenu* 31 (1967), pp. 261-79 [in Hebrew].

Jastrow, M., *A Dictionary of the Targumim, the Talmud Babli and Yerushalmi, and the Midrashic Literature*, 2 vols., New York, 1967.

Jean, C.F., and J. Hoftijzer, *Dictionnaire des inscriptions sémitiques de l'ouest*, Leiden, 1965.

Jespersen, Otto, *Efficiency in Linguistic Change*, Denmark, 1949.

Joüon, P. Paul, *Grammaire de l'Hébreu Biblique*, Rome, 1923.

—'Notes philologiques sur le texte hébreu d'Ezéchiel', *Biblica* 10 (1929), pp. 304-12.

Kasovski, Ch.J., *Thesaurus Thosephthae*, 6 vols., Jerusalem, 1932-61.

—*Thesaurus Mishnae*, 4 vols., Jerusalem, 1956-60.

—*Ozar Leshon Targum Onkelos Concordance*, 2 vols., Jerusalem, 1986.

Kaufman, Stephen A., *Akkadian Influences on Aramaic*, Chicago, 1974.

Kaufmann, Y., *History of the Religion of Israel*, 4th edn, 4 vols., Jerusalem, 1937-56 [in Hebrew].

Kautzsch, E., *Grammatik des Biblisch-Aramäischen*, Leipzig, 1884.

—*Aramäismen im Alten Testament untersucht*, Halle, 1902.

—edn, *Gesenius' Hebrew Grammar*, 2nd edn, trans. A.E. Cowley, Oxford, 1910 (reprinted edn, 1974).

Keil, C.F., *Ezekiel. Commentary on the Old Testament*, Grand Rapids, reprinted edn, 1973.

King, Robert D., *Historical Linguistics and Generative Grammar*, Englewood Cliffs, 1969.

Kiparsky, Paul, 'The Role of Linguistics in a Theory of Poetry', in *Language as a Human Problem*, pp. 233-46; ed. M. Bloomfield and E. Haugen; New York, 1974.

Koehler, L. and W. Baumgartner, *Lexicon in Veteris Testamenti Libros*, Leiden, 1958.

König, F.E., *Historisch-kritisches Lehrgebäude der Hebräischen Sprache*, 3 vols., Leipzig, 1881-97.

Kraeling, E.M., *The Brooklyn Museum Aramaic Papyri*, New Haven, 1953.

Kraetzschmar, R., *Das Buch Ezechiel*, Göttingen, 1900.

Kräutlin, Jonathan, *Die sprachlichen Verschiedenheiten in den Hexateuchquellen*, Leipzig, 1908.

Kropat, A., *Die Syntax des Autors der Chronik*, BZAW 16, Giessen, 1909.

Kugel, James, *The Idea of Biblical Poetry. Parallelism and its History*, New Haven, 1981.

Kuhn, K.G., *Konkordanz zu den Qumrantexten*, Göttingen, 1960.

Kutscher, E.Y., 'Biblical Aramaic', *EM* 1, Jerusalem, 1953 [in Hebrew].

—'Dating the Language of the Genesis Apocryphon', *JBL* 76 (1957), pp. 288-92.

—'The Language of the Hebrew and Aramaic Letters of Bar Cosbah and his Contemporaries. Part one. The Aramaic Letters', *Leshonenu* 25 (1960), pp. 117-33 [In Hebrew].

—'The Language of the Hebrew and Aramaic Letters of Bar Cosbah and his Contemporaries Part two. The Hebrew Letters', *Leshonenu* 26 (1961), pp. 7-23 [in Hebrew].

—*Words and their History*, Jerusalem, 1961 [in Hebrew].

—'Aramaic Calque in Hebrew', *Tarbiz* 33 (1964), pp. 118-30 [in Hebrew].

—'Mittelhebräische und Judisch-Aramäisch im neuen Koehler–Baumgartner', *Hebräische Wortforschung* [SVT 16], pp. 158-75; Leiden, 1967.

—'The Dead Sea Scrolls', *EncJud* 16.

—'Mishnaic Hebrew', *EncJud* 16.

—*The Language and Linguistic Background of the Isaiah Scroll (1QIsaa)*, Leiden, 1974.

—*Studies in Galilean Aramaic*, Jerusalem, 1976.

—*A History of the Hebrew Language*, ed. Raphael Kutscher; Jerusalem, Leiden, 1982.

Labov, William, 'The Social Motivation of a Sound Change', *Word* 19 (1963), pp. 273-309

—'The Social Setting of Linguistic Change', in *Current Trends in Linguistics*, by Thomas A. Sebeok, Vol. 11, Paris, 1973.

Lambert, Mayer, *Traité de Grammaire Hébraïque*, Hildesheim, 1972.

Lambdin, T.O., 'Egyptian Loanwords in the Old Testament', *JAOS* 73 (1953), pp. 145-55.

Landes, George M., 'Linguistic Criteria and the Date of the Book of Jonah', *Eretz-Israel* 16 (1982), pp. 147-70.

Landy, Francis, 'Poetics and Parallelism. Some Comments on James Kugel's "The Idea of Biblical Poetry" ', *JSOT* 28 (1984), pp. 61-87.

Lass, Roger, *On Explaining Language Change*, Cambridge, 1980.

Leahy, T., *A Study of the Language of the Essene Manual of Discipline*, Ph.D. dissertation, Johns Hopkins University, 1958.

—'Studies in the Syntax of 1QS', *Biblica* 4 (1960), pp. 135-57.

Lehman, Winfred P., *Historical Linguistics. An Introduction*, New York, 1962.
—'Saussure's Dichotomy between Descriptive and Historical Linguistics', in *Directions for Historical Linguistics*, pp. 3-20; ed. W.P. Lehman and Yakov Malkiel; Austin, 1968.
Lemke, Werner E., 'The Synoptic Problem in the Chronicler's History', *HTR* (1965), pp. 349-63.
Levenson, Jon D., *Theology of the Program of Restoration of Ezekiel 40–48*, Missoula, 1976.
Levine, Baruch, *Survivals of Ancient Canaanite in the Mishnah*, Ph.D. dissertation, Brandeis University, 1962.
—'MELŪGU/MELŪ: The Origins of a Talmudic Legal Institution', *JAOS* 88 (1968), pp. 271-85.
Levy, J., *Neuhebräische und Chaldäisches Wörterbuch über die Talmudim und Midraschim*, 4 vols., Leipzig, 1876-89.
Licht, J., *The Hodayot Scroll*, Jerusalem, 1957 [in Hebrew].
Lidzbarski, M., *Ephemeris für semitische Epigraphik*, Giessen, 1909-15.
Lieberman, Saul, *Hellenism in Jewish Palestine*, New York, 1962.
Lightfoot, David W., *Principles of Diachronic Syntax*, Cambridge, 1979.
Lotz, John, 'Elements of Versification', in *Versification. Major Language Types*, pp. 1-21; ed. W.K. Wimsatt; New York, 1972.
Lowe, W.H., ed., *The Mishnah on which the Palestinian Talmud Rests*, Cambridge, 1883.
MacDonald, J., 'The Particle 't in Classical Hebrew', *VT 14* (1964), pp. 264-75.
Mansoor, M., 'Some Linguistic Aspects of the Qumran Texts', *JSS* 3 (1958), pp. 40-54.
Marcus, David, *A Manual of Babylonian Jewish Aramaic*, Washington D.C., 1981.
Margoliouth, D.S., 'Language of the Old Testament', in *A Dictionary of the Bible*, Vol. 3, pp. 25-35; ed. James Hastings; Edinburgh, 1900.
Margolis, Max L., *A Manual of the Aramaic Language of the Babylonian Talmud*, München, 1910.
Mathews, Kenneth Alan, *The Paléo-Hebrew Leviticus Scroll from Qumran*, Ph.D. dissertation, University of Michigan, 1980.
Melammed, Ezra Zion, *Bible Commentators*, 2 vols., Jerusalem, 1975 [in Hebrew].
Merrill, Eugene H., *The Language and Literary Characteristics of Isaiah 40–55 as Anti-Babylonian Polemic*, Ph.D. dissertation, Columbia University, 1984.
Metmann, Leo, *Die hebräische Sprache. Ihre Geschichte und lexikalische Entwicklung seit Abschluss des Kanons*, Jerusalem, 1904.
Milgrom, Jacob, 'Priestly Terminology and the Political and Social Structure of Pre-Monarchic Israel', *JQR* 69 (1978), pp. 65-81.
Miqra'ot Gedolot, 5 vols., Eshkol edition, Jerusalem, 1976 [in Hebrew].
Morag, Shelemo, 'Qumran Hebrew: Some Typological Observations', *VT* 38 (1988), pp. 148-64.
Moran, W.L., 'The Hebrew Language in its North-West Semitic Background', *The Bible and the Ancient Near East Essays in honor of W.F. Albright*, New York, 1961, pp. 54-72.
Moscati, S., *An Introduction to the Comparative Grammar of the Semitic Languages*, Wiesbaden, 1964.

Mukařovsky, Jan, 'Standard Language and Poetic Language', in *Linguistics and Literary Style*, pp. 40-56; trans. Paul L. Garvin; ed. Donald C. Freeman; New York, 1970.

Newson, Carol, *Songs of the Sabbath Sacrifice. A Critical Edition*, Atlanta, 1985.

Nida, Eugene A., 'Implications of Contemporary Linguistics for Biblical Scholarship, *JBL* 91 (1972), pp. 73-89.

Nöldeke, Th., 'Aramaisms', *Zeitschrift der Deutschen Morgenländischen Gesellschaft* 57 (1903), pp. 412-20.

—*Kurzgefasste Syrische Grammatik*, Leipzig, 1880.

—*Compendious Syriac Grammar*, London, 1904.

O'Conner, M., *Hebrew Verse Structure*, Winona Lake, 1980.

Oesterley, W.O.E. and Theodore H. Robinson, *An Introduction to the Books of the Old Testament*, New York, 1958.

Paul, Hermann, *Prinzipien der Sprachgeschichte*, Tübingen, 1960.

Payne-Smith, R., *Thesaurus Syriacus*, Oxford, 1879-1901.

Peretz, Y., *The Relative Clause*, Tel-Aviv, 1967 [in Hebrew].

Polotsky, H., 'Semitics', in *The World History of the Jewish People*, Vol. I. *The Dawn of Civilization*, pp. 99-111; ed. E.A. Speiser; Tel-Aviv, 1964.

Polzin, R., *Late Biblical Hebrew. Toward an Historical Typology of Biblical Hebrew Prose*, Missoula, 1976.

—'Notes on the Dating of the Non-massoretic Psalms of 11QPsaa', *HTR* 60 (1967), pp. 468-76.

Qimron, Elisha, 'The Language of the Second Temple in the Book of Psalms', *BM* 23 (1978), pp. 139-50 [in Hebrew].

—'The Vocabulary of the Temple Scroll', *Annual for the Study of the Bible and the Ancient Near East* 4 (1980), pp. 239-62 [in Hebrew].

—'The Dating of the Book of Jonah', *BM* 81 (1980), pp. 181-82 [in Hebrew].

—*The Hebrew of the Dead Sea Scrolls*, Atlanta, 1986.

Rabin, C., 'The Historical Background of Qumran', in *Scripta Hierosolymitana* 4, pp. 144-61; Jerusalem, 1958.

—*The Zadokite Documents*, 2nd edn, Oxford, 1958.

—'Foreign Words', *EM* 4, Jerusalem, 1962 [in Hebrew].

—*The Syntax of the Biblical Language*, Jerusalem, 1967 [in Hebrew].

—'Hebrew', in *Current Trend in Linguistics*, ed. Thomas Sebeok, Vol. 6; Paris, 1970, pp. 304-46.

—'Hebrew', *EM* 6, Jerusalem, 1971 [in Hebrew].

—'Hebrew and Aramaic in the First Century', in *The Jewish People in the First Century* , 2 vols., Vol. 2, pp. 1007-39; ed. S. Safrai and M. Stern; Assen: van Gorcum, 1976.

Rendsburg, G., 'Late Biblical Hebrew and the Date of "P" ', *JANES* 12 (1980), pp. 65-80.

—'A New Look at Pentateuchal HW', *Biblica* 63 (1982), pp. 351-69.

Revell, E.J., *A Structural Analysis of the Grammar of the Manual of Discipline*, Ph.D. dissertation, University of Toronto, 1962.

Riffaterre, Michael, 'Describing Poetic Structures. Two Approaches to Baudelaire's *Les Chats*', in *Structuralism*, pp. 188-230; ed. Jasques Ehrmann; New York, 1970.

Robertson, David, *Linguistic Evidence in Dating Early Hebrew Poetry*, Missoula, 1972.

Rooker, Mark F., 'The Diachronic Study of Biblical Hebrew', *JNSL* 14 (1988), pp. 199-214.

—'Ezekiel and the Typology of Biblical Hebrew', *HAR* 12 (forthcoming).

Rosenthal, F., *A Grammar of Biblical Aramaic*, Wiesbaden, 1974.

Ryssel, Carlous V., *De Elohistae Pentateuchici Sermone*, Leipzig, 1878.

Rubenstein, A., 'A Finite Verb Continued by an Infinitive Absolute in Biblical Hebrew', *VT* 2 (1952), pp. 362-67.

—'Notes on the Use of the Tenses in the Variant Readings of the Isaiah Scroll', *VT* 3 (1953), pp. 92-95.

Samuels, M.L., *Linguistic Evolution*, Cambridge, 1972.

Sappan, Raphael, *The Typical Features of the Syntax of Biblical Poetry in its Classical Period*, Ph.D. dissertation, The Hebrew University, 1974 [in Hebrew].

Saussure, Ferdinand de, *Course in General Linguistics*, trans. Wade Baskin, New York, 1959.

Saydon, P.P., 'Meanings and Uses of the Particle *'t*', *VT* 14 (1964), pp. 192-210.

Schlesinger, Michael, *Satzlehre der Aramäischen Sprache des Babylonischen Talmuds*, Leipzig, 1928.

Schneider, M.D., 'The Literary Hebrew Language', *Leshonenu* 6 (1935), pp. 301-26 [in Hebrew].

Segal, M.H., 'Mishnaic Hebrew and its Relation to Biblical Hebrew and to Aramaic', *JQR* 20 (1908), pp. 647-737.

—*A Grammar of Mishnaic Hebrew*, Oxford, 1927.

—*Introduction to the Bible*, 2 vols., Jerusalem, 1964 [in Hebrew].

Segert, S., 'Die Sprache der moabitischen Königinschrift', *Archiv Orientalni* 29 (1961), pp. 197-268.

—*Altaramäische Grammatik*, Leipzig, 1975.

—*A Basic Grammar of the Ugaritic Language*, Los Angeles, 1984.

Selle, F., *De Aramaismis libri Ezechielis*, Leipzig, 1880.

Shapira, D.S., 'The Literary Sources of the Book of Ezekiel', *Sinai* 66 (1969-70), pp. 1-12 [in Hebrew].

Smend, R., *Der Prophet Ezechiel*, Leipzig, 1880.

Soden, W. von, *Akkadisches Handwörterbuch*, Vols. I-III, Wiesbaden, 1965-81.

—'Aramäische Wörter in neuassyrischen und neu- und spätbabylonischen Texten. Ein Vorbericht', *Orientalia* N.S. 35 (1966), pp. 1-20, 37 (1968), pp. 261-71.

Sperber, A., *The Bible in Aramaic*, Leiden, 1959-73.

—*A Historical Grammar of Biblical Hebrew*, Leiden, 1966

Stankiewicz, Edward, 'Linguistics and the Study of Poetic Language', in *Style in Language*, pp. 69-81; ed. Thomas A. Sebeok; New York, 1960

Sturtevant, E.H., *Linguistic Change*, Chicago, 1917.

—*An Introduction to Linguistics*, New Haven, 1947.

Sukenik, A.L., *Hidden Scrolls*, Jerusalem, 1948 [in Hebrew].

Tadmor, Hayyim, 'The Historical Inscriptions of Adad-Nirari III', *Iraq* 35 (1973), pp. 141-50.

Tigay, Jeffrey H. 'An Empirical Basis for the Documentary Hypothesis', *JBL* 94 (1975), pp. 329-41.

Torczyner, H., *Lachish I. The Lachish Letters*, London, 1938.

—'The Aramaic Influence on Hebrew', *EM*, Jerusalem, 1950 [in Hebrew].

—*The Language and the Book*, Jerusalem, 1954 [in Hebrew].

Torrey, C.C., *Pseudo-Ezekiel and the Original Prophecy*, New Haven, 1930.

198   *Biblical Hebrew in Transition*

Tov, Emmanuel, 'Determining the Relationship between the Qumran Scrolls and the LXX. Some Methodological Problems', in *The Hebrew and Greek Texts of Samuel*, pp. 45-67; ed. Emmanuel Tov; Jerusalem, 1980.
Trever, John C., 'Completion of the Publication of Some Fragments From Qumran Cave I', *RQ* 5 (1965), pp. 323-44.
—*Scrolls from Qumran Cave I*, Jerusalem, 1974.
Tsevat, M., *A Study of the Language of the Biblical Psalms*, Philadelphia, 1955.
Tucker, Gene M., *Form Criticism of the Old Testament*, Philadelphia, 1971.
—'Editor's Foreword', in *The Old Testament and the Literary Critic*, pp. vii-viii; by David Robertson, Philadelphia, 1977.
Ullendorf, E. 'Comparative Semitics', in *Current Trends in Linguistics*, ed. Thomas A. Sebeok, Vol. 6, *Linguistics in South West Asia and North Africa*, pp. 261-73; Paris, 1970.
—*Is Biblical Hebrew a Language?* Wiesbaden, 1977.
Ulrich, Charles, *The Qumran Text of Samuel and Josephus*, Missoula, 1978.
Vogt, E., 'Zur Geschichte der hebräischen Sprache', *Biblica* 52 (1971), pp. 72-78.
Wagner, M., *Die lexikalischen und grammatikalischen Aramäismen im alttestamentischen Hebräisch*, BZAW 96, Berlin, 1966.
Walker, N. 'Concerning the Function of 'ʾ', *VT* 5 (1955), pp. 314-15.
Wallis, E.A.W. and L.W. King, *Annals of the Kings of Assyria*, London, 1902
Watson, Wilfred G.E., 'Verse-Patterns in Ugaritic, Akkadian, and Hebrew Poetry', *UF* 7 (1975), pp. 483-92.
—*Classical Hebrew Poetry*, Sheffield, 1984.
Weingreen, J., 'The Construct-Genitive Relation in Hebrew Syntax', *VT* 4 (1954), pp. 50-59.
Weinrich, Uriel, *Languages in Contact*, New York, 1953.
—'William Labov, and Marvin I. Herzog, 'Empirical Foundations for a Theory of Language Change', in *Directions for Historical Linguistics*, pp. 95-188; W.P. Lehmann and Yakov Malkiel; Austin, 1968.
Widdowson, H.G., *Stylistics and Teaching of Literature*, London, 1975.
Williams, R.J., *Hebrew Syntax. An Outline*, Toronto, 1967.
Williamson, H.G.M., 'The Composition of Ezra i-vi', *JTS* 34 (1983), pp. 1-30.
Wright, G.A., *An Investigation of the Literary Form, Haggadic Midrash, in the Old Testament and Intertestamental Literature*, Ph.D. dissertation, Catholic University of America, 1965.
Yadin, Y., *The Scroll of the War of the Sons of Light Against the Sons of Darkness*, Oxford, 1962.
—*The Temple Scroll. English and Hebrew*, 3 vols., Jerusalem, 1983.
Yamauchi, Edwin M., *Mandaean Incantation Texts*, Ph.D. dissertation, Brandeis University, 1964.
Yoder, Perry B., 'Biblical Hebrew', in *Versification. Major Language Types*, pp. 52-65; ed. W.K. Wimsatt; New York, 1972.
Young, G. Douglas, 'Ugaritic Prosody', *JNES* 9 (1950), pp. 124-33.
Zeitlin, S., *The Zadokite Fragments*, Philadelphia, 1952.
Zevit, Ziony, 'Converging Lines of Evidence Bearing on the Date of P', *ZAW* 94 (1982), pp. 481-511
Zimmerli, W., 'The Special Form- and Traditio-Historical Character of Ezekiel's Prophecy', *VT* 15 (1965), pp. 515-27.
—*Ezekiel*, 2 vols., Philadelphia, 1979, 1983.
—*I Am Yahweh*, trans. Douglas W. Stott; Atlanta, 1982.

Zuckermandel, M.S., *Tosephta Based on the Erfurt and Vienna Codices*, Jerusalem, 1970.

INDEX OF BIBLICAL REFERENCES

INDEX OF EXTRA BIBLICAL REFERENCES

INDEX OF AUTHORS CITED

DATE D'